Don B. Morlan, Eastern Illinois University

George E. Tuttle, Jr., Illinois State University

An Introduction to Effective Oral Communication

The Bobbs-Merrill Company, Inc.
INDIANAPOLIS

To Sue and Joann

The Bobbs-Merrill Company, Inc.
4300 West 62nd Street
Indianapolis, Indiana 46268

First Edition
First Printing 1976
Designed by Irving Perkins

Library of Congress Cataloging in Publication Data

Morlan, Don B
An introduction to effective oral communication.

1. Oral communication. I. Tuttle, George E., joint author. II. Title.
PN4121.M63 808.5 76–21856
ISBN 0–672–61408–1

Contents

Preface

An Introduction to Effective Oral Communication is designed as an introductory text written primarily for the student. It is prepared so that the reader will learn about oral communication principles and theory as well as achieve a minimum level of skill development.

Some of the most distinctive features of this text are drawn from contemporary educational theory intended to aid the student. First, learning objectives—identified as goals—are placed at the beginning of each chapter to give the reader direction. They make the reader aware of minimum information and skills which he or she should expect to possess when the chapter is completed.

Second, summary probes are placed strategically throughout each chapter rather than just at the ends of chapters. Summary probes throughout the text require immediate review of a few particular concepts. The immediate reinforcement should increase retention. Summary probes found at the end of chapters usually call for synthesis or application of principles or skills from the entire chapter. Some of the probes found at the end of chapters will relate specifically to learning objectives stated at the beginning of the chapter.

Third, research probes, which are to be found in the Learning Experience sections at the ends of chapters, are distinctive because of their emphasis on experimental and experiential learning. The research probe suggests an experience or experiment to provide deeper understanding of a particular concept.

Finally, this text is written with the reader in mind. We have made every effort to prepare a text at a reading level appropriate for most college freshmen. Where terms with special meaning are used, the terms are explained. Many of the examples used are likely to be within the past or immediate experiences of the intended readers. Portions of the text have been field tested by readers with appropriate reading levels.

We wish to extend special acknowledgment to Wanda Wiley for her careful editing of the manuscript for technical purposes. Her conscientious attention to detail has made a major contribution to the text. R. Glen Wiley, Bruce Wheatley, Jon Hopkins, and Clayland Waite—all colleagues in the Department of Speech-Communication at Eastern Illinois University—were especially helpful in making materials available in preparation of the text and providing helpful assessment. Bob Corn of Eastern Illinois University completed the photography used in the text. Julie Lewis and Craig Schmitt, graduate assistants in Speech-Communication at Eastern Illinois University, served as photographic models.

Acknowledgment is made to the following publishers and individuals for permission to use materials or information:

University of Illinois Press for use of the Schramm communication model from Wilbur Schramm, *The Process and Effects of Mass Communication*. Copyright © 1955 by the University of Illinois Press. Used with permission.

Holt, Rinehart, and Winston for use of the Berlo communication model from David K. Berlo, *The Process of Communication: An Introduction to Theory and Practice*. Copyright © 1960 by Holt, Rinehart, and Winston, Inc. Adapted and reprinted with permission.

Bobbs-Merrill Company for use of the Miller communication model and extracted copy from Gerald R. Miller, *Speech Communication: A Behavioral Approach*. Copyright © 1966 by Bobbs-Merrill Company, Inc. Used with permission.

Journalism Quarterly for use of the Westley and MacLean communication model. Reprinted with permission from the *Journalism Quarterly* 34 (1957), 31–38.

McGraw-Hill for use of the poem from *The Blind Men and the Elephant*. Illustrations © 1963 by Paul Galdone. Used with permission.

Advertising Age for permission to use the chart depicting advertising volume for 1973–74 from the September 15, 1975 issue of *Advertising Age*. Copyright 1975 by Crain Communications, Inc.

New York Times for permission to use two radio program schedules. Copyright 1924 and 1940 by the New York Times Company. Reprinted with permission.

National Association of Broadcasters for permission to reprint from the Television Code, Eighteenth edition, published by the Code Authority of the National Association of Broadcasters June 1975.

WTHI, Channel 10, in Terre Haute, Indiana, for permission to reprint their advertising rate card. Printed with permission of Bill King, sales manager.

Introduction

A study of human communication can be both a complex task, and, at the same time, a very simple one. Human communication is complex because it involves virtually every action and experience of the human existence. Anytime we are in the physical presence of other people, we are expressing communicative messages whether we intend to or not. Complexity abounds in our subject matter because it is virtually impossible to isolate specific events in human communication.

The study of communication is simple in the sense that we should need no extensive creation of motivation for academic inquiry into the area. The often-heard question resounding from classroom walls, "What good will this course do me?" should not apply to a study of human communication. We, the authors, can assure you of two undeniable facts: first, you *are* human, and, second, your success in whatever you do in the future will relate directly to your ability and agility in communicating effectively.

The approach in this text is to view human communication in four specific settings, referred to as communicative events in human existence. Our four events form an orderly progression from less formal to more formal situations.

The first communicative event to be discussed will be your communicative behavior in interpersonal settings. By interpersonal we mean those situations which find you face to face with other human beings. By far the greatest amount of human communication falls within this category. Much of our interpersonal communication is deliberate and calculated for specific effect. An even greater amount of our interpersonal communicative behavior is unintentional and, many times, unknown to us. If someone is watching you as you read this text, you are transmitting communicative messages to him manifested in your physically observable reactions to what you read.

Our second communicative event consists of human interaction in small group settings. We are all members of various kinds of groups. Each of us holds a position in several social groups, work groups, and family groups. Fluent and rewarding continuation in our group roles depends on our ability to communicate within these groups and to make alterations in our communicative behavior as we move from one group to another.

The third communicative event of concern to us finds each of us in situations where we are confronted with the task of transmitting messages to larger groups of people, or in a one-to-many setting with ourselves filling the role of the "one." We will refer to this communicative event as public speaking. Even though we might assume that we will be in the role of public speaker less often than the sender in either interpersonal or small group communication, we frequently find ourselves in the role of receiver of public communication. Our approach to public speaking is not only sender-oriented, but we will demonstrate a great concern for the problems facing us as receivers of public communication. While you may not be able at this point to envision yourself in situations as the speaker in public, you can easily picture yourself receiving such public messages.

Our fourth and final communicative event will lead us into the area of mass media. We are a media-oriented society. While most of us will never be senders in a media situation, our role as receivers of media messages cannot be overstated. No doubt you have already been exposed to a barrage of media messages. To remain unknowing of some basic concepts of media communication in a society so influenced by media is to remain unaware of a most effective and, sometimes, dangerous tool of certain elements of that society.

As you progress through this textbook, consider it as a four-step journey into human communicative behavior. Material contained in each step should be retained and applied in the next. You should regard all the information that follows as it applies to you as both a sender and a receiver in each of the four events. What follows is of vital importance to you and your future success at interacting with other human beings. Please, don't take it lightly.

I

Interpersonal Communication

ONE

GOALS **After completing this chapter you will be able to:**

1. Define "interpersonal communication".

2. Apply significant parts of communication models to actual communication situations.

3. Distinguish several aspects of communication which are unique to humans.

Communication Theory

Communication process and performance are inseparable. Knowing process alone might make one knowledgeable but still unable to communicate meaning effectively with other humans. Acquisition of performance skills might make one interesting as a show piece but probably not a very effective communicator of meaning with other human beings. It is the person who knows how to blend process with performance skills who will be more effective in communicating meaning with other humans.

Every person using the term *interpersonal communication* believes they are addressing the most urgent conditions of the human experience; yet the descriptions seem so varied. Clearly, each author must have a unique meaning for the term *interpersonal communication* which often goes unstated. Like the classic example of Babylon, we are confounded by many varied tongues. Rather than simply add one more foreign tongue to an already confused situation, this section will attempt clarity first. A definition of *interpersonal communication,* not *the* definition, but *a* definition, will be developed as a reference for the subsequent discussion of factors which will affect the outcome of communication. The reader should be cautioned that no definition of interpersonal communication will be universally accepted, but a study of what happens should make some relative sense—relative to the frame of reference in the particular definition.

Man is distinct from other forms of animal life by the relatively unique sophistication of ability to communicate. Man shares physical mechanisms such as vocal folds, resonators, and articulators with other forms of animal life; however, the psychomotor capacity is greater than in most other forms. Even man's ability to symbolize is shared; however, the sophistication of man's capacity to symbolize abstractly is not shared by other animals. It appears that man's most distinctive communication feature is what Alfred Korzybski has labeled "time binding."[1]

Time binding refers to the ability to transmit knowledge through symbols from generation to generation. This gives man control over change and environment to a greater degree than any other form of life. You are fortunate not to have to experience all that has been experienced by all humans throughout history. Much of the past experience has been preserved and passed on through communication. We can be grateful that each generation does not have to discover the wheel again.

Functions of Communication

Man is fortunate that oral communication serves three distinct functions in social relationships: utilitarian, aesthetic, and therapeutic.

Gerald Miller has observed that oral communication allows humans to understand, control, and alter their environments while at the same time it provides the most effective means of maximizing rewards and minimizing punishment from the environment.[2] How often do we say something for the effect we want to create in a listener? In all walks of life we praise and blame for results. Communication to fulfill needs in daily life is a *utilitarian* function.

Oral communication on television, the stage, or through oral reading is an artistic expression which will provide enjoyment, pleasure, or information. This communication fulfills an *aesthetic* function.

Diagnosis of a problem to "reduce tension" in a group is rehabilitative. People trying to find common ground through oral expression are fulfilling a *therapeutic* function. This would include a a panel discussion, as well as an encounter group.

DEFINITION

The most useful mode of communication is clearly oral communication. The findings of Nichols have been replicated and validated.[3] It is clear that normal discourse of the average American is divided as follows:

Listening	42%
Speaking	32%
Reading	15%
Writing	11%

It is little wonder that years of failing to study seriously and systematically the oral communication process has left man generally unable to communicate effectively.

We will define *communication* as the "process of creating a meaning." *Oral communication,* then, will be defined as the process of creating a meaning through speech. Oral communication has occurred when the oral stimuli, as it was initiated and intended by a sender, corresponds closely with the stimuli as it is perceived and responded to by the receiver.

The term *interpersonal* is used in this book to refer to oral communication in one broad type of setting where stimuli are exchanged. That setting has five distinct characteristics: (1) the stimuli occur in a face-to-face setting; (2) the stimuli are sent and received by all parties; (3) the stimuli are both verbal and nonverbal; (4) the face-to-face relationship occurs in close proximity; (5) there is considerable dialogue. Simply put, this means two or more people are standing or sitting in close proximity and facing each other. Each one speaks briefly and listens a great deal to others. The words and actions of each person speaking are noticed by the others. The only "audience" is the group of people in close proximity. Voices are likely to be conversational rather than loud.

This limitation of in*ter*personal communication suggests that in*tra*personal communication is not identical because intrapersonal communication is within the self. However, as we shall soon discover, the intrapersonal communication process is fundamental to interpersonal, as well as other forms of communication. Also excluded from the definition of interpersonal communication are the following situations: public address before a congregated audience; one person communicating to many via a form of media; and the actor on the stage. One may correctly argue that certain principles are fundamental throughout all the communication situations. That argument is not contradictory to the definition of *interpersonal* as given here. What we have, then, is a situational definition of interpersonal communication with arbitrary parameters for the sake of systematic study.

SUMMARY PROBES

1. **How do you define communication?**
2. **How do you define interpersonal?**
3. **How does man differ from other forms of animal life in terms of communication behavior?**

COMMUNICATION MODELS

In order to study the "process" aspect of communication we often refer to models. To create a frame of reference for discussion of communication barriers, we also refer to models. Communication models come from many different sources for different purposes. Philosophers want a graphic representation of an abstraction. Electrical engineers want a diagram of information exchange. Mathematicians want to quantify a symbolic process. We will review several significant models, each having at least one important feature to expand our understanding of the communication process. Then, we can synthesize our own representation model.

Aristotelian Model

The first and most basic model is the Aristotelian model. Aristotle in his *Rhetoric* established three elements basic to any communication act: speaker, message, listener. The relationship of the three parts was primarily a one-direction relationship as shown in Figure 1.1. The three parts of the Aristotelian model are basic to nearly all other communication models.

Figure 1.1 **Aristotelian Model of Communication**

Schramm Model

The Schramm model is more complex and particularly noteworthy for the notion of "field of experience."[4] Schramm's model is diagramed in Figure 1.2.

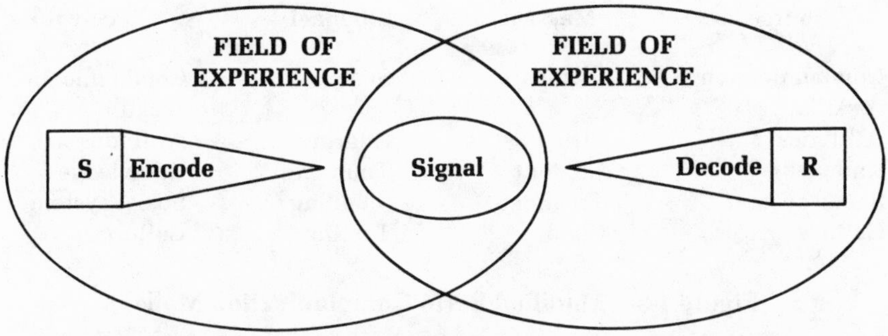

Figure 1.2 **Schramm's Communication Model**

The field of experience refers to things which occurred to you throughout your life to give meaning to symbols. It also includes those things about yourself of which you are aware at the time of communication. It is important to note that communication occurs, only, when the signal falls within the overlapping areas of the two fields of experience. Unless two individuals have shared similar experiences, they will not have shared meaning for symbols or signals. The source encodes a message using signals which have meaning to the receiver. The receiver decodes a message by taking meaning from his own field of experience.

It is virtually impossible for two humans not to have some area of overlapping experiences. Perhaps they are not aware of just how much they share in common. It is possible that two individuals may *believe* they have nothing in common. But, if they understand the notion of the field of experience, they will begin a search for the areas of overlap in their fields of experience in order to communicate. It is, also, virtually impossible for two humans to have identical fields of experience. Even identical twins have been treated differently at various points in their lives.

The source is the speaker's mind. The encoding process is that which occurs when the idea is translated into words. The signal is the actual message. The decoding process involves attaching meaning to language symbols. The destination is the listener or receiver's mind. The field of experience is the total make-up of past and present experiences and influences.

You can apply the model to an ordinary communication experience. If you say to a vendor at a baseball park, "I'll take two beers," you hope the fields of experience have been similar enough so that the vendor passes you a "real" beer rather than a root beer soda.

Source	Message	Channel	Receiver
Communication skills	Elements	Seeing	Communication skills
Attitudes	Structure	Hearing	Attitudes
Knowledge	Content	Touching	Knowledge
Social system	Treatment	Smelling	Social system
Culture	Code	Tasting	Culture

Figure 1.3 **Modified Berlo Communication Model**

Berlo Model

A third model which makes a contribution by an emphasis on the interdependence of variables is the Berlo model.[5] The Berlo model focuses on the nature of the sender and receiver interacting through the characteristics of the message and the channel. The Berlo model, represented in Figure 1.3, is organizational in nature.

Miller Model

Gerald Miller's model is noteworthy for its emphasis on the relationship of physical behavior and verbal behavior. Figure 1.4 is a diagrammed adaptation of the Miller model.[6]

Miller's own description is helpful to a full understanding of the model:

> It can be seen that the Source-Encoder constructs a message concerning some Referent. In order to avoid confusion, it should be pointed out that the term, 'Referent' is employed in a broader sense than is usual. Specifically, the Source-Encoder constructs a message that may 'refer to' a wide range of objects, acts, situations, ideas, or experiences. . . . The total message that is encoded consists of at least three principal factors: Verbal Stimuli, Physical Stimuli, and Vocal Stimuli. Although these are linked with the Source-Encoder by three separate arrows, the joining of these arrows with dotted lines indicates that all three dimensions of the message are encoded simultaneously, and that the message functions as a unit.
>
> The message is transmitted to a Receiver-Decoder, who responds in some way to its verbal, physical, and vocal elements. As indicated, the first motive of the Source-Encoder is to gain the Receiver's attention. Once his attention is focused on the message, the Receiver-Decoder supplies a set of meanings for it, and certain nonevaluative (Compre-

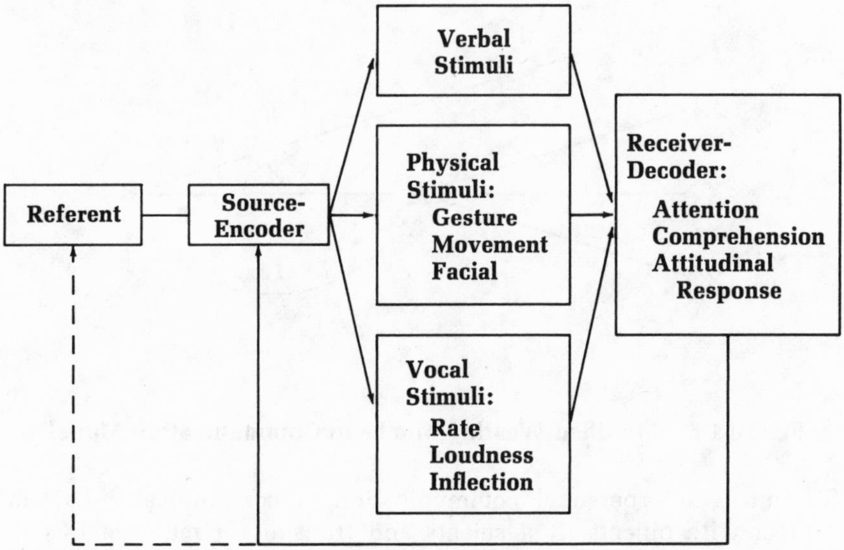

Figure 1.4 **Miller Communication Model**

hension) and evaluative (Attitudinal) responses occur. The extent to which these responses are consistent with the Source-Encoder's purpose is dependent upon the total meaning resulting from the particular combination of the three types of stimuli. The arrows extending from the Receiver-Decoder to the Source-Encoder and to the Referent incicate that the Receiver-Decoder may respond jointly to at least two categories of stimuli: those linking the Referent itself (primarily the verbal stimuli) and those associated with the individual who is encoding statements about the Referent (primarily the Physical and Vocal Stimuli). Obviously, the Receiver-Decoder's responses to both Source-Encoder and Referent will interact to determine the meaning he assigns to the situation.

Whereas it would be psychologically difficult to respond to the Referent without also responding to the Source-Encoder the converse does not necessarily hold, i.e. the Receiver-Decoder might focus his entire attention on the Physical and Vocal Stimuli encoded by the Source and largely ignore the Verbal Stimuli relating to the Referent.[7]

Westley-MacLean Model

The Westley and MacLean model, although quite complex, is important in its simplified form for an inclusion of the element of feedback.[8] A simplified form of the model is presented in Figure 1.5. The basic elements of the model are objects (X's) and people (A and

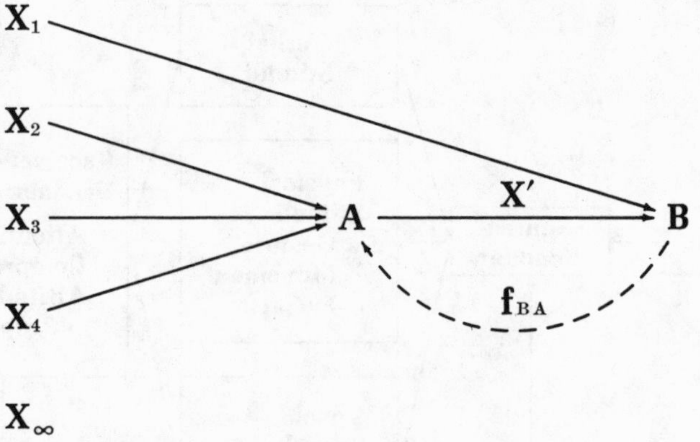

Figure 1.5 **Modified Westley-MacLean Communication Model**

B). During interpersonal communication, a communicator (A), in contact with objects (X's) selects and transmits a message (X') to communicator B. Person B may or may not have the same objects in the environment, but nonetheless, B transmits feedback (f_{BA}) to A. Conversation can provide an example: Person A: "Is my tie on straight?" Person B: "It looks straight but it isn't the right color."

It is now possible to begin extracting the important elements from these models into a synthesis which should give greater meaning to oral communication. A source in a field of experience emits a message with verbal and nonverbal stimuli in the presence of a receiver. The receiver decodes the stimuli arriving at meaning from his or her experiences. Immediately, the receiver begins to provide both verbal and nonverbal feedback. The feedback itself, then, becomes a message from a new sender. The original receiver has become the sender, and the original sender has become the receiver. Feedback, which became a message, had original meaning within a field of experience, and in turn took on meaning in the new field of experience. The circular or spiral effect continues as long as the individuals continue to operate within a shared field of experience. Then, the oral communication is transactional in nature.

We have gone from theoretical models to descriptions. Next, consider two examples. Imagine you are driving on a major highway moving generally with a small amount of traffic. Soon you hear the wail of a siren and observe through the rear-view mirror the flashing lights of a police car and an officer waving you off the road. After stopping, the officer walks over to your car. His first words are, "Let me see your driver's license." Let us interrupt the scene at this point and analyze the situation from a communication point of view. The way you perceive the officer *walking* is conditioned in part by your past experiences with the police. If your experience was positive, perhaps with "Officer Friendly" in school or through a close acquaintance who is a police officer, you will not feel threatened, and the officer's walk will not appear threatening to you. On the other hand, if you have been "busted" several times, the approaching officer's stride will seem threatening to you. How you feel, based on your past experience, will affect your decoding of the command, "Let me see your license."

The officer's perception of you will, also, be conditioned by his past experiences with motorists. If he has encountered friendly motorists, he expects cooperation and will be inclined to make a simple request, possibly even saying, "please." On the other hand, if he has been verbally and physically attacked by motorists, he is likely to make the command more forcefully. Clearly, how you give feedback at the point of initial communication will affect the future direction of the communication. The approach, the perception, the command, and the response are four points at which the communication outcome could be modified. By projecting further into the possible continuing interaction, it is easy to speculate that there would be many more points where the communication outcome could go wrong for either individual.

Let us consider a very different circumstance involving more of a trust-mistrust circumstance than a fear-unfearful circumstance. Imagine you are a grain dealer in a small community. You notice a wholesale representative drive up, get out, and walk into your store. He walks in and says, "Good morning, may I help you today?"

You respond, "Not today." Again, perception will be influenced by fields of experience—yours and the wholesale representative's. The message is shaped by your previous experience with the last wholesale representative and with your last experience with this representative. His "help," then, may be decoded by you to mean anything from "helpful" to "cunning." The representative's previous experience that day with other retailers and previous experience with you will affect how he decodes your response.

COMMUNICATION BREAKDOWN

Preceding examples in this chapter illustrate what might happen within the receiver of communication stimuli to pose barriers to communication. When the receiver's perception comes from a different field of experience than does the source's perception, the barrier is sufficient to cause a breakdown in communication. A communication breakdown is a failure of the human communication system. The breakdown results from overpowering barriers that inhibit factors in the communicative attempt. It is difficult to predict exactly when a barrier will become so strong that it will cross the breakdown threshold.

Throughout this book various communication barriers will be identified. Each one has the potential to cross the breakdown threshold. The number of barriers, and hence, breakdowns, is almost infinite. At this point, we will identify categories of communication barriers with illustrative examples of each category.

Many barriers and breakdowns affecting oral communication originate within the source. Using the Berlo concept of source as a category, we can consider the following as typical breakdowns: (1) failure of the source to select words whose common meanings correlate with the idea intended; (2) unusual organization of the subordinate parts to an idea; (3) sound production which is too soft; (4) failure to utilize feedback for corrective purposes.

Other barriers and breakdowns to effective oral communication originate within the receiver. Using the Berlo concept of receiver as the category, we can consider the following as typical breakdowns: (1) failure to listen; (2) jumping to conclusions after hearing only a part of a message; (3) hostility toward a source.

Additional barriers and breakdowns to effective oral communication originate outside both the source and the receiver. Typical breakdowns in the external category are: (1) distance between the source and the receiver; (2) interruptions from outside noises, commonly referred to as interference; (3) size of a group; (4) quantity of information in the communication channel.

Breakdowns as described above may occur at any point in the communication process. As sender and receiver you should be constantly aware of their presence and their potential destructive effect on communication between two human beings.

SUMMARY PROBES

1. **Why do we use communication models?**
2. **What is one unique feature of each of the following communication models:**
   a. **Schramm**
   b. **Berlo**
   c. **Westley-MacLean**
   d. **Miller**

3. In what way would the synthesized communication model be helpful in explaining each of the following communication situations:
  a. A major league umpire ejecting a manager from the game.
  b. United Nations Ambassador from the United States addressing the Security Council.
  c. Manager of a department store conducting an interview with a prospective employee.
  d. You presenting a formal speech to a class.

LEARNING EXPERIENCES

1. Prepare an analysis of your communication during one day from 8:00 a.m. until bedtime. Set up your worksheet on fifteen-minute intervals, with five columns as in Figure 1.6. Total the time spent for each activity. What percent of your time was spent on each? How do your percentages compare with those shown in this chapter?

2. Build your own visual model of communication behavior that you observe over a seven-day period. Make it in the form of a mobile or some other visible and tangible form that will help others understand your device. Bring the model to a class meeting and share it giving necessary explanation.

3. Make a list of communication breakdowns which you have experienced in each of the following areas: (a) the message; (b) reception of the message; (c) interpretation of feedback; (d) sending the message. How many of these could have been avoided?

	Speaking	Listening	Writing	Reading	Other
8:00 A.M.					
8:15					
8:30					
etc.					

Figure 1.6 **Communication Activity Log**

TWO

GOALS **After completing this chapter you will be able to:**

1. Exert better control over selection of things to which you will attend and listen.

2. Improve your ability to sort information you receive.

3. Understand the importance of controlling marginal stimuli which distort a message.

4. Form a more realistic picture of how your values and beliefs affect stimuli you receive.

5. Communicate to other people's fields of experience.

6. Recognize the relationship between intrapersonal communication and interpersonal commmunication.

7. Listen more effectively.

Intrapersonal Variables Affecting Oral Communication

Intrapersonal communication is the communication process which occurs within a person. The signals or cues may arise from many sources, but when they are received, there is a communication which is internal. There are several parts of the process about which a great deal is known, or at least accepted—self-concept, perception, listening, thought, and memory. This chapter will consider these five variables of intrapersonal communication. These variables affect how the individual communicates with the self; and, just as important, how they prepare to encode and decode communication with others. In the case of encoding and decoding, the intrapersonal communication process becomes interrelated with the interpersonal communication process.

Extrasensory means of communication, even if valid, would be communication between individuals or between entities unknown, rather than within the individual. There is so much sensationalism publicized about the extrasensory means of communication and so little scholarly study that any attempt at this time to suggest that instruction is possible would be foolish. Therefore, the extrasensory means of communication are excluded from this text.

In this chapter we will consider the relationship of five intrapersonal variables: self-concept, perception, listening, thought, and memory. These are processes which occur within the individual, but clearly affect all communication transactions.

SELF-CONCEPT

How we view ourselves will make a difference in the way we receive communication symbols and construct communication symbols to send. Research has suggested that there is a relationship between one's self-image as a communicator and his success as a communicator.[1] The extent to which one is willing to reveal information about himself may be positively correlated with amounts of interpersonal exchange.[2] It has further been observed that a positive relationship exists between attitude toward self-disclosure in interaction and complexity of construct usage in forming interpersonal impressions.[3] Stated simply, how we view ourselves will affect the outcome of communication intrapersonally and with others.

Self-Esteem

Self-esteem, a part of self-concept, is clearly related to our role as a receiver of communication. Individuals who have low self-esteem or confidence in themselves are easier to sway with persuasive appeals than those who are highly confident. The person with low self-esteem is quick to doubt himself and accept what others say. The high self-esteem person will have greater resistance to persuasion because such a person does not doubt his value system or his reasoning power.

Dogmatism

A second important aspect of the self is the degree of dogmatism. (Dogmatism refers to the degree of rigidity or flexibility in approaching people or ideas.) It is not just an idea or momentary feeling, but rather a relatively stable trait as a perspective for viewing many things. When one is dogmatic, he will hold a particular view regardless of any specific evidence. We commonly use the term *closed-minded* to refer to a highly dogmatic person. In contrast, the common term *open-minded* usually refers to the person who is not highly dogmatic. For further discussion of dogmatism see Rokeach[4] and Bettinghaus.[5]

Another dimension to dogmatism is to think in terms of latitudes of acceptance and rejection. A latitude of acceptance is the range of positions out of a possible scope of positions toward an issue that a person is willing to accept. For example, one white person might be willing to accept integrated armed services, integrated factories, integrated schools, integrated housing, but could not accept mixed marriages. Another white person might be able to accept only integrated armed services. As a second example, an individual might be able to accept women receiving equal pay with men and women in sports, but could not accept women in a private men's club. Another individual might be able to accept all of the above. Research by Sharif, Sharif, and Nebergall[6] has determined that an individual who has a narrow latitude of acceptance is a highly dogmatic individual.

The extent of one's dogmatic nature may be likely to have an effect on how the person communicates intrapersonally to decode messages. Research is not conclusive, but does suggest that a highly dogmatic receiver is difficult to persuade unless confronted with a source they consider believable, and low dogmatic receivers tend to listen to the substance of a message.

Is it good or bad to be dogmatic with a narrow latitude of acceptance? The answer has to be personal. Does one want to be a thinking individual or one subject to the direction of others without doing much thinking themselves? Philosophically, we might consider one a higher ideal than the other. If one wants peace with his environment as a higher priority than idealism, then another answer might be made.

Ego Involvement

A third aspect of the self which affects communication is ego involvement, or the strength of feeling on an issue. Research has suggested some relationships do exist between ego involvement and how people formulate positions on issues. If you are highly involved emotionally and personally with an issue, you are likely to have a wide latitude of rejection. The effect is that when you hear a persuasive message which deals with a topic in which you are involved, you will be likely to reject the position of the message.[7]

When we become highly involved, we may find ourselves trying to decode messages and encode other messages when our feelings are inconsistent with one another, or when feelings are inconsistent with facts. Then we can easily make a decision that is cognitively inconsistent. The cognitive consistency theory is dependent on an assumption that we strive to maintain internal consistency among our personal beliefs, feelings, and actions.[8] This assumption seems to be the psychological counterpart of the physiological theory of homeostasis controlling body functions. Several individuals have developed theories from the cognitive consistency concept. We will consider three special theories: balance, symmetry, and dissonance. Each has added some useful information to help increase our understanding of how we communicate intrapersonally.

Balance. Fritz Heider developed a balance theory which sought to explain the pattern of attraction.[9] The theory, when placed in model form, depicts a series of relationships between a person, P, and another person, O, and an object, X. The relationship is pictured in Figure 2.1. Heider theorized that if person P likes person O and

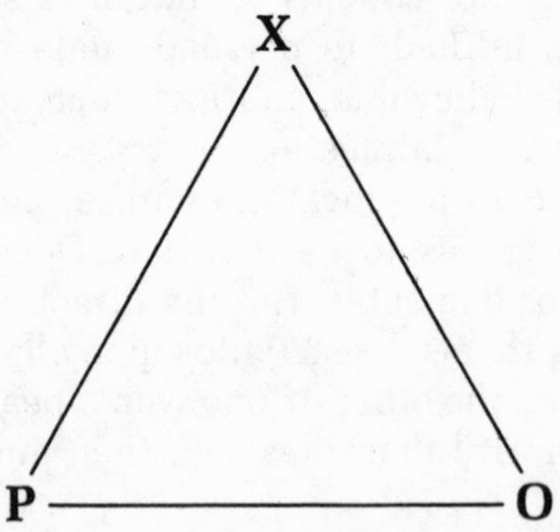

Figure 2.1 **Person-Object Relationship**

person O likes X, person P will tend to like object X also. If P and O both dislike X, there is still a balance between their feelings. However, if P and O do not have the same feeling toward X, the object, there will be inbalance. There will also be inbalance if P dislikes O and they have the same feelings toward the object X.[10]

Symmetry. Newcomb developed a related theory called *symmetry* to explain the attitudes of individuals to each other in relation to an object.[11] According to the symmetry theory, two individuals will "strain" to develop similar attitudes when they communicate about an issue. The two individuals, if they have any attraction toward each other, will be likely to communicate about an issue and their positions will become more identical or balanced toward the issue.

An application of symmetry would be an explanation of how you and a friend might change your positions slightly on some candidate for political office. You would be inclined to discuss the candidate and slowly bring your respective positions of like or dislike toward the candidate closer together. Each of you will intrapersonally process your feelings toward the issue heavily influenced by your feelings toward the other person. In your intrapersonal processing, you will seek to maintain balance.

Dissonance. When two elements are in direct opposition, an inbalance in feeling will exist. The inbalance is called dissonance. Dissonance theory states that the person feeling dissonance will consciously seek to remove the dissonance by modifying one element or the other to create balance.[12] For example, you like rich foods, but gaining weight is not healthy. The dissonance resulting will cause one to modify feeling toward one element or the other. At the time of the Watergate revelations, many Republicans suffered severe dissonance. Their feelings toward the President were not in balance with the evidence. President Nixon's decision to resign resolved many severe dissonant feelings toward the impeachment proceedings.

There are several underlying notions of dissonance theory which help explain how we process data, relate it to our emotions, and arrive at feelings on issues or people. Four of them are:

1. The existence of dissonance creates tension and we will be motivated to reduce that tension.
2. When dissonance exists, we try to reduce it, and we avoid situations which would increase the dissonance.
3. The greater the dissonance, the greater the effort to reduce the inbalance.
4. The amount of dissonance depends upon the importance of the elements and the relationship between the elements.

The three theories—balance, symmetry, dissonance—should help you understand how you are ego involved in the messages sent as a source and in the messages decoded as a receiver. Consider the following questions:

1. What can you do as a communication source to guide receivers to select the response you seek to your communication symbols?
2. How can you as a receiver give response to communication symbols which will accurately reflect your ego involvement without seeming overly egotistical?

What we consider to be ourselves is a product of our environment. Feedback is the vehicle of exchanging views of the self. To improve exchange of information about self, we must be willing to make some disclosure of the self. To disclose oneself is to reveal something of the "private" self. Speech is a means of providing self-affirmation since others constantly observe our communication behavior and try to sift out information and clues by which they can shape and confirm their image of us. What we are is a part of our intrapersonal communication system, as well as our interpersonal communication system.

Since self-disclosure is a factor in our communication, nondisclosure may also be an important factor. Sometimes an individual will consciously seek to conceal the self. In fact, most of us probably have large fears about revealing too much about our inner selves. When that is the case, we speak for the purpose of concealment. We do not want others to know the role we are playing, our motivations, or our values.

SUMMARY PROBES

1. **In what way does ego involvement affect decision-making?**
2. **What is dogmatism?**
3. **How is dogmatism related to the self-concept?**
4. **How does dogmatism affect the field of experience of two communicators?**
5. **What is the relationship(s) between three forms of consistency theory—balance, symmetry, and dissonance?**
6. **What aspect of self-concept do you associate with each of the following: Heider; Newcomb?**
7. **How is self-concept related to your role as a communication receiver and as a communication source?**

PERCEPTION

Self-concept and perception are so closely related, it is difficult to treat them separately. Arbitrarily, we may point out that self-concept refers to the "what we are" that causes us to hold certain views; whereas perception refers to the "fact of holding unique views" toward stimuli in the environment. Self-concept may be causative while perception is effect.

There are many ways by which we perceive. The five senses provide input into the brain for processing. However, not all input is used: the brain selects information by extracting certain stimuli and ignoring other stimuli. Perception, then, is in part achieved by selectivity and attention, both intentional and unintentional. How we select the stimuli and retain information is partly due to our concept of ourselves and our concept of the other person.

Selectivity

Walking down Michigan Avenue in Chicago on a Saturday afternoon one will be confronted with thousands of stimuli—cars passing, people walking, buildings, traffic policemen, boats on Lake Michigan, a speaker on a soap box in Grant Park. Most of the sources of the stimuli are moving or changing. At any given moment it is impossible for the brain to process all of the stimuli. Instead, certain stimuli are selected.

Why we select can be an interesting investigation. Much of the selectivity is a product of the field of experience identified in the Schramm communication model. The ability of a farmer to determine whether a particular morning is a good day for cutting hay is not comprehensible to a city dweller. However, the farmer can receive the same stimuli of dryness in the air and bright sunshine and process that into a judgment based on selective perception.

The selectivity from the stimuli seems to be due to complexity, intensity, and redundancy. Up to a certain point, the more complex a set of stimuli, the more attraction it has. Power and force of stimuli attract. Repetition tends to make selection of stimuli unavoidable.

Attention

Selection is clearly influenced by attention to stimuli. Attention is the process of selecting and then focusing on the selected stimuli. What makes us focus our attention to certain stimuli and not to others? The conditions responsible for focusing are what Bryant and Wallace called the Laws of Attention.[13]

The first condition is intensity. Among competing stimuli, the stronger, the more intense stimulus will be preferred to the weaker. An intense light holds attention more than a dull light. Language which evokes images will be preferred to bland language. A "festering sore" will hold attention more with a receiver than an "abscess."

The second condition is size. Among competing stimuli which vary in size, the larger is preferred to the smaller. In communication the term *size* may mean physical space or length of time. A full gesture commands more attention than a small twitch of the wrist. Adequate development of an idea commands greater attention than a single word or phrase which is meant to represent a whole train of thought.

The third condition is change. Among competing stimuli, the moving one is preferred to the one at rest. It is easy for us to recognize that a voice with fluctuation in rate, pitch, and volume commands more attention than a monotone. A body in motion will command attention; thus, movement and gesture are a powerful stimulation from a speaker.

The fourth condition is pattern and organization. Among two or more collections of stimuli, the group which is organized will be preferred over the group which is disorganized. The individual items must be cognitively related to one another, or in a logical order. In other words, a large group of related stimuli focus attention, whereas a large group of unrelated stimuli distract or go unnoticed.

The fifth condition is familiarity between two stimuli, one familiar and the other strange; the familiar one will be preferred. When looking at two pictures of a house, the one most similar to your house will most likely capture your attention, all other things being equal. Certainly what is familiar will vary greatly from culture to culture. It is this condition which makes it possible to transfer information which becomes familiar. Then, the speaker can again move from the familiar to the unfamiliar. The process may continue as long as a source and receiver don't become tired.

To understand how perception affects communication, we must consider three aspects of the person perception variable. First, we should consider the principal determinants of our experiences of another person's emotional states and personality. Second, we must consider the way in which an impression of another person is formed. Third, we must consider the processes for attributing lasting perceptions to other people.

Our ideas about another person vary considerably according to whether they come from overt characteristics of the person or from inferences on our part about the person. Historically, we have tended to view person perception as a perception of emotions of another or as a perception of a personality.

Some research has suggested that accurate information for person perception is available through the means of facial expression, paralinguistic cues, eye contact, words, and context of words. Facial expression and eye contact seem to have some universality across cultures.

After considerable research and speculation, it is generally agreed that neither method gives a very accurate means of person perception. It seems more useful to search for the underlying process of what is happening when one person forms an impression of another.

The second concern is how we form an impression of another person. That is determined more by how cues are added together than by listing cues. Here, the relationship to perception of self—ego, wants, needs—contributes to selectivity. We tend to select that which will be useful; thus, selection is utilitarian. Existing attitude sets toward issues will affect perception of people if they are not already known.

The third concern is determining the processes for attributing lasting perceptions to other people. This concern has led to a search for patterns in which stable stereotypes interact in predictable fashion. Miller has observed that the dialect of a person affects stereotyping.[14] Recent research by Delia and others has identified complexity of the individual as a factor in the formation of evaluative integrated impressions.[15] In another research investigation, Wheeless observed that exposure to information affected stability of the perception.[16]

SUMMARY PROBES

1. **How do we form perceptions of other people?**
2. **How does perception affect opinion formation?**
3. **What are five conditions which affect attention?**
4. **How is selective perception related to the field of experience in intrapersonal communication?**

LISTENING

As self-concept was interrelated with perception in the intrapersonal communication process, so perception is also interrelated with listening. Listening is active. Listening is complex. Listening involves auditory and visual activity by a receiver. Listening is the part of the oral communication process we do most of the time. We listen to many kinds of stimuli. Our interest here is limited to listening to oral communication.

We may define listening as a subprocess of the communication procedure involving hearing, understanding, and remembering. One of the most common communication problems is to equate hearing and listening. We might hear someone make a request, but the stimuli may not be able to compete with Howard Cosell's description of a great touchdown on a football telecast. If we do not "attend" to the request, we cannot understand and certainly cannot remember. Therefore, we would be guilty of not listening. The process is intrapersonal, within oneself. The stimuli are external, and thereby link listening to interpersonal communication.

In order to be an effective listener, you should first realize that there is purpose to your listening behavior. You are probably trying to do one or more of the following: (1) listen for information; (2) listen for enjoyment; (3) listen to evaluate critically.

Listening for Information

When a definite answer to a specific question is sought, we are listening for information. This is a significant part of learning. However, we must be careful not to allow our feeling or motives to misprocess the stimuli received in response to a question. An overeager salesman may ask if you want to buy the car you are looking at. You answer, "yes," and he may write out a sales contract. No doubt you will be more embarrassed than the salesman when you reveal you can't afford the car.

Listening for Enjoyment

Aesthetic listening is a way of enlarging our personal enjoyment of life. As adults we have learned the personally rewarding value of listening to music, listening to stories on stage, listening to social conversation. This is purposeful humanistic listening which is very important to our personal cultural existence.

Listening to Evaluate Critically

The most intellectual form of listening is making critical evaluation. Reasoning is a required part of this type of listening. The rational function of the brain must operate at a high level of complexity.

Critical evaluation must not be confused with the common notion of being negative. When you listen critically, you are attempting to discern whether a speaker distorts information for his own purpose. Essentially, that means comparing what is heard with some criteria for judgment.

When someone speaks to persuade, you must make a critical evaluation of the support material presented by that person. Speakers often present examples. For reasons of economy, they will present one or two examples and suggest or imply a generalization. Indeed, the example may illustrate some concept. It is your task as listener to question whether the example was appropriate to the point claimed, and second, whether the one example was used in place of an argument.

Statistics are often presented and usually considered highly respectable as support material. We are impressed by numbers. However, you must be cautious of statistics. It is easy to succumb to card stacking—slanting of facts to prove a point. In discussing the effect of a metropolitan police task force to combat crime, a speaker may provide statistics which demonstrate that murders in St. Louis, Chicago, Detroit, and Philadelphia have declined. Yet, what about statistics not cited? What of the statistics of murder in the fast-growing suburban regions around each of these cities? What of the statistics for other crimes against people—assault, rape, and attempted murder?

Another danger posed by statistics is the bandwagon effect—the unstated argument implied with statistics that "everybody's doing it." A speaker might provide data which states that 60 percent of all automobile drivers ignore seat belts, and then make the claim that seat belts should not be included as standard equipment in automobiles. Critical listening would cause one to consider whether the actions of masses of people was the essential factor in making a judgment about including seat belts as standard equipment.

Quotations are frequently given as support by speakers. The ideas of feelings of a highly credible source make a claim become more believable. Testimony is given in court to establish the character of a defendant. Sometimes nonverbal behavior is added to make a "plain folks" propaganda appeal. A gubernatorial candidate recently walked the entire 400-mile length of a state asking for votes, as he walked through every little town and hamlet. It worked.

The critical listener must ask if testimony is from a source knowledgeable about the subject for which testimony is given. Furthermore, the critical listener must ask if the qualified source giving testimony is honest and not giving known false information.

Comparison is often used as support by speakers. The comparison is an examination of the similarities between two different things. Sometimes the opposite, contrast, is used. The validity of comparison and contrast depend upon accuracy of the examination and selection of meaningful characteristics to compare or contrast. A critical listener would also want to question whether the inference suggested from the comparison does, in fact, follow from the facts compared.

In order to improve intrapersonal communication, you will want to strive consciously to become a listener for information, a listener for pleasure, and a critical listener. You will certainly agree, now, that listening is far more than hearing, that listening is active, that listening is necessary.

Improving Your Listening

Most people must consciously cultivate good listening habits if they expect to be successful at any of the three types of listening. This section will review some guidelines which have been found helpful to many people in improving their listening process. They may be helpful to you.

Prepare to Listen. Determine what your expectations are for listening. Are you listening for pleasure, information, or to be critical? Create a mental mood for the type of listening. Do everything possible to remove distractions in the physical environment. Sit where you can hear and where you will not be bothered by distractions. Don't be uncomfortable, but don't be too comfortable.

Control the Emotions. It is easy to become irate at the words and ideas of a speaker. A conscious effort should be made to withhold evaluation until comprehension is complete. Effective listeners maintain an open mind. Think about the words or phrases which are most upsetting to you and make an effort to remain calm when you hear those words. If you can do that, you will "desensitize" yourself.

Listen for Ideas and Patterns of Reasoning. Good listeners focus on ideas. They search for reasoning and support. They strive to find relationships. The poor listener just listens for facts.

Listen to Difficult Material. Recognize that listening to certain kinds of material which is difficult will be necessary. Make a conscious effort to listen to lectures on public issues, panel discussions, public speeches.

Avoid Being Critical of Delivery. There is a time and place to make judgments about someone's delivery of a message but don't allow that to occur at the same time you are trying to find meaning in the message. It is true that the source of a message has a responsibility to make the presentation of the message as clear as possible, but you have a responsibility to listen for meaning, ignoring any distractive elements of delivery.

Use Spare Time Wisely. The difference between speaking time and comprehension time is considerable. Use that time to relate information to previous concepts presented by the speaker. It is suggested that you use the spare time to: (1) anticipate what the speaker is likely to say; (2) note the adequacy of support for each point; (3) mentally review each point presented; (4) listen for subtle nuances in a message—"hidden meanings."

SUMMARY PROBES

1. **What is critical listening?**
2. **How should you as a listener treat statistics and testimony presented by a speaker?**
3. **In what way is listening active?**
4. **What can you do to improve your listening?**

THOUGHT

The thought process is the way we relate data, perceived through listening and seeing, in order to arrive at judgments and conclusions. No matter what the subject may be, there are essentially two avenues of thought open for arriving at a decision. One method we call rational, and the other we call irrational.

Rational Thought

A rational decision is a product of thought which has gone through a logical sequence. We call this reasoning. John Dewey,[17] in

How We Think, presented an analysis of how we reason. The analysis is just as valid today as it was in 1910. First, there is awareness of some difficulty or unsatisfactory condition which needs to be changed. Second, a criteria is established for measuring possible ways to satisfy the need. Third, an analysis is made of the cause of the difficulty. Fourth, there is a survey of possible ways of satisfying the need and thereby eliminating the condition. Fifth, there is a review of the ways to satisfy the need leading to a solution or a "best method." Sixth, a plan is made to act upon the choice.

As an example, you might process as follows: (1) you are warm; (2) you decide the temperature is going to remain high; (3) you decide to rank criteria such that physical comfort takes higher priority on this day than making money; (4) you consider putting in overtime working at some task in an air-conditioned building, sitting on a cake of ice, or taking a swim; (5) taking a swim seems the most relaxing; (6) you proceed to plan where to swim and do just that. This is a rational decision. The mind may go through the stages so rapidly that it may not even be conscious of the act in each stage.

Deductive Reasoning. When we reason deductively, our mind rigidly follows the laws of formal logic. We begin with a generalization and then proceed to a specific conclusion. If we could freeze our steps when we reason deductively, they might appear like the following example:

Major premise: Statistics show that passengers with seat belts fastened in auto accidents are less likely to be killed.
Minor premise: Our seat belts are fastened.
Conclusion: We are less likely to be killed if we are in an auto accident.

The conclusion of one deductive chain may become a part of the major or minor premise of a subsequent chain of reasoning as the following example illustrates:

Major premise: Insurance rates will decrease if there is less casualty risk involved in an accident.
Minor premise: We present a smaller casualty risk because our seat belts are fastened.
Conclusion: Our insurance premium should decrease.

When we reason deductively, it is important that both the premises be true. Perhaps, the most common error made when using this form of thought is mistakenly to assume validity of the major premise. Sometimes we make the error of drawing a conclusion which is not composed of one part from the minor premise and one part from the major premise. The first kind of error, the most common kind, is illustrated in the following example:

Major premise: All athletes use drugs.
Minor premise: He is an athlete.
Conclusion: He uses drugs.

Whenever you hear any statement including the word "all," you should proceed with extreme caution. Premises in a chain of reasoning which contain the totality of "all" are usually highly suspect.

Inductive Reasoning. The second form of rational thinking is inductive reasoning. It is the reverse of deductive reasoning. One begins with specifics and progresses to a generalization or from several generalizations to a higher order generalization which unifies all the other generalizations.

Generalizations are drawn from several specific instances. If an instructor didn't give any A's during any of the last four terms, one will possibly conclude that the instructor is not likely to give an A this term. Again, if automobile accidents have increased sharply on the day after a snow storm in December, and twice on similar occasions in January, you would probably generalize that if there is a snowfall in February, accidents will increase sharply the following day.

You must be careful that inaccurate generalizations are not made when processing information with this inductive form of reasoning. Do you have enough specific instances upon which to base the probability? One or two specific instances will not be sufficient. With just one or two specific instances the conclusion will be just a guess rather than a reasoned generalization. Are the conditions similiar to those under which the specific instances occurred? If they are not basically similar, then again, the conclusion would be a guess rather than a reasoned generalization.

Causes and effects are related inductively. You might be reasoning from cause to effect or from effect to cause. You will attempt to draw a conclusion which answers one of two questions: why or what? Why has a certain thing happened? What is the cause? If we do a certain thing, what will the effect be? Again, you will be trying to make projections into the future based on the specific cause and effect relationships of the past.

You must be careful when processing information with a cause-effect reasoning process. Are there possible causes that are omitted or ignored? Are the apparent causes strong enough to produce the alleged effects? Are there exceptions to the observed cause-effect or effect-cause relationships? Are there other possible causes? Such faulty reasoning has resulted in the following common stereotypes:

1. Electing a Democratic president will lead to a war.
2. Electing a Republican president will lead to a depression.
3. Walking under a ladder is bad luck.
4. An apple a day will keep the doctor away.

As a receiver of communication you will want to apply the tests of reasoning to the messages you receive. You will communicate intrapersonally—with yourself—to examine the validity of the deductive or inductive conclusions presented to you. You will make judgments about the credibility of the source of the message, based upon your analysis of the reasoning process you employ internally.

As a source of communication, you will probably choose to use either the deductive or inductive reasoning process to be persuasive. In doing so, you will make some assumptions about how your receiver will process the information intrapersonally when it is decoded. As a persuasive source, you will need to employ a shortened form of the process for the sake of time. The shortened form presented must be derived from a full and complete process which is accurate. Further discussion and additional examples of deductive and other forms of reasoning are included in Chapter Twelve.

SUMMARY PROBES

1. **What is the distinction between inductive and deductive reasoning?**
2. **In what way is reasoning an intrapersonal communication process?**
3. **What are the tests of deductive reasoning?**
4. **What are the tests of inductive reasoning?**

Irrational Thought

Irrational thought is a process which is *not* reasoning; therefore, it is correct to use the term *unreasonable*. Unfortunately, we have ascribed rather strong negative connotations to the term *unreasonable*. Irrational thought is a valid means of thinking and, thus, a valid means of communicating intrapersonally. Unfortunately, we know very little scientifically about how these processes work. In fact, some scientists are still unconvinced that the irrational thought processes are processes at all. Whether they are processes or not is questionable, but that they exist as ways of knowing can hardly be questioned. Included in irrational thought are transcendental thinking and intuition.

Transcendental thought is not a new concept. In this country, the fundamental belief in transcendental thought as a way of knowing truth was articulated over one hundred years ago by Ralph Waldo Emerson and Henry David Thoreau. It is a belief that the five senses are not sufficient for gathering and perceiving data, but that there is a stage of knowing which enables one to transcend to an ultimate truth. As professed by Emerson, it does not deny that the senses are part of the knowing process, but it departs from reasoning by the way the data is ultimately treated.

Intuition as a means of knowing does not require the gathering of data through the senses. It does not require the conscious mind to relate one fact to another. Intuition is to know without process.

Until more can be known about the consistency, accuracy, and predictive validity of the irrational means of thought, the rational processes of thinking must be accepted and advocated as superior means of decision-making for individuals and for collections of individuals in society. Therefore, this book will continue to describe communication, interpersonally, in small groups, in large groups, and to masses as it has for intrapersonal communication—from the assumption of the superiority of rational thought.

MEMORY

Memory is essential to communicating intrapersonally. We cannot make rational decisions about the now and the future without reference to the past. As a receiver of communication, we cannot perceive in a meaningful way or engage in inductive or deductive reasoning without reference to experiences of the past. Memory is the making of an impression, its retention, and its subsequent recall and recognition.

From the time Aristotle identified memory as a classical canon for communication to the present-day efforts to study information processing, the value of man's memory has been recognized. Some facts are known: the brain is composed of billions of nerve cells which appear either to emit or not to emit impulses; the brain works with the central nervous system to receive electrical impulses; the impulses reaching the brain may or may not make an impression upon a brain cell; the impression, if made, may or may not be stored. If the impression is stored, it may or may not be subject to later recall. There are many if's in the exact process. You probably know from your own experience that some people recall more than others. The maximum limit to recall isn't known. Gerard has given the following illustration:

> I have been told of a bricklayer who under hypnosis described correctly every bump and grain on the surface of a brick he had laid in a wall 20 years before. Guesses have been made as to how many items might be accumulated in memory over a lifetime. Some tests of perception suggest that each tenth of a second is a single frame of experience for the human brain. In that tenth of a second it can receive perhaps ten thousand units of information, called bits. In 70 years, not allowing for any reception during sleep, some 15 trillion bits might pour into the brain and perhaps be stored there.[18]

At least three factors operate as variables in what any individual is able to recall. Time is clearly one of the most important variables.[19] We all know how rapidly we forget information. For example, after hearing a speaker, we remember less of the message two weeks later than we did two hours after the communication was received. Some studies indicate that after only 20 minutes we will recall only 60 percent of a verbal message. After one day, we may do well to be able to recall one-third of the oral message. It also seems that the time point in our life may affect recall. Experiences during youth are more vividly fixed than experiences during later years.

A second factor is the intense vividness at the time the message is received. Thus, a four-year-old child's experience of being burned by grease from a hot stove may be one of the few things recalled from the first four years of life because the physical image is vivid. Likewise, the damnation message of a revivalist preacher may be the only verbal experience recalled because the message was so intense.

A third factor affecting the recall is the inhibitory function of the brain. There are many physical and psychological reasons why the brain may block the recall of information.

Implications for Receivers of Communication

Even though the potential for recall seems unlimited, the normal recall of most humans is quite restricted. It is not likely that you will be able to recall more than five or six items from any given event. What is recalled is a matter of focus and organization at the time of perception. Thus, the suggestions for effective listening are designed to help the receiver of an oral message focus and organize the oral stimuli being presented.

The implication for the source in communication is clear. He should be aware that organizing the message will help the receiver. The message should be planned so that there are no more than five or six main points throughout.[20] That does not mean omitting material, but it does mean regrouping some material into subgroups of larger ideas. If this is done, the source will increase the likelihood that the message will be recalled by the receiver twenty minutes after hearing the message. Likewise, anything you as the source can do to relate the ideas you are trying to communicate to feelings, emotions, beliefs, and values of the receiver through vividness or intensity will increase the likelihood that the ideas will be recalled twenty minutes after hearing the message.

SUMMARY PROBES

1. **What steps would you take to prepare yourself as a receiver of a message from a speaker?**
2. **How are listening and perception related to thought?**
3. **What is the relationship of ego to your intrapersonal communication when you consider the question of purchasing a new car?**
4. **How will you as a source use the concept of field of experience to process the message you intend to send?**
5. **How will you as a receiver use the concept of field of experience to process the message you receive?**
6. **How is your intrapersonal communication process important to communication with others—i.e., in-**

terpersonal communication, small group communication, communication to a large group, communication to a mass audience?

7. **What are dissonant feelings?**
8. **How do you resolve dissonant feelings?**

LEARNING EXPERIENCES

1. Arrange for someone to give you a signal to begin a three-minute time period and another signal to end the three-minute time period. At the first signal, stop, look, and listen. Make a list of all the stimuli that are competing for your attention. Compare your list with the lists of several other people doing the same exercise. How many differences do you find?

2. With one other class member, take a walk around campus or down a city street. As you walk, allow your senses to be alert to what is happening. Be aware of the physical sensations you come in contact with. As you experience these sensations, think about your past experiences with them. Compare your past experiences with those of the other person and consider how your perceptions now differ.

3. Think of a person who impressed you one way at first, but impressed you differently later. What was responsible for the change in perception? Did the person actually change? Was it just your perception that changed? Which is more accurate?

4. Set up a class discussion on a controversial topic. The discussion should be unstructured, except that before each participant speaks he must summarize what has been said by the previous speaker. If the summary is thought to be correct, the process continues. If the summary is thought to be incorrect, the others are free to interrupt and clarify the misunderstanding.

5. Set up a class discussion on a controversial topic. One member makes a declaratory statement. The responding member acknowledges the message in the following way, "You feel . . . about . . . ?" The sender simply answers "yes" or "no." Then the respondent may declare something which is to be acknowledged by the first sender. This process continues until the group has complete understanding of one another's point of view.

6. In a group of three or four, describe in detail two or three roles you play during any given day. Explain how you think you are projecting an image of person communication in each role. Use the following variables and situations:

Variables	Situations
1. Language	1. at home
2. Appearance	2. with parents
3. Attitude	3. on the job
	4. with a teacher

THREE

GOALS **After completing this chapter you will be able to:**

1. **Recognize nonverbal acts as symbols.**
2. **State the relationships between verbal and nonverbal symbols.**
3. **Describe the effect of certain nonverbal symbols in communication situations.**
4. **Increase your awareness of the forms by which you can communicate nonverbally.**
5. **Communicate more efficiently through refinement of the nonverbal symbols you send.**
6. **Understand the role of inconsistency between verbal and nonverbal symbols.**
7. **Function more efficiently as a receiver of nonverbal symbols in interpersonal settings.**
8. **Recognize the cultural variables which affect nonverbal communication.**
9. **Formulate judgments about the rhetorical aspects of nonverbal communication in terms of:**
    a. **the limits of propriety.**
    b. **ethics of manipulation.**

Nonverbal Variables

Somewhere in the forgotten past, Homo sapiens struggled with crude forms of speech. During the eons, the crude form evolved into the sophisticated verbal language which we all came to know during our early childhood. Long before the days of language, Homo sapiens probably communicated through a series of gestures, movements, and actions. Ritualistic dance may very well have been the earliest art form by which humans communicated beliefs and feelings among themselves and with their deity. Even though oral language has evolved with Homo sapiens to a high level of sophistication, the use of nonverbal symbols has not diminished. But the function of the nonverbal communication has changed. This chapter will consider the functions of nonverbal communication, the forms of nonverbal communication, and suggestions for improving your efficiency and effectiveness as a sender and receiver of nonverbal communication.

DEFINITION AND SIGNIFICANCE

Nonverbal communication is usually defined as any form of communication which is not specifically verbal as expressed in words. The definition includes several obvious classes of symbols in the form of stimuli given such as body movement and vocal variation. The definition also includes several less obvious symbols in the form of arrangement of stimuli, such as time, space, and color.

There are some forms of stimuli which are within the definition of nonverbal, but over which man can have very little control, such as the weather and the rising of the sun. Stimuli over which man has little control will be considered in this text because they are important and may have an influence on the other forms of nonverbal stimuli as well as upon those which are verbal.

The psychologist, Albert Mehrabian,[1] has posited a formula purported to represent how much impact each communication component has on receivers: total impact = 0.07 verbal + 0.38 vocal + 0.55 facial. You may doubt the wisdom of drawing conclusions from the social scientists' efforts to intrude upon an art form with calculator and tape measure. Regardless of whether or not the formula is accurate, you can easily recognize that nonverbal symbols have a great impact on human communication through empirical observation around you. Did you ever notice in a high school classroom that students had various ways of raising their hands? Sometimes the hand would shoot up rapidly. A person responding that way was usually eager or certain of an answer, or both. Sometimes the hand would go up haltingly, suggesting uncertainty. Did you ever notice how some people would make the teacher think the hand had been raised a long time by supporting the elbow and letting the hand droop at the wrist?

If you were to ask a personnel manager of some company what was the most revealing part of an interview, the personnel manager would probably reply, "the handshake."

If you have ever watched people walk into a department store where you worked, you may have become aware of their communication before a single word was uttered. By the way they dressed, walked, handled the merchandise, and by several other kinds of nonverbal symbols you processed the communication and made inferences about their intent and purpose. You might have judged them a likely customer, a looker, or perhaps a potential shoplifter.

During a poker game, you may have observed closely the actions of other players. How rapidly they arranged their cards may have revealed an urgency to play. A player who has just discovered the fourth ace in a five-card hand finds it hard to conceal a twinkle in the eye. Deliberate caution in placing a bet may have caused you to assume that the person was faking when he later proceeded with a large bet.

Which facial expressions communicate joy? surprise? anger? sadness? Would you agree facial expressions can communicate across cultures?

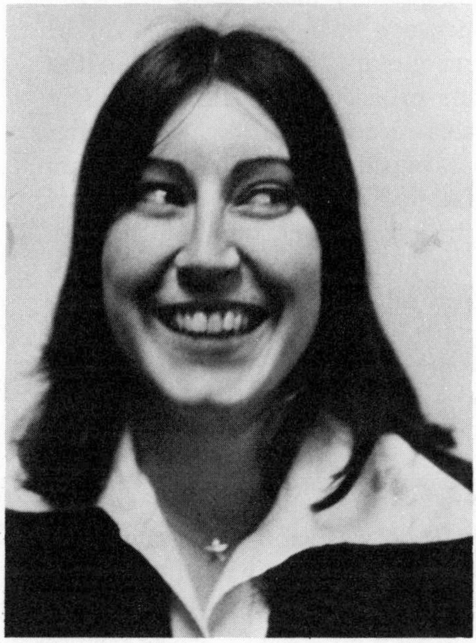
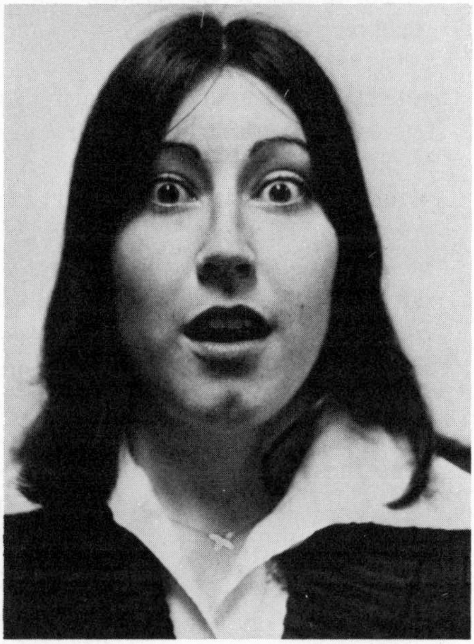

FUNCTIONS

Ever since Birdwhistell began to study nonverbal communication, there has been a growing interest in the subject. From scientific studies like those of Birdwhistell[2] and Mehrabian,[3] to books written for popular circulation like those of McGough[4] and Fast,[5] the interest seems to be in trying to understand nonverbal communication and to improve people's ability to function as senders and receivers of the nonverbal stimuli. Just what are the functions of nonverbal communication? There are at least three important categories of functions: (1) support for verbal communication through consistency; (2) replacement of verbal communication; (3) contradiction of verbal communication through inconsistency.

Support for Verbal Communication

When nonverbal symbols support verbal symbols, the message is amplified. The stronger message is more likely to catch the attention of the receiver. The consistency of the two stimuli will convey a clarity of meaning. In the absence of consistency, the receiver is likely to be puzzled. For example, if you are wrinkling your brow and using words about how much you enjoy the dinner, the host will be confused by the contradictory symbols. Almost invariably, the receiver will believe the visual message rather than the verbal message. The old adage, "seeing is believing," is testimony to the general value system operating in the processing of stimuli. This is true because one of the characteristics of nonverbal communication is that the message is perceived as being highly credible. The same principle applies to a speaker observed denouncing government spending with words but speaking in a monotone without gestures or movement of any kind: The visual image is not consistent with what we expect from a highly concerned individual. Therefore, receivers would be likely to pay very little attention to the words. If the speaker had demonstrated the depth of feeling by hand gestures, by pauses, and by rate change for emphasis and clarity, then the receiver would have been more inclined to believe and possibly even heed the source.

The late Senator Everett Dirksen was, perhaps, the best example in the twentieth century of consistency between the verbal and nonverbal codes for communicating a depth of feeling or belief. Receivers in the Senate, through the mass media, or in face-to-face communication had little difficulty knowing what Senator Dirksen's position or depth of feeling was on any issue from nuclear testing to marigolds.

Replacement of Verbal Symbols

Sometimes silence "speaks louder than words." Edward T. Hall has written a strong argument for the influences of time and space in what he called *The Silent Language.*[6] He described how the speed implementing nondiscriminatory labor practice guidelines was a message revealing the attitude of certain municipal government agencies. That description is a clear indication of the role time plays in the nonverbal process. Hall also pointed out that what occurs in the organization and use of space provides important leads as to the specific cues responsible for cultural shock. Condon has suggested that nonverbal symbols work across cultures.[7]

Sign language is a well-known means by which nonverbal communication replaces verbal communication. The sign may be an object arranged by someone—a flag, a picture, a highway marker with two lines crossing inside a circle, a black power raised arm and fist. The sign may be gestures used alone to replace words; such as the sign language of the deaf or the sign language of certain American Indian tribes. The sign may be a complex set of actions involving the whole body and objects as in pantomime or silent films.

Contradiction of Verbal Communication

The third function of nonverbal communication is to contradict the verbal message. This may seem confusing. Just a few paragraphs ago, it was pointed out that nonverbal and verbal symbols needed to be consistent to convey meaning. However, there is a legitimate function served when in certain instances nonverbal symbols do contradict verbal symbols. That function occurs when a source wants to convey the message of having mixed feelings. Occasionally, social expectations dictate certain ways of acting which are strongly at odds with true feelings. At these times, it is common to send inconsistent messages paying lip service (verbal communication) to social convention, while nonverbal messages betray true feeling. For example, you may have seen someone play the role of a good hostess by offering a guest a third piece of dessert and observed that the smile on the hostess's face which was present the first and second times was missing the third time. You can draw your own obvious conclusions as to whether the guest (receiver) accurately processed the meaning in the inconsistency between nonverbal and verbal messages.

SUMMARY PROBES

1. **How do you define nonverbal communication?**
2. **How important is nonverbal communication to human communication?**
3. **What are the three functions of nonverbal communication?**
4. **List five examples where misunderstanding of the nonverbal message might have some effect on communication.**

TYPES OF NONVERBAL COMMUNICATION

This chapter will discuss seven categories of nonverbal communication: paralanguage, body movement, tactile, space, time, sign, and physical conditions.

Paralanguage

Paralanguage refers to vocalizations which are not words but which may convey meaning or add to the meanings of words. You may have heard that it isn't "what you say, but how you say it that counts." This testifies to the importance in a message of vocal cues which aren't quite words. The paralanguage nonverbal symbols consist of vocal modifiers, vocal differentiators, vocal identifiers, and voice quality.

The voice can be modified considerably in rate, pitch, volume, and to a lesser degree in quality;[8] We have a considerable body of stereotype meaning associated with these paralanguage cues.[9] Addington conducted extensive research into the relationships between stereotyped judgments and vocal cues.[10] Among his findings are the stereotypes listed in Table 3.1.

Vocal pause, sometimes called "trough noises" by certain theorists because of their likeness to sounds of hogs eating at a trough, have

Table 3.1 **Simulated Vocal Cues and Personality Stereotypes**

Cues	Speakers	Stereotyped perceptions
Breathiness	Males	Younger; more artistic
	Females	More feminine; prettier; more petite
Nasality	Males	A wide array of socially unacceptable characteristics
	Females	A wide array of socially unacceptable characteristics
Orotundity	Males	More energetic; healthy, artistic, proud, interesting
Increased rate	Males	More animated and extroverted
	Females	More animated and extroverted
Increased pitch variation	Males	More dynamic, feminine, aesthetically inclined
	Females	More dynamic and extroverted

been the embarrassment of many speakers. The same vocal pauses appear in conversation and often convey some meaning. When person A asks person B if he would like a piece of chocolate cake, a reply of "uh-huh" will be recognized as affirmative and yet it isn't a word. A reply of "um" would be clearly indicative of uncertainty. The same vocal pause, "um," in the context of a sentence would probably be decoded by a receiver and be processed as a sign of apprehension. There are some contemporary vocalizations which are words but have no meaning. Phrases like, "you know," and "okay" are really just contemporary versions of trough noises. They creep into conversation without any attached meaning.

What is the meaning to you of paralanguage forms of nonverbal communication? As a sender of communication, you will want to observe as many of the following suggestions as possible:

1. Omit vocal pauses which do not carry meaning. Don't hesitate to let there be three seconds of silence.
2. Use a variation in rate, pitch, and volume to add emphasis and clarity to the vocal symbols.
3. When using vocal variations, be sure the meaning you are sending with the nonverbal symbols is consistent with the meaning of the verbal symbols, unless you want to convey uncertainty.
4. Avoid overdoing vocal variation. Usually, you will not want the communication to call attention to itself and away from the ideas of the message.

As a receiver of communication, you will want to attempt to relate the nonverbal message to the verbal message. The following suggestions may be helpful:

1. Consciously listen to the verbal message and look at the visual message.
2. If there are inconsistencies in the nonverbal and verbal messages, attempt to determine if the source intends to suggest uncertainty or is just misleading.
3. Reserve personality judgments based on the paralanguage stimuli received. They may well be inaccurate.

Body Movement

A considerable portion of nonverbal communication relates to body movement. Space and time refer partly to movement of the body in a setting. Birdwhistell pioneered the study of communication through bodily movement with his study of *kinesics*.[11] This text will consider selected body movement categories of eye contact, gesture, posture and motion.

Eye Contact. One of the most pervasive stereotypes in American culture is that one's honesty can be judged by how he establishes eye contact. If you can't look at a person "eyeball to eyeball," you will be suspect of devious motives. A number of con men have fleeced unsuspecting customers with a good "acting" job of eyeball-to-eyeball sincerity. The success of their con games is testimony to the wide acceptance of eye-contact honesty in our value system.

Eye contact is the source of considerable communication between men and women. The sincerity of a man's proposal of marriage may be more in the eyes than in the words. There is a considerable degree of "trust" through eye contact established between individuals in interpersonal communication situations, although culturally bound rules govern the communication: it is sometimes deemed inappropriate for men and women who are strangers to attempt to use the channel of eye contact to reinforce the verbal messages they are transmitting.

Eye contact is a means of seeking feedback. When one person who is speaking comes near the end of an utterance, looks at another individual, and pauses, the second individual is likely to process the eye contact as a request for information or at least a response.

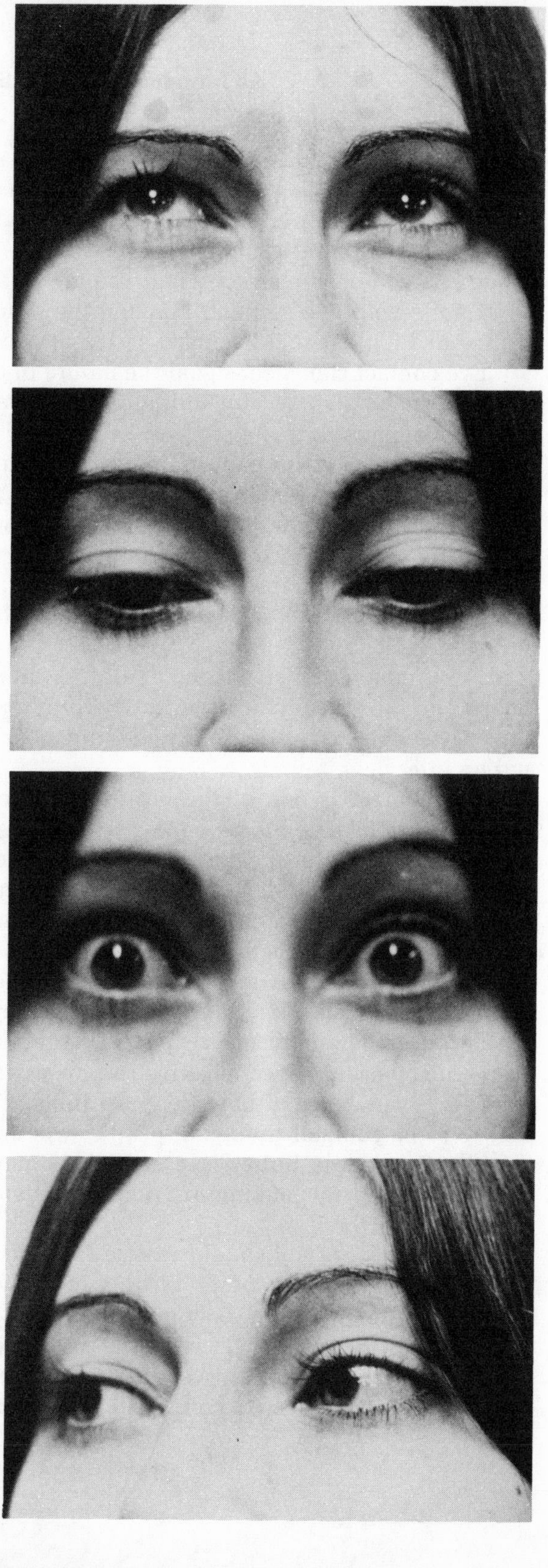

What do the eyes communicate?

Eye contact also occurs to signal that the communication channel is open. When you seek eye contact with a waitress in a restaurant, you are indicating the communication channel is open and you want to say something. The reverse may also be true; as you try to signal, the communication channel is closed. If you meet a long-winded person on the street when you are in a hurry, you are likely to try and avoid eye contact. Looking the other way is a signal the communication channel is closed as far as you are concerned.

Eye contact can, also, signal the nature of a communication relationship, such as a need for affiliation, involvement, or inclusion. It is not uncommon to make more eye contact with people you like. In fact, research by Mehrabian indicates the function may be different in males than it is in females: "In sum, findings which relate degree of eye contact to attitudes in nonthreatening interpersonal situations suggest that males show greater variability in their eye contact with their addresses relative to females and that they more consistently exhibit greater degrees of eye contact with liked than disliked addressees."[12]

Eye contact may signal the end of an interpersonal transaction. Knapp and others concluded, after eighty interviews, that the breaking of eye contact was the first sign, verbal or nonverbal, of desire to end an interview.[13]

Eye contact is one of the best ways to establish interpersonal communication with one person or with a larger audience. The contact suggests that the speaker cares about his effort to communicate. A receiver will find it difficult to be inattentive if he is the object of eye contact. As a communicator in a small group of two to four people and as a speaker before a large audience, you may find it difficult to direct your eyes to the receivers. Perhaps, you fear they will be able to see "inside" you. It is not always easy to look people in the eye because some may not respond favorably to your ideas. However, remember that even negative responses are important feedback, providing knowledge of how to adjust the message. It may be necessary to force yourself to look at people; you may find it very uncomfortable for awhile but it is essential. It may be helpful in larger groups to begin by looking at friendly individuals, then moving to other parts of the group.

As a receiver, you should realize that the nonverbal symbols of eye contact, like many other aspects of nonverbal communication, are culturally bound. For example, you would not expect a Japanese businessman to look at you while he speaks or while you speak to him. In the Japanese culture, eye contact is a sign of disrespect and is felt to be unnecessary to communicate meaning. As a businessman, your honesty and integrity would be suspect if you attempted to establish eye contact in a conference with a Japanese businessman.

Gesture. The second category of body movement is gesture, the action of the hands, arms, shoulders, and head. Like most nonverbal communication, gestures are learned and vary considerably from culture to culture. Over thirty years ago, Efron observed that the sharp contrasts in gestural styles of eastern European Jews and southern Italians slowly disappeared and were assimilated into American norms when they migrated to the United States.[14]

Birdwhistell and others searched for standardized norms for gestures. They reasoned that if meanings were consistent, it would be possible to educate sources to use certain gestures for certain meanings and to educate receivers to encode a gesture accurately. Can we trust the conclusion which states that a card player who steeples a hand with a fist has a strong hand? Or, is the card player deceiving us? Or, perhaps, the player is just nervous. When the Russian leader clasps his hands over his head, can we trust that to mean a sign of friendship and unity of the nations as the gesture would mean in the Russian culture? The problem with gestures is a problem of unreliability. They usually emerge from unconscious feelings. As suggested earlier, a gesture might indeed represent truer feeling if it could be verified the gesture came from the subconscious mind. However, the uncertainty about validity produces the reliability problem for the receiver.

In the interpersonal communication situation, gestures can exist alone, but frequently they lead to touch. Then, the kinesthetic and tactile forms of nonverbal communication interact with each other and both interact with the verbal message. As a receiver of communication, you may have to make a validity judgment about the source before you can properly decode the nonverbal message.

As a source of communication, you should realize that accurate gestures are better than no gestures and that inaccurate gestures are probably worse than no gestures. You may be able to use gestures to *describe* (as the hands showing the size of a fish), to give *emphasis* (as the clenched fist pounding or the extended index finger jabbing the air), to suggest feeling of *acceptance and rejection* (as the open hand and arm movements toward or away from the body).

Posture and Motion. The third category of body movement is posture and motion. Body movement and attitudes have been studied in the context of liking or disliking another person. Mehrabian for example, found that the relationships vary according to culture and sex.[15] He also found a slight variation in liking or disliking between communicators. There was a slight decrease in directness or orientation of males and females toward intensely liked addressees. In another study Mehrabian and Williams found general support for their hypothesis that the degree of liking when communicating nonverbally to a receiver is directly correlated with intended persuasiveness of the communication.[16]

Posture types have been categorized by some which reflect sex and culture variables. A sample of over 100 posture types are available in Knapp's *Nonverbal Communication in Human Interaction.*[17]

Tactile

Communication through touch is being widely recognized for what many people knew long ago—a means of communicating feeling without words. Thus, teachers have discovered that elementary school children in particular feel a warming praise from a slight touch on the shoulder and politicians believe it is essential that they convey strong character through a firm handshake.

Culture defines the meanings given to touch. As children grow into adults, the desire to touch and to be touched remains, but the rules that are stressed control the desire within each culture. At social occasions, men will certainly shake hands with each other, but women might not shake hands. Touching men and women carries sexual overtones. The extent of touch and the meaning of touch will develop differently in other cultures. Two Frenchmen will greet each other with a kiss. Russian comrades will hug twice—once on each shoulder. These acts seems "strange" to Americans.

The desire to communicate through touch seems universal regardless of culture. Tactile experiences are the very first experiences which evolve as a person grows. One of the very first experiences of the unborn human embryo is the sensation of touch. Further, as soon as the newborn's breathing passages are free of mucous, the physician often places the baby on the mother's abdomen. Some researchers are suggesting that the first touch after birth may affect an entire personality. They argue that caressing strokes rather than firm strokes (as might be necessary if the baby was slow to take his first breath) would be a first step to developing a humanized individual.

In American society, infants and children receive much attention through touch and handling. Warmth, caring, loving, and firmness are all conveyed by parents who know the importance of doing so. As children approach the teen years, they are less likely to seek or receive touching contact from parents. In later teen years, a new sensitivity seems to emerge—a sensitivity to peers' touching. For adults, the need for contact accelerates during times of stress.

Thus, the need for contact seems to be present in all humans. The way of satisfying that need will vary from culture to culture. Within each culture, how one touches in relation to the norms will communicate deep feelings.

Space

The study of space relationships is called *proxemics*. All things have physical boundaries around them separating one from another. Considerable research establishing the known limits of territoriality of animals and birds has been completed. It is generally accepted that one subject of animal and bird communication is related to territoriality. Humans are reluctant to admit that territoriality has any bearing on human communication, but the validity of the concept of human territoriality must be accepted. A homeowner's concept of the degree of privacy he wants for his property will affect his attitude toward people who cross his property, i.e. paperboy, mailman, neighbor children.

The normal conversational distance between strangers will illustrate the importance of the dynamics of space. If person A gets too close, then person B backs up instantly. If A gets too close again, B will back up again. It is not uncommon to see someone backed all the way across a room.

The vocal message can be qualified by the distance involved in the conversational zone. Hall has observed norms in American society and summarized the following shifts in voice as associated with specific distance ranges.[18]

1. Very close (3–6) inches)	Soft whisper, top secret
2. Close (8–12 inches)	Audible whisper; very confidential
3. Near (12–20 inches)	Indoors, soft voice; outdoors, full voice; confidential
4. Neutral (20–36 inches)	Soft voice, low volume; personal subject matter
5. Neutral (4½–5 feet)	Full voice; information of nonpersonal matter
6. Public distance (5½–8 feet)	Full voice with slight overloudness; public information for all to hear.
7. Across the room (8–20 feet)	Loud voice, talking to a group.

The interaction distance norm will be less for Latin Americans than it is in the United States because the Latins feel they must be very close to communicate. In conversation with them, you would probably back away repeatedly unless you are Latin yourself. On the other hand the interaction distance norm will be greater for Englishmen than it is in the United States. An Englishman would probably back away from you if you tried to move within three feet to converse.

Time

The arrangement of time may be used as a means of communication. Economic advisers to the president may suggest that economic news should be released during prime-time television if the news is positive, and early in the morning if it is bad. Plant managers in the United States are fully aware of the significance of a communication made during the morning or afternoon which takes everyone away from his work. Socially, a girl probably feels insulted if she is asked for a date at the last minute. Suburbanites are conscious that people invited for a dinner party will probably arrive ten to thirty minutes late, so a hostess would not feel insulted if the guests do not arrive at the designated time.

Even in the United States, time may be viewed differently by whites and blacks. A black person may use time as a means of communicating protest against the white society by ignoring the white man's clock. North American Indians have a sense of time completely at variance with the clock-bound habits of the average person. For some tribes, events begin when a sense of readiness exists.

The implication for interpersonal communication is to be conscious that time does communicate. The task as a source is to let time communicate what you intend. The task as a receiver is to process accurately what is intended by the users of time.

Sign

Object language refers to the display of material things—clothes, hair style, shoes, make-up, machines, and paintings. Well-known objects such as a flag, a swastika, and a wedding ring communicate relatively clear meanings.

Compton has conducted research which indicates close relation-

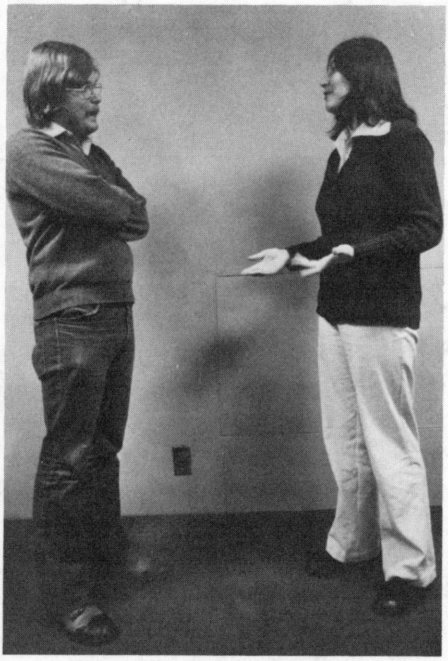

Distances for conversation vary from one culture to another. Which picture would you guess represents English? Which typifies Latin Americans?

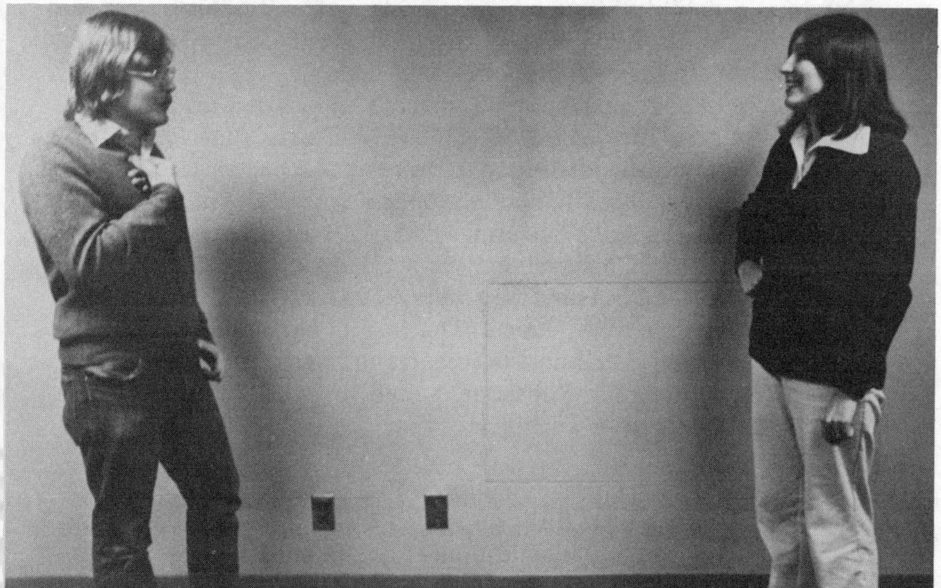

ship exists between selection of clothing and expression of one's self.[19] Experiments in which the same individual gave an identical message but changed only clothing style have demonstrated the effect of clothing on attitude toward source credibility. Even wearing eyeglasses seems to produce favorable judgments regarding source intelligence and industriousness.[20]

The implications for a source in an interpersonal communication situation are obvious: You need to dress and appear in a manner consistent with the audience, the image you seek to create, and the message you will seek to transmit or exchange.

Physical Conditions

The physical conditions of a communication environment will provide a considerable amount of information about the person or persons responsible for arranging the situation.

Long before scientific behavioral research, it was suspected that climate was a factor in human behavior. It was hypothesized that a relationship existed between climate and crime. The National Advisory Committee on Civil Disorders gave official sanction to the notion that hot summer nights contributed to rioting in ghetto areas. Recognizing the probability of such a relationship, the city of Chicago, as well as other cities, have allowed fire hydrants to be opened when summer temperatures become extremely high.

Surrounding objects will also have an influence on perception. The presence of certain kinds of objects, like early American furniture, will communicate something to you about a particular office. A living room of elegant white leather-covered furniture will communicate to you that the room is formal or possibly for show purposes. That experience will communicate something about the one who arranged the setting. Maslow and Mintz experimented with "ugly," "beautiful," and "average" rooms. The results indicated a strong relationship between visual-aesthetic surroundings and the nature of the human interaction.[21] Subsequent studies by Wong and Brown reported more effective performance in rooms which are "beautiful."[22]

In interpersonal communication situations, the control of environment is the responsibility of a host. In an interview, the interviewer usually controls the conditions. For example, a name plate on the desk may communicate formality or informality, depending on the style and appearance of the name plate. Pictures on the walls may suggest a friendliness or formality. The type of magazine on a table will communicate to a person entering the setting something about the interviewer. A religious magazine will communicate something different from an issue of the National Rifle Association magazine. In these interpersonal situations, the host will control the meaning.

SUMMARY PROBES

1. **What is one example of each of the following forms of nonverbal communication: paralanguage, body movement, tactile, space, time, sign, physical condition?**
2. **How is culture related to proxemics, touch, gesture?**
3. **What would each of the following mean to you as receiver of the message:**
   a. **A sloppily dressed person interviewing for a job?**
   b. **A hug from a person you just met?**
   c. **Eye contact from a person talking to you?**

IMPROVING NONVERBAL COMMUNICATION

This section will consider means by which you can be a more effective receiver, as well as sender, of nonverbal communication symbols. Several implications have been made throughout the discussion of specific forms of nonverbal communication. These implications suggest specific ways to be more effective. Here, the purpose will be to offer broader suggestions which may be applicable to several specific forms and nonverbal communication.

The first step to improving your role as a source or receiver of nonverbal communication is recognition of the impact of the nonverbal symbols. Hopefully, by this time you have recognized the importance of consistent nonverbal and verbal symbols.

The second step is to recognize three important principles of nonverbal communication as developed by William D. Brooks.[23] They help to explain the difference between nonverbal and verbal communication:

1. Nonverbal symbols are perceived to have very high validity. The nonverbal symbols will be believed when they are contradictory to

the verbal symbols. A blush or frown are considered to be strong indications of feeling, whereas words might be considered just that—words.

2. Nonverbal channels are especially effective for communicating feelings, attitudes, and relationships. In courtship, love, or combat, nonverbal communication is the most effective way to communicate. Trust can be reflected through several forms of the nonverbal symbols. The full range of attitudes can be communicated with great confidence and accuracy.
3. One cannot communicate. The opposite of verbal behavior is silence. Even the silence itself is a nonverbal communication. There is no such thing as nonbehavior. Every sound, movement, silence, and pause contributes to nonverbal communication. It is frightening to realize that with the verbal code you can stop, reflect, organize the message you want to transmit, but, with the nonverbal code, such hesitation to send stimuli is impossible.

The third step is for you to become familiar with the special effect of culture on several of the nonverbal communication forms, i.e. proxemics, touch, gestures, time.

Step four is for you to begin developing greater sensitivity to the stimuli around you. Several learning experiences at the end of this chapter are designed to help you increase your sensitivity.

LEARNING EXPERIENCES

1. Explain how background pictures, specifically designed as nonverbal communication, add to or detract from a verbal message in the following situations:

a. A backdrop of psychedelic colors and designs behind a speaker's platform for a political candidate.

b. A burning cross at a Ku Klux Klan rally.

2. Select a photo or cartoon and locate music which would support the message.

3. Select one or two nonverbal rules of conduct and break those rules in an interpersonal communication situation. What was the effect?

4. Divide into pairs and enact an argument between: (a) a girl and her boyfriend; (b) a parent and child; (c) taxi driver and customer; (d) boss and employee. As you enact the argument, you may use only the words "strawberries taste better with sugar," or "onions for breakfast."

5. Conduct your own experiment. Step 1: prepare a ten-minute emotional message on any topic to be given to two groups of six people each. Step 2: prepare a ten-item quiz over the material. Step 3: with group A, state the message in a monotone fashion. Step 4: with group B, state the message in a dynamic manner. Step 5: give each group the quiz. Step 6: compare the scores. What happened?

6. Select some classical theme, such as "good will win and evil will lose," and either alone or with a small group improvise a story around it without using words. Try creating the story line itself, without using words to communicate with each other. Discuss how nonverbal cues could have been improved.

7. Martin Luther King said, "We will try to persuade with our words, but if words fail, we will try to persuade with our acts." To what "acts" was he referring? Discuss the meaning of his statement.

8. Conduct your own experiment. Step 1: during a sixty-minute viewing of a television program, chart the difference and frequency of sign language used without words during the program and during the commercials. Step 2: total up the numbers. Step 3: ask five people how often they think sign language will occur in a sixty-minute television viewing. Step 4: compare the average of the five survey responses with your sample.

9. For a period of two hours assume you are mute. Since you cannot speak, use only nonverbal symbols such as gestures, signs, and pictures to communicate. Note which of your nonverbal cues seemed successful. Discuss the results with another person who has been trying the same activity. What symbols were successful for both of you? Which symbols can you improve in order to increase the effectiveness of your interpersonal communication?

10. In an attempt to learn more about gestures and how to execute them, observe the gestures of a speaker noting the facial and body expressions. Write a report on your observations telling whether gestures were natural, overused, underused, and how they might have been improved.

11. Take a survey at a party of the different classes of gestures. Do the same survey using a public speaker. Compare the different classifications.

12. Write five to ten sentences in which gestures of the hand would be needed to communicate the meaning. Practice stating the sentences and using the most appropriate gesture.

13. List five different occupations in which nonverbal symbols are an essential part of the communication needed for the job.

14. Conduct your own experiment as follows: enter an elevator and move to the back; allow several people to get on, allow them to locate their positions, speak to one person and move one step toward that person; repeat the behavior 10-15 times; compare the reactions of different types of people to the invasion of their private territory.

15. Conduct another experiment: enter into conversation with a group of three to four people, select one individual and move one step toward that individual as you converse. Repeat the behavior with several groups; draw any apparent conclusions about how different people react.

FOUR

GOALS **After completing this chapter you will be able to:**

1. Distinguish between meanings and symbols for the meanings.

2. Recognize that meanings lie within people.

3. Use words as relative symbols rather than absolutes.

4. Communicate to the world as it really exists.

5. Utilize several guidelines for more effective selection of communication symbols to send a message.

6. Recognize your own feelings and needs that affect the way you process messages received from a speaker.

Language Variables

The essence of human oral communication is language. Language is power. If a person is bitten by a rattlesnake in a remote Arizona wilderness, a radio communication system will allow a doctor in Tucson to tell the victim what to do until help arrives. The doctor has power over life and death through the words. However, the power is limited by the nature of the relationship between objects, language, and people in a changing world. If the victim is an inexperienced camper from Los Angeles, the terminology of the doctor may not be familiar. Demonstration organizers during the turbulent sixties had power over people's behavior with words. An evangelist preacher has power with words to bring individuals to witness before an altar. The sophistication of human oral communication comes from the elastic and relative characteristics of language. Unfortunately misunderstanding occurs from these same two characteristics. This chapter will consider the meanings of language, the adjustment of language to the world, and guidelines for using language in interpersonal communication.

MEANING OF LANGUAGE

Language, as used here, means the verbal form of communication in which word symbols are used for abstractions. Abstractions are organized categories of our perception of stimuli. The abstracts take on reality as words. The words are merely convenient labels which help us classify things and concepts. The word *tree* enables us to create several categories of characteristics known from memory or perceived through observation.

One category might include the following among its characteristics: produces a thick exterior layer of cells, grows extensions from the central core of growth, and sends fibers growing into the soil. Every tree in the world has its own label. Sometimes it is convenient to limit the categories to specific classes of trees. Even so, the word chosen, *elm* refers to millions of specific objects usually identified as "that" elm. Since the words are symbols for categories of characteristics, it is reasonable to conclude that there will be a limited number of words to represent an infinite number of things. The word, then is the tool for communication.

Categorizing permits reduction of complexity in communication about the environment. Classes of things may be referred to by a word. Aristotle emphasized that rhetoric is concerned with classes of things rather than with individual things and he abstracted by comparing and contrasting key critical characteristics of things. Through abstraction, language loses specificity and precision. Therefore, communication can occur when, and only when, source and receiver are fortunate enough to use a word symbol which has categorical characteristics within the shared field of experience (see Schramm's communication model in Chapter One).

When words become spoken, there is a greater probability of confusing the categories. When oral language is used, there is an infinitely larger number of meanings available to the listener to chose from than is available to the reader of written language. The meanings become subject to a greater number of varying factors such as change of voice, syntax, action, and dress.

Therefore, even though spoken language provides power to the source, the danger exists that the strength will be weakened by limitations on the specificity of language.

SUMMARY PROBES

1. **How is language defined?**
2. **How can language give power to a speaker?**
3. **In what way is power through the spoken word limited?**
4. **What are some categorical characteristics of the word symbol "computer, death"?**

LANGUAGE AND THE WORLD

How does your conception of things have meaning? Is your process for ascribing meaning a learned process? If the process is learned, how? To know the functioning process of oral language in a social structure is fundamental to oral communication.

There are at least four fundamental perspectives to studying the process. The four do not completely support nor completely deny each other.

The behaviorist view of B. F. Skinner is that learning language, like any other behavior, results from operant conditioning. The Skinnerian view maintains that as a child utters correct syllables, the child is rewarded by the parents. The reward becomes a reinforcement if it is pleasant. Reinforcing the desired behavior of sound formation and use means the sounds are more likely to appear in the future.

To the infant, the parent's voice soon becomes the symbol for reinforcement. Imitating the voice becomes a pleasant experience. Thus, words are "learned." Later, early words become the base for conditioning the meaning of other words.

The Skinnerian theory would argue that there are many words for which no object exists.[1] The theory would further argue that humans do not consciously remember the process of giving meaning to words. In essence, the words have no meaning themselves. The words are merely stimuli.

An opposing view is that developed by Noam Chomsky.[2] He doubts that operant conditioning can account for the complex sentences a child can construct although he has never heard them before. Chomsky argues that humans are endowed with certain behavior which includes a structure of language. Therefore, the acquisition of complex sentences is a result of innate ability.

A third view is that acquisition of language is just a product of maturation:[3] learning language is not related to need, but simply to maturation. Piaget's closely related view extends the maturation concept into stages of intellectual growth.[4]

The fourth view, the semantic, is a perspective rather than a single theory. The semantic perspective has two important focuses: One focus deals with the meanings words have; whereas, the second deals with the impact words have on people. The semantic focus explains that once a community of people accept a name for an object, the meaning has become conventionalized at least with that community. Osgood suggests that words represent a replica of our behavior toward objects, events, and processes.[5] Blankenship points out that the semantic meaning of a word emerges from three sources: its denotation, its connotation, and its social and linguistic context.[6] The importance of the social and linguistic context is the point of Ogden and Richards's observation: ". . . it is actually through their occurrence together with things, their linkage with them in a 'context' that symbols come to play that important part in our life which has rendered them not only a legitimate object of wonder but the source of all our power over the external world."[7]

The focus on receiver's response is the contribution of semantics to the conditions of a changing environment. This particular focus, general semantics, posits that (1) meanings of words lie within people (both senders and receivers); (2) the interaction of words in context with their changing environment is the most productive means of studying language in oral communication. Consider several key concepts which constitute the general semantics focus.

Alfred Korzybski, the acknowledged founder of the general semantics focus, postulated a considerable number of conclusions, observations, and suggestions about how man behaves verbally in society. Several of these postulates have been extracted by Stuart Chase.[8] The following four principles are from the general semantics writings of Korzybski, Hayakawa, Lee, and Johnson.

Things Are Constantly Changing

Nothing is static. Consider your own life of a few years and note how many things around you have changed. Buildings are torn down. New motels replace cornfields. One day, federal assistance is denied the cities. The next day, assistance is given. People's referents change. Symbols for the referents have emerged—*input, output, radiation fallout*. All of these are new terms. Knowing the changes of the last two decades, think of all the changes over centuries. Even values change although they need not. The fact is that certain things change from "good" to "bad" and back to "good" and so on. Consider how strange the following words would sound to a group of young people today: *statue of liberty play; white lightning; it's groovy; blood, sweat, and tears,* (no, not a rock group). The continual struggle of people to reject change has been an identifiable human condition responsible for the popularity of the television show "All in the Family."

When a person disregards the change in the people, conditions, values that are being judged, then the general semanticist says that person has made a *frozen* evaluation. The frozen evaluation can be major barriers to communication between people. Refer to the communication process models of Chapter One. The Berlo model suggested that beliefs and attitudes as well as conditions were factors affecting the source and receiver. The Schramm field of experience concept would suggest the experiences of life relative to a word symbol must undergo some similarity of change in both source and receiver.

It Is Impossible to Know Everything

Earlier it was pointed out that attention is a major factor in perceptions. Clearly, everything about the wooded object we call a tree could not be noted by any receiver. Therefore, you must accept as fact the conclusion that any picture your mind receives by any or all senses is not complete. No matter how the world is described, there will be some distortion.

Failure to recognize this principle is a barrier to successful interpersonal communication. Many people receive the words and, believing their perception to be complete, they misunderstand. The assumption of certainty causes one to overlook the fact that the message given in return as feedback may be misunderstood.

Meanings Are in People, Not Words

A word might have a pleasant sound, but otherwise it has no meaning in and of itself. The meaning is in the people sending and receiving the word. Therefore, the meanings of complex language are not in the words but in the people using the words. The word *cool* is an example. Even in the sentence, "We had a cool swimming party," the meaning is still not in the context. To an eighteen-year-old it probably refers to like versus dislike of what went on at the party. To a fifty-year-old it probably refers to the temperature of the water. S. I. Hayakawa has pointed out:

> Symbols and things symbolized are independent of each other; nevertheless, we all have a way of feeling as if, and sometimes acting as if, there were necessary connections. For example, there is the vague sense we all have that foreign languages are inherently absurd: foreigners have such funny names for things, and why can't they call things by their right names? This feeling exhibits itself most strongly in those tourists who seem to believe that they can make the natives

of any country understand English if they shout loud enough. Like the little boy who was reported to have said, "Pigs are called pigs because they are such dirty animals," they feel that the symbol is inherently connected in some way with the thing symbolized. Then there are people who feel that since snakes are "nasty, slimy creatures" . . . the word "snake" is a nasty, slimy word.[9]

Words have so many meanings which already have been conventionalized, that it would be nearly impossible for a word by itself to have a definite meaning when it stands in isolation. Berman points out that the 500 most used words in English have at least 14,000 different conventionalized meanings.[10] The concept that meanings are in people is dramatically illustrated in the following poem:

The Blind Men and the Elephant

It was six men of Indostan
To learning much inclined,
Who went to see the Elephant
(Though all of them were blind),
That each by observation
Might satisfy his mind.

The first approached the Elephant,
And happening to fall
Against his broad and sturdy side,
At once began to bawl:
"God bless me! but the Elephant
Is very like a wall!"

The Second, feeling of the tusk,
Cried, "Ho! What have we here
So very round and smooth and sharp?
To me 'tis mighty clear
This wonder of an Elephant
Is very like a spear!"

The Third approached the animal,
And happening to take
The squirming trunk within his hands,
Thus boldly up and spake:
"I see," quoth he, "the Elephant
Is very like a snake!"

The Fourth reached out an eager hand,
And felt about the knee
"What most this wondrous beast is like
Is mighty plain," quoth he!

"Tis clear enough the Elephant
  Is very like a tree!"

The Fifth, who chanced to touch the ear,
  Said, "E'en the blindest man
Can tell what this resembles most;
  Deny the fact who can,
This marvel of an Elephant
  Is very like a fan!"

The Sixth no sooner had begun
  About the beast to grope.
Then seizing on the swinging tail
  That fell within his scope,
"I see," quoth he, "the Elephant
  Is very like a rope!"

And so these men of Indostan
  Disputed loud and long,
Each of his own opinion
  Exceeding stiff and strong.
Though each was partly in the right
  They all were in the wrong.[11]

Words Have Various Levels of Abstractions

An abstraction is the idea we have of things (or the referent for a word symbol). Abstractions vary in degree of complexity. Through culture, environment, and context, many words are placed on *different levels of abstraction* depending on how *real* the referent is, that is, how easy it is to visualize, understand, or communicate.

When you try to define a term, you probably move down the ladder of abstraction from complex to concrete. By trying to move up the ladder of abstraction, your receiver will become confused. Hayakawa gave the following example of a probable dialogue for defining the word symbol *red:*

"What is meant by the word *red?*"
"It's a color."
"What's a color?"
"Why, it's a quality things have."
"What's a quality?"
"Say, what are you trying to do, anyway?"[12]

The questions asked by the receiver have pushed the original speaker up the ladder of abstraction. Try that little experiment sometime on a friend.

By moving down the ladder of abstraction you might arrive at the following definition of *red:*

> "What is meant by the word *red?*"
> "Well, the next time you see some cars stopped at an intersection, look at the traffic light facing them. Also, you might go to the fire department and see how their trucks are painted."[13]

It is possible to identify several levels in the ladder of abstraction. A typical ladder might appear as in Table 4.1.

Table 4.1 **Levels of Word Abstraction**

Level	**Word**
7	Food
6	Foul
5	Chicken
4	Hen
3	Rock Cornish hen
2	A particular hen which can be seen and touched
1	Microscopic, cellular and atomistic structure

The source and receiver in a communication situation must be encoding and decoding word symbols at the same level of abstraction or there will be a communication breakdown.

Some meaning can be provided through the context surrounding the word. Research has shown that meaning is found in the context. Nouns in particular, take on meaning from the context of a sentence.[14] DiVesta and Ross discovered that imagery of nouns is more related to associate learning than adjective imagery: the receiver perception of the noun *gorilla* is more likely to influence imagery than any of the colorful adjectives which might accompany the word in an utterance.[15]

SUMMARY PROBES

1. **What is the operant conditioner?**
2. **How does Chomsky challenge Skinner?**
3. **How do you distinguish between semantics and general semantics?**
4. **What is meant by the statement, "things are constantly changing"?**

5. **According to general semantics, where are meanings to be found?**
6. **What is a "level of abstraction"?**

GUIDELINES FOR USING LANGUAGE IN INTERPERSONAL COMMUNICATION

In order to improve communication through oral language, seven suggestions should be considered to help avoid the dangers inherent in the process of using word symbols.

Words Have Consequences Because They Have Meanings

The meanings are interpreted differently by different people. Goals, beliefs, values all affect perception of a word symbol. Because the word you choose will have effect, people will feel or act in response to your word. You must be prepared to accept the consequences for your words. Therefore, you will want to exercise great care so that your word choice will be likely to produce the consequences you wish with a given receiver.

Avoid the Dangers of Bypassing

Person A makes a statement. Person B hears but fails to process and make a response to that idea. Instead, person B makes a statement which was in his or her mind as Person A spoke. The first idea is simply bypassed or allowed to go without processing as thought. Bypassing is a likely consequence of just "hearing" rather than listening.

Bypassing is not something you do intentionally. Listeners frequently decide they know what is to be said before it is said. Have you ever been in a conversation with someone you know very well and found yourself falling into the habit of assuming you know what the person will say? If so, you may have made an error of not listening but constructing a response to what you expected to hear. Interpersonal misunderstanding can occur between people who are very close. The answer is to remain vigilant to the need to *listen* to what people actually say even if it turns out to be exactly what you expected.

Think Etc. After a Statement

The symbol, etc., will remind word users that characteristics are left out when the word is used. By thinking etc. after a statement, you will be reminded that characteristics have been omitted. Not all has been told. A car dealer may tell you about the low price and gas economy of a particular car. If you are an experienced buyer, you must be realistic and realize that not all characteristics can be discovered about the car. Any decision in life has to be made with an etc.

Use Indexing to Break Up False Identification

Indexing will allow you to break up stereotyping and fixed ideas into manageable units: Think of John Brown as different from John Smith as different from John Doe. By indexing you will mentally group but maintain flexibility of the components of a group. Stereotypes do not form if mental grouping is flexible. As a source of communication, you will want to recognize the notion of indexing by avoiding stereotyping like the following: "Business leaders are ruthless; look at J. D. Rockefeller," and then praising the social responsibility of Andrew Carnegie.

Use Mental Dates

You should use mental dates to remind yourself that objects are in process, in a state of constant change. Korzybski's time signal of mental dating should cause you to stop and reflect on what a situation is *at a given time*. Some people, for instance, are still mentally fighting a war with Japan which ended more than thirty years ago. Other people still resent Tennessee Valley Authority even though its functions have changed. Probably, you are young enough not to have developed attitudes based on nonexistent conditions, unless, for example, you have been conditioned by television movies to what the American Indian was like 100 years ago. If you were so conditioned, you will have a difficult time processing information communicated by an American Indian you might encounter lecturing in a college classroom, or working fifty stories high on a high rise construction job, or selling insurance for a major company.

Place Mental Quotes Around Highly Abstract Terms

Word symbols like *water* are relatively close to their object as compared to the word symbols like *liquid*. As pointed out earlier, it is necessary to use abstractions. The problem is that as both source and receiver in interpersonal communication you must be aware of the abstract nature of the words.

Communication must be conducted on the same level of abstraction. If it is necessary to step down, both source and receiver must be willing to move down to the same level. Failure to operate on the same level has often resulted in communication breakdowns between architects of public buildings and public taxing bodies. When an architect says a job is "complete" he usually is thinking of a systems concept. He means all of the *major parts* of the process are completed to a high degree. The public taxing board member thinks in terms of doors on hinges and light switches. Whether you are a source or a receiver, remember to place mental quotes around words in a higher level of abstraction.

Avoid Signal Responses as a Receiver

Signal responses are quasi-automatic responses. The behavior responding to a word symbol is the product of habit or conditioning alone. No thinking occurs. It is important to control your interpersonal communication so as to avoid responding to signal reactions with other signal reactions unless you wish to so react. An appropriate response to a signal is to pause for a few seconds and evaluate the situation. That way your response to the signal can reflect thinking. Hopefully, your response will be at a level of abstraction which allows the communication to continue rather than break down. Remember, engage brain before opening mouth or making a move.

SUMMARY PROBES

1. **What can you do to avoid the dangers of bypassing?**
2. **How do levels of abstraction pose dangers to oral communication?**
3. **What can you do to avoid communication breakdowns which occur from abstracting?**
4. **How does general semantics help improve interpersonal communication?**

5. What are the most recent "good" and "bad" words which have entered our vocabularies?
6. If an earthquake occurs, how is your power limited with words? In what way will the words give you power?

LEARNING EXPERIENCES

1. In a group of five or six people, compile a list of words which are potentially explosive with various audiences (i.e. abortion, busing, detente, urban guerrilla).

2. Describe the ways in which you are different today from what you were yesterday.

3. Observe several conversations. How often can you notice bypassing, stereotyping, projection?

4. In the list below, certain words need to be regarded with caution because their habitual use could indicate a failure to recognize change. Substitute some words from the second list that indicate awareness of change.

Static (No Change)	Dynamic (Change)
never	sometimes
forever	at present
always	today
finished	continuing
(continue list)	(continue list)

5. Place a pen or pencil in front of you. How many attributes of that instrument can you list in five minutes? (What is it made of? What can it be used for?) Analyze the attributes. Which would identify that particular instrument and no other?

6. Present a speech to the class discussing a personal experience in which you and another person had difficulty communicating because you had different meanings for words or phrases you used.

7. Make a list of words, then read the list to another person. Have the other person write down immediate responses to the words. Then discuss the reasons for the responses. You might try this activity with a small group of people in order to have more responses to compare and discuss.

8. Racism and religious prejudice, two of the major problems in American society today, involve some degree of communication breakdown. Make a list of the possible ways in which semantic problems between receivers and senders as discussed in this chapter could contribute to these two social problems.

FIVE

GOALS **After completing this chapter you will be able to:**

1. **Write a definition of dyadic communication.**
2. **Relate the dyadic communication situation to the potential for breakdowns in the communication process.**
3. **Explain how transactional analysis may help make communication more effective.**
4. **Apply the transactional analysis approach to an analysis of your own communication behavior.**
5. **Deal with crossed and ulterior transactions.**
6. **Improve your ability to use questions effectively in interview situations.**
7. **Describe the functions of different types of interviews.**
8. **Improve your verbal and nonverbal symbols in an interview situation.**

Dyadic Communication

A recent survey revealed that the most frequent situations in which most people perform communication acts are in one-to-one and small groups.[1] In one sense, both situation categories are interpersonal in nature. Many of the source and receiver variables are the same or very similar for both categories. However, because of a few small, but important differences, the one-to-one or dyadic situation will be discussed separately. The definition of *interpersonal communication* used in this text excludes communication in groups of three or more; larger groups will be discussed at length in Part Two.

Most decisions by humans affecting themselves, as well as others, take place in the dyadic relationship. Certainly, you have consulted with your doctor about some illness or condition. Somewhere in high school, you probably had many important dyadic contacts with a teacher, counselor, or administrator with decisions regarding your work, future, or immediate behavior. You have probably had countless one-to-one interactions with a parent. Perhaps, you have been interviewed upon entering a hospital or clinic. By now, you have possibly interviewed someone for information you need in a paper or for a news item in a school publication. You may already have been interviewed by a prospective employer regarding a job. On the job, you may have been given instructions, or you may have given instructions to another person. Everyone has been in a one-to-one communication with a friend. Your dyadic friendship communications have probably been in several different degrees of intimacy depending on the friendship and the situation. It is clear that dyadic communication situations are very frequent in our lives.

The question is often raised, "How effective are our interpersonal communication relationships?" If the views of critics are accurate, you are fortunate, indeed, if you are not one of the majority of humans who feel their interpersonal relationships are inadequate. If you are one so fortunate, how can you be sure you aren't like the Missouri mule—wearing blinders and seeing only a few feet in front? Maybe your interpersonal communications aren't as effective as you think. Gustav Ichheiser charges that in many of our day-to-day communication transactions, we operate in "reciprocal ignorance of each other."[2] The feeling of inadequacy is possibly responsible for the popularity of transactional analysis.

Your personal, professional, and business interpersonal communications can be favorably altered by: (1) viewing interpersonal communication as a transaction; (2) playing a role in which you practice those features of transactional analysis which will make positive contributions to the communication transaction. The next portion of this chapter will deal with those two means. The third and final part of this chapter will deal with the means of improving your skill to communicate in selected formal interview situations.

COMMUNICATION AS TRANSACTION

Communication involves meaning. Communication as transaction, then, deals with the formulation of meaning through transactional communicative acts. The transactions involve the notion of simultaneous happenings which exert influence over each other. Each participant is simultaneously the sender and the receiver of stimuli. Each person influences and is influenced by the other person. Out of the interaction and influence, the communication stimuli—both verbal and nonverbal—have meaning.

Some proponents of the transactional notion suggest that the term necessitates viewing sender and receiver as participators and viewing the communication act as more complex than action-reaction.[3] The view suggested, here, is that the concept of transaction refers to the fact that one set of stimuli has an effect on the next set of stimuli, rather than referring to what names the individuals are given or the speed at which the stimuli are presented.

Intimacy

Intimacy is one of the most important characteristics of dyadic communication. The informality of the dyad allows the uniqueness of each person to be presented.[4] The closest intimate communications are generally not accepted in larger public communication. Have you observed the reactions of people who encounter a romantic pair kissing and hugging on a heavily traveled sidewalk? Some people giggle while others reflect indignation and disgust. Both reactions arise from the feeling that intimacies are not for display in public but rather reserved for the dyadic situation. There is a similar feeling toward the various verbal acts.

Because intimacy is a characteristic reserved for the dyadic situation, then it follows that dyadic communication has the potential to be most rewarding and most disappointing, most ecstatic and most agonizing. By the same token, disagreement that arises through dyadic communication is usually rather cautious and tempered. Most individuals are aware of the destructive potential of the disagreement and seek to camouflage the disagreement. If you are like most people, and a disagreement emerges with another person in a dyadic situation, you will engage in some kind of role playing to protect your ego and the ego of the other person.[5]

Completeness

A second characteristic of the communication in the dyadic situation is completeness. The dyad tends to be more complete and less divisible. Two people can provide a united front, as many married couples do. We think of two people as a complete unit when we think of pairs. The strength of many marriages is because two individuals can collectively resist outside pressures. With larger groups, there is always a weak link somewhere which can be worked on to create division.

The dyad is complete because it cannot be further subdivided from within. If two people in a dyad cannot get along, the options are limited to two: adjust or break the dyad. If one withdraws, the relationship ceases completely. Therefore, the two members are completely interrelated in the dyadic situation.

Uniformity

A third characteristic of communication in the dyad is that the communication symbols tend to be more uniform in complexity, abstractness, and style. Two individuals who maintain a dyadic relationship will have certain common goals, values, and ideas. They will tend to communicate at the same level of abstraction out of recognition that more meaning can be exchanged that way. The common purposes may spread to more similar word choices, syntactical patterns, even delivery patterns.

The three characteristics are not always present to the same degree in each dyadic situation. It is not important, here, to dwell on whether they are dependent or independent communication variables. It is important to know that they are common characteristics to most dyadic situations in varying degrees. It is also important to be aware that all three of the above characteristics can be affected to some degree by the nature of the communication symbols, verbal and nonverbal, which are selected. The symbols, as the conveyors of meaning, are the extension of thoughts and feelings. Assuming you are consistent with verbal and nonverbal symbols, it is worthwhile to examine the nature of the language we commonly use in the analysis of the communication transaction.

IMPROVING COMMUNICATION WITH TRANSACTIONAL ANALYSIS

There are several perspectives which could be used for examining communication transactions in the dyadic setting. The most current interest is in transactional analysis. Because it is popular, provides a utilitarian way of examining communication transaction, and has a philosophical base behind the terminology, transactional analysis will be used.[6]

Transactional analysis provides a language classification system according to the maturity level of states of being represented through words. The three ego states in the classification are parent, adult, and child.

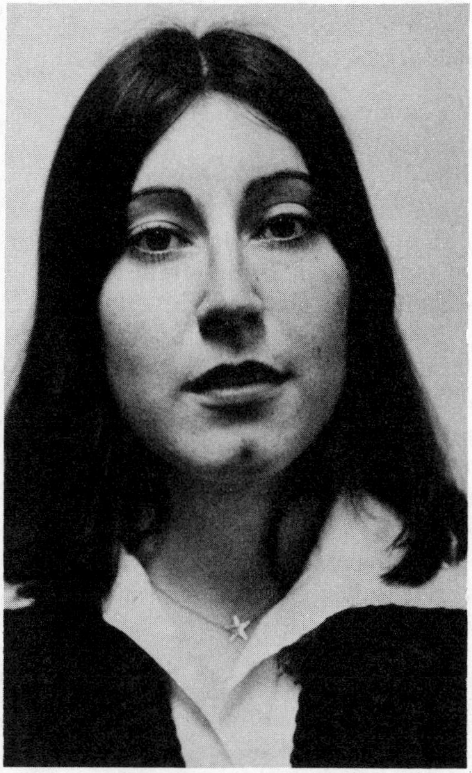

Transactional analysis suggests there are three ego states. Can you determine which picture represents parent? adult? child?

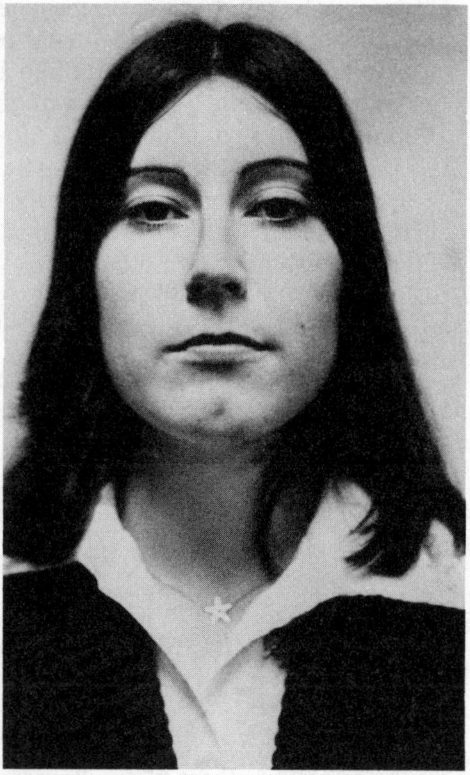

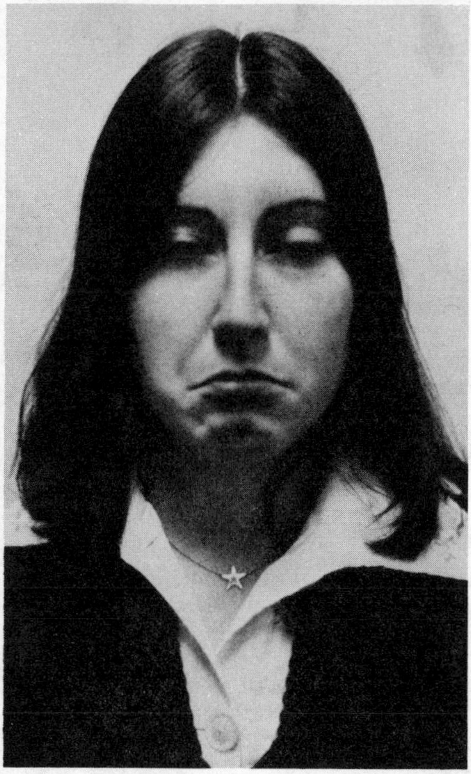

The parent state contains all the admonitions, rules, and laws the child has heard from parents and authority figures during his life. This includes all the "no's" directed to the toddler, the looks of pain on a mother's face when clumsiness brings embarrassment to the family. These rules are preponderant in the parent state and perceived as truth. The state itself is not perceived as being either good or bad. In the parent state, one reasons from a priori rules.

The child state contains all the thoughts of the self. It contains the recordings of early experiences, and responses to the experiences. The child ego state may be either a natural childlike state or an adapted childlike state using responses taught a certain way. Examples of the natural childlike state are, "Let's go fishing." and, "Whee, we won!" Examples of the adapted childlike state are, "He hates us, let's go fishing!" and "If I don't get a new desk, I'll quit."

Naturally, the three states are not so clear cut as the above descriptions suggest. They actually overlap as suggested by the model in Figure 5.1.

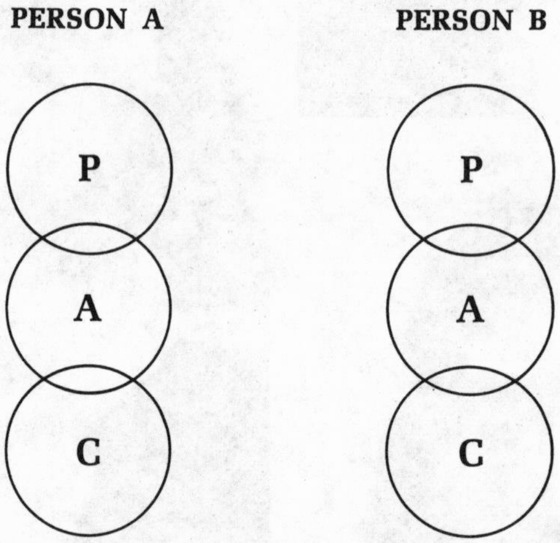

Figure 5.1 **Transactional Relationships**

Transactions between individuals can be complimentary, crossed, or ulterior. Complimentary transactions (Figures 5.2 and 5.3) facilitate communication, whereas crossed transactions (Figure 5.4) are communication breakdowns.

Ulterior transactions imply hidden meanings. People often say one thing and mean another (Figure 5.5). What they say overtly in a

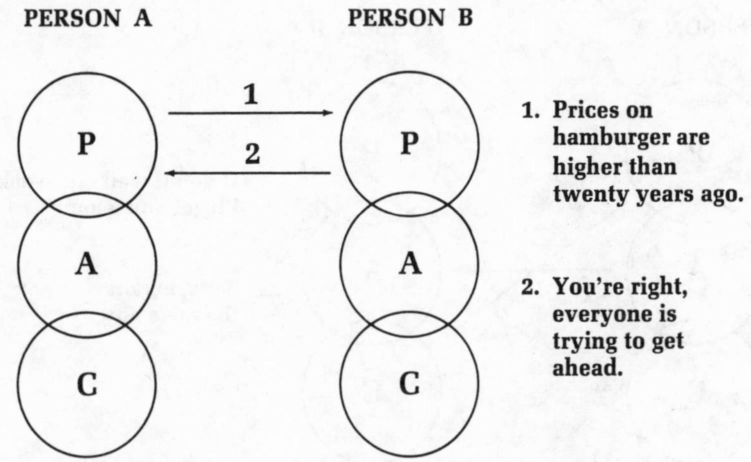
PERSON A
PERSON B
P
A
C
1
2
P
A
C
1. Prices on hamburger are higher than twenty years ago.
2. You're right, everyone is trying to get ahead.

Figure 5.2 **Complimentary Transactions**

social level is contrary to what they are saying intrapersonally. The ulterior transaction must be understood and accepted or modified for the communication transaction to continue in any meaningful way. The ulterior transaction cannot be ignored. In Figure 5.5, person B must respond to the overt stimulus but must act according to the hidden meaning or say something which will change the level of the ego state wording.

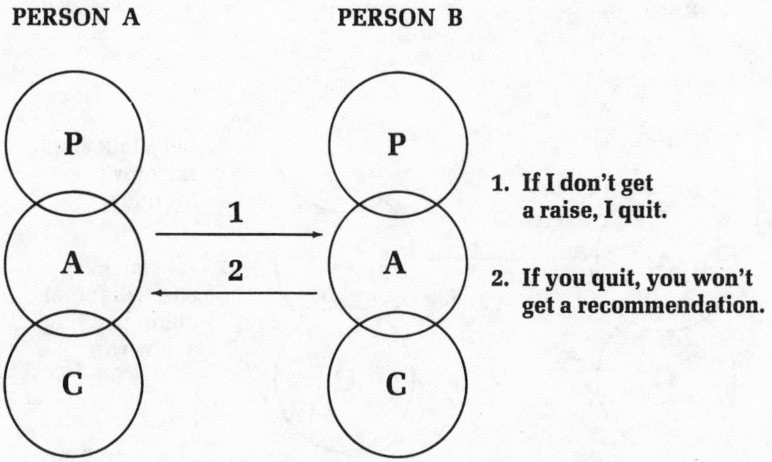
PERSON A
PERSON B
P
A
C
1
2
P
A
C
1. If I don't get a raise, I quit.
2. If you quit, you won't get a recommendation.

Figure 5.3 **Complimentary Transactions**

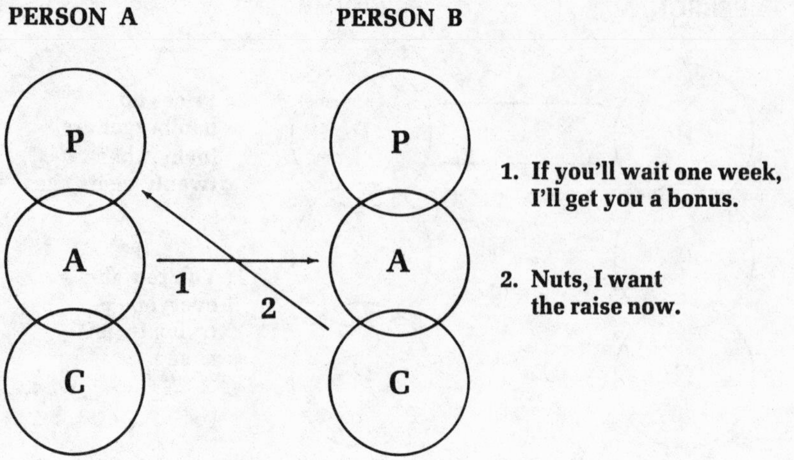

Figure 5.4 **Crossed Transaction**

The ulterior transactions are made by people who are trying to play games with one another. Eric Berne has suggested that much of our interpersonal communication transactions are part of some game being played for offensive or defensive purposes. Berne has analyzed over thirty-five different games that people play.[7] Examples are found in Table 5.1.

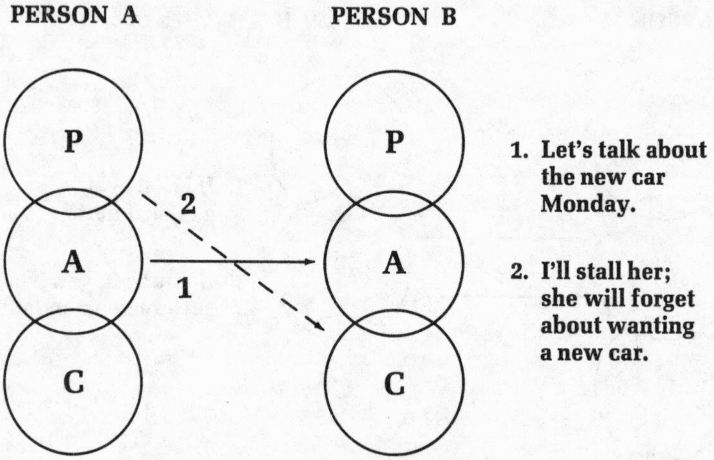

Figure 5.5 **Ulterior Transactions**

Table 5.1 *Gamesmanship*

Theme	**Name of the game**	**Purpose**
Blaming others	"If it weren't for you"	You're Not O K
Saving others	"I'm only trying to help you"	You're Not O K
Getting even	"Now I've got you, you S.O.B."	You're Not O K
Getting sympathy	"Look how hard I've tried"	I'm Not O K
Provoking putdowns	"Kick me"	I'm Not O K

You can contribute to the end of game playing and thereby allow people to communicate with complimentary transactions, hopefully as adult to adult. You might refuse to play the game, or you might refuse to provide the payoff or the satisfaction.[8]

When applying the terminology of transactional analysis to an examination of communication behavior, it is important to remember that people cannot be classified by chronological age, nor can they be locked into one classification category. In fact, everyone changes from one ego state to another. The changes are apparent in manner, appearance, work, and gestures. During one hour, any individual may change from one ego state to another ego state several times.

As you listen to another person communicating, recall that they have formulated their message out of data perceived from three different ego states. You are confronted with the challenge to respond with language from an appropriate ego state or engage in transitionary language, designed to invite the other person to change to another ego state.

Certainly, you will not always be successful in attempts to create perfectly complimentary transactions, nor can you be assured that the complimentary transactions themselves will produce harmonious human relations. In your role as an adult reading this text, you can perhaps accept the notion of human error in the pursuit of humanism. The philosopher Elton Trueblood has observed:

> The fact that we do not have absolute certainty in regard to any human conclusions does not mean that the task of inquiry is fruitless. We must, it is true, always proceed on the basis of probability, but to have probability is to have something. What we seek in any realm of human thought is not absolute certainty, for that is denied us as men, but rather the more modest path of those who find dependable ways of discerning different degrees of probability.[9]

SUMMARY PROBES

1. **What is an ego state?**
2. **What are the characteristics of parent, adult, and child ego states?**
3. **What are the characteristics of the dyadic communication?**
4. **Which is most helpful—complimentary transactions, crossed transactions, ulterior transactions?**
5. **What can you do about games people play?**

INTERVIEW

The interview is one form of dyadic communication familiar to most people. One survey revealed that in three midwest communities 93 percent of those surveyed had participated in an interview regarding a job.[10] An interview is a communication between two parties, both of whom speak and listen from time to time. At least one of the two parties has a preconceived and serious purpose for the transaction. The actual interview may have more than two individuals if several of them are acting as one party (as in a group interview or board interview). The fact that one party has a preconceived and serious purpose clearly distinguishes the interview from the casual encounter on the street or in the halls.

The fact that parties constantly change roles as speaker and listener gives the interview its transactional nature. If either person in the interview finds that he is talking without interruption, that person probably is not getting through to the receiver. Both individuals not only speak and listen, but also engage in moment-to-moment adaptations. Memorized speech is impossible in an interview.

Types of Interviews

Interviews can be conducted for any of a great number of reasons. For our purposes, we will identify nine specific types of interviews.

Information Seeking. The information-seeking interview is a situation in which the first person, the interviewer (R), seeks information from another person, the interviewee (E). Census takers for the federal government, market researchers, opinion pollsters are obvious examples. However, anytime you are seeking information for a class or any project and you go to someone who is an expert, you are engaging in the information-seeking type interview. In this type, the interviewer maintains most of the control over the interview, in terms of questions asked and often in terms of time. Most of the questions are asked by the R who controls the extent and duration of tangent discussions.

Information Giving. The information-giving interview is usually a situation in which one person is giving instructions or directions to another. A typical example is the motorist who pulls into the filling station to ask directions. Either person in the information giving interview may initiate the interview. The plant foreman may want to be certain a new procedure is being followed. A sales manager may want to provide salespersons with information about a new product. Questions may be asked by the person giving the information to determine if the receiver understands. Those questions are seeking feedback with which to judge understanding of the message.

Problem Solving. Such interviews involve information and persuasion just like problem solving in other situations. This type occurs when two store employees, regardless of their respective rank or classification, meet face to face and try to resolve a problem. Typical problems might be displaying advertising for a product or allocating space for new product lines. Either person may initiate the interview, but it may be very difficult to determine who is dominating. Whereas other types of interviews rely heavily upon primary and secondary questions planned partly in advance, the problem-solution type relies more on questions which relate to the reflective thinking process discussed in Part Two of this book.

Counseling Interview. The counseling interview may be persuasive as one person tries to get another to change his behavior, or it may be nonpersuasive in which the objective is to provide a situation for one person to gain insight into himself. The problems in counseling interviews are strictly personal problems. Open and nondirected questions are prevalent in the counseling interview.

Employment Interviewing. This type of interviewing is familiar to just about everyone. This is a separate category of interview because of its immediate goal—employment. Actually, it is a combination of several other types. For example, information is sought, information is received, the E tries to persuade the R to act favorably. Sometimes the R also tries to persuade the E to act favorably.

Receiving Complaints. This is a specialized interview found most commonly in business. An irate customer usually begins with an angry demand, "I want my money back." Eventually, specific closed questions must be asked and answered by both parties to determine the source of the irritant to the customer.

Reprimanding. The reprimanding interview is also a specialized type in business and education. When behavior modification is desired, one party will initiate and probably control the interview. Although there will be considerable dialogue with both parties speaking and listening, the R will clearly control the direction and duration of the interview. You may recall being part of one of these interviews in the principal's office in high school.

Appraisal. Appraisal interviews provide information to the E regarding how a job is being performed and offer guidelines relative to future performance. The appraisal interview has become common in merit systems in industry, business, and education. It is related to the counseling interview when it deals with student academic progress. Some teachers, for example, choose to hold such interviews to review student's academic progress periodically.

Persuasive. Persuasive interviews are common to business. Anytime a prospective customer and a salesperson meet to discuss possible purchase of a car, major appliance, house, farm, machinery, and so on, the two parties are participating in a persuasive interview. It is still a dyadic communication even when a husband and wife meet with a salesman. The two of them constitute one party in most cases. In such an interview, the purposes of the two parties are different. One wants to make a sale at the most profit, while the other wants to buy at the lowest price. Great risk of communication breakdown from misperception of questions is possible. Language may be a problem with the dangers of bypassing, stereotyping, and "allness" threatening to interfere.

SUMMARY PROBES

1. **How do you define an interview?**
2. **What are the different types of interview? Give a specific example of each type.**
3. **How common are interview situations?**

Question and Answer Process

The essence of any interview includes the questions asked and answers given. Therefore, in a serious interview with a serious purpose, it is important to plan the kinds of questions to be asked, as well as some of the specific questions. Before any other progress can be made in improving interviewing, it is necessary to develop skill in the question-and-answer process. For that purpose, you will need to know about questions and their uses. Following is a description of five basic types of questions.

Open Question. Open questions allow the respondent complete latitude for response. Only the topic has been controlled by the one asking the question. Examples of open questions are:

What are your goals in life?
What do you expect to be doing five years from now?
Why did you leave your last job?
What did you like about your last job?
What can you tell me about yourself?

The intent of the question is to allow the one asking to make inferences from the response. How you respond to an open question may reveal your personal priorities. If you choose to talk about money first and helping people second, then, you have revealed something about yourself. The open question, also, allows the one asking to make inferences about your ability to think clearly and organize thoughts—in other words, your verbal sophistication.

Closed Questions. Closed questions allow the respondent very little latitude for response. In fact, the closed questions may be composed so carefully that the respondent has only three or four possible responses. The multiple-choice questions asked on written exams are carefully worded closed questions. Examples of closed questions are:

What was your salary on your last job?
How long have you lived at this address?
Do you favor Humphrey or Kennedy for the Democratic nomination?

The closed question is used to obtain specific information. Closed questions save time and increase accuracy but tend to discourage completeness.

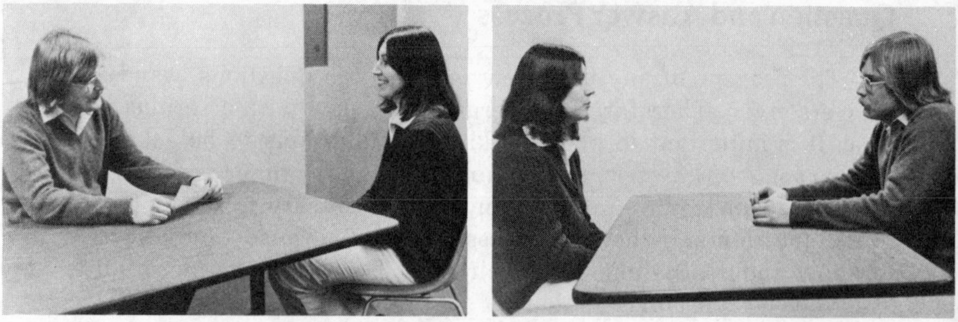

Employment interviews can be formal or relaxed. One determinant is the location of physical barriers between R and E. Which of the above interviews is most relaxed?

A market survey interview involves an R asking questions and an E responding.

Primary Questions. Primary questions are questions which introduce an entire subtopic. Usually, it will be an open type question which can be followed by several other related questions.

Secondary Questions. Secondary questions are probing and inquiring questions. They are intended to gain specific information and they may probe more deeply for attitudes or beliefs which have emerged in answer to primary questions. Often, sounds will also serve as probing secondary inquiries. Even silence can be used to urge a person to continue but sometimes, if the interviewee (E) is slow to answer, an inexperienced interviewer (R) may rush to rephrase a question or ask another question.

The following portion of an interview illustrates the use of primary and secondary questions:

	R: Good afternoon, Mr. X. Would you be willing to aid a survey of religious practices by answering a few questions?
	E: Of course, I'll be glad to help.
Primary Question	R: Do you believe the Christian religion exerts a strong influence on social consciousness?
	E: I think . . .
Secondary Question	R: How have your Catholic friends responded to the Papal Encyclical on birth control?
	E: They seem to . . .
Secondary Question	R: Do you feel the World Council of Churches has made any progress toward reducing world hunger?
	E: From what I have heard. . . .

Mirror Question. Mirror questions are actually a summary or conclusion stated by an R and put as a question for an E to respond to with a yes or no and a brief amplification. Examples of the mirror question include:

You say that gas prices should be controlled?
Is it correct, then, that you feel a tax increase is necessary?

The mirror questions are often used as internal summaries of a subtopic in much the same way internal summaries are used within a speech.

Questions should be the result of some preplanning. No matter what type of interview is to occur, both parties should have given some thought and preparation to what primary questions need to be asked. In fact, some speculation should be made about possible secondary questions, although many of the secondary questions will emerge from the transaction.

The answers to questions should follow the form of the questions asked. If an open question is asked, it isn't very informative or helpful to provide a one-word response or a very short response. If a closed question is asked, it isn't very helpful to the communication transaction to provide a long-winded answer in which you expose all of your philosophy and its foundations. Sometimes, an explanation is necessary to give the conditions responsible for a short answer. If this happens to you, be very certain the gain in clarity is worth the loss of time. Then, ask if you may explain your answer. Generally, you will be given that courtesy if it isn't abused.

Failure to give thought to questions and answers may cause an interview to be a waste of time or possibly be the source of misleading information. In the informational interview, information is useless when the data and the meanings are omitted, or when statements are distorted.

The admonition to prepare must be accompanied by the admonition to be flexible. Since the interview is so transactional in nature, many meanings will be exchanged through small verbal and nonverbal symbols. These small symbols will be unplanned; thus, feedback responses to those small symbols will be unplanned.

Therefore, anytime you participate in interviews as interviewer or interviewee, make an effort to observe the following guidelines:

1. Determine a purpose.
2. Analyze the purpose to plan the kinds of primary questions you will ask or likely be asked.
3. Analyze the possible questions to plan some basic points of response to those questions.
4. During the interview, as an R, develop primary questions with relevant secondary questions.
5. During the interview, as an E, fit your responses to the questions.
6. Be flexible during the interview.

Conducting an Information-Seeking Interview

The information-seeking interview, like all interviews, must have an opening, a substantive part, and a closing. During the opening segment, an effort is usually made to establish rapport between the two parties. There should be an effort to establish confidence, trust, and clear purpose. Some light discussion of areas of common interest would be appropriate for some types of interviews. Statement of purpose would be appropriate for all types of interviews.

During the second stage, the substantive question and answers are given. All subtopics are explored at length to the satisfaction of both parties and primary questions and related secondary questions are asked and answered.

During the final stage, the interview is brought to a close. The R should review information through a few summary statements and key mirror questions. The R should thank the E for assistance. The E should indicate acceptance of the thanks. There should be agreement by the R and the E on whether further interviews will be necessary.

When planning questions for the information-seeking interview, you will need many specific closed questions designed to obtain desired data. For example, the admittance interview at a hospital should be concerned with specific past medical history, allergy to drugs, and insurance data. An interviewer who has planned carefully will ask an open question about what concerns the patient may have. That would give the nonsmoking E a chance to indicate if he would be bothered by being in a room with a person who smokes. To the extent the hospital can feasibly accommodate the situation, the knowledge gained from the answer to such an open question would help the hospital provide better service to the patient.

In some instances, it might be well for the R to inform the E ahead of time of the data sought. A person representing a Concerned Citizens Group for Education seeking information about a school district's indebtedness would be wise to let the business manager know ahead of time what they seek. The questions and answers during the interview might be more productive both in information exchanged and feelings preserved between the two parties and the groups each party represents.

Conducting an Employment Interview

During the employment interview there are two broad purposes: (1) the applicant wants to obtain a good job; and (2) the employer works to obtain a good employee. To obtain those ends there are four things which will likely happen: (1) the applicant will seek to find out as much as possible about the company; (2) the applicant will try to sell himself for the job; (3) the employer will seek to find out as much as possible about the applicant; (4) the employer will try to sell the company to the applicant. The interview will contain information seeking, information giving, and persuasion during the transaction.

If you are applying for a position, there are three factors you should consider carefully: (1) preparation of the résumé; (2) preparation of topics for questions and answers; (3) communication variables.

Preparation of Résumé. Begin preparing the résumé with an outline of your background and education. From the outline, the formal résumé may be prepared to be sent to prospective employers before the interview. The résumé should contain the following information:

Personal Information
Name
Present address
Permanent address
Present telephone
Permanent telephone
Date of birth

Education
Field of major study and related fields
Any special recognition as a student
Certification, diploma, degree earned (include date).

Work Experience
Summer jobs
Full-time jobs

Activities
School activities
Church and community activities

References
Names and addresses of two or three
people who know you and your interests and can
attest to your character.

Be sure the résumé is carefully thought out and carefully typed. It will be your first contact with the prospective employer and may be an important factor in whether you are able to get to the next step, the interview.

Preparation of Topics. You should prepare topics for consideration during the interview. Ask yourself, "If I were the employer, what would I want to know?" Several studies reveal that major areas of concern to employers are ability, desire to work, social-emotional maturity, and character. Determine what you will want to know about the company, the job, the people you would work with, the community. Certainly you will want to plan on finding answers to questions like the following:

1. What will I be expected to do?
2. Is there a training program?
3. Can a person learn and grow on this job?
4. What are the chances for promotion?
5. What is the beginning pay?
6. How does one increase his pay?
7. What are the fringe benefits?

A word of caution is in order. You may be very interested in the pay and fringe benefits (who wouldn't be?); but reserve that question until late in the interview. The information will be provided if the interviewer knows his or her job. If it isn't provided, you should ask.

Communication Variables. The third factor is communication variables. Word choice is a very important communication variable. You should recall the problems with words and meanings. Careful word choice should minimize those problems. You will want words which allow for a completed transaction in the same ego state and at the same level of abstraction used by the interviewer. Nonverbal symbols are also very important to the interview transaction. Thus, most personnel managers will readily admit that the first and most lasting impression is made through the handshake. Nonverbal symbols by you as well as those by the R will provide clues to sincerity, interest, and commitment.

SUMMARY PROBES

1. **What are the three parts of any interview?**
2. **How are open and closed questions used in an information-seeking interview?**
3. **Why should questions be planned?**

4. **What are crucial factors for successful employment interviewing?**
5. **What kind of things would prospective employers want to know?**
6. **What kind of things would applicants want to know?**
7. **How do you compare or contrast open and mirror questions?**
8. **What information is essential for a good résumé?**
9. **How do nonverbal symbols affect interviews?**
10. **Why are dyadic communications transactions?**

LEARNING EXPERIENCES

1. Make a diagram to show which ego states are operating in each of the following transactions:

Example: A wife who is grieving for a lost friend is comforted by a sympathetic husband. The diagram would appear as in Figure 5.6. Draw or reproduce the figure and add arrows to show transactions outlined below.

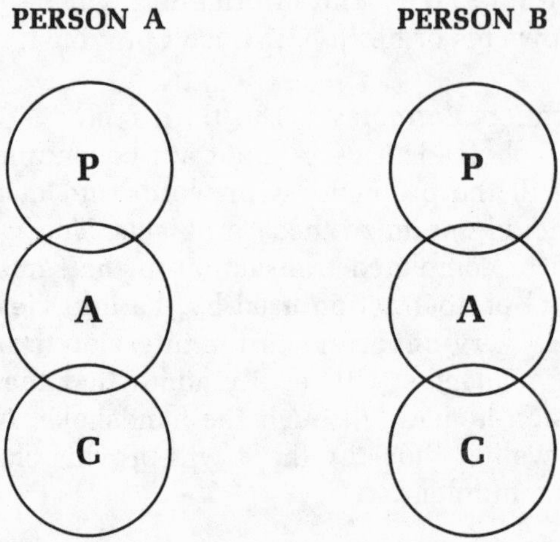

Figure 5.6 **Transactional Relationships**

a. A husband who asks where his cuff links are is told by his wife that she hasn't seen them, but she will help him hunt for them.

b. When a young man tells his father he has a report to finish that night, his father instructs him to go to bed.
c. A man who wants to quit smoking asks his wife to destroy his cigarettes when she finds them or to "come on strong" when he lights up.

2. Explain which ego state is operating in each of the following transactions:

a. To a stimulus concerning a piece of modern art:
Response: "Good grief! What's it supposed to be?"
Response: "That costs $350,000 according to the price tag."
Response: "Oh, what a pretty color!"
b. To a lecturer using four-letter words:
Response: "I wish I dared to talk like that."
Response: "I wonder why he chooses those words to use, and what their effect is on this audience?"
Response: "Using those words shows a weak vocabulary."
c. To a stranger putting his arm around you:
Response: "I wonder why he is doing it?"
Response: "I'm scared."
Response: "Never let a stranger touch you."

3. Write a dialogue between two businessmen illustrating crossed transactions.

4. Keep a diary of dyadic communication you observe during a day. Describe efforts being made to avoid playing games.

5. Give an example of and diagram a complimentary, crossed, and ulterior transaction, based on actual transactions in group or dyadic communication.

6. In each of the following, give an example of how your parent, child, and adult would respond:

a. A coworker is late for work on a day when you both were to finish a vital assignment.
b. A good-looking man or woman smiles at you at the water fountain.
c. An unknown seven-year-old boy comes to the door and asks you if you would like to help him win a trip to Disney World by buying a certain newspaper.

7. Research a well-known company and then prepare an outline of questions (primary and secondary) you would want to ask if you had an interview for a job with that company.

8. Conduct two information-seeking interviews. In one, ask primary open questions. In the other, ask primary closed questions. Write a comparison of the two experiences.

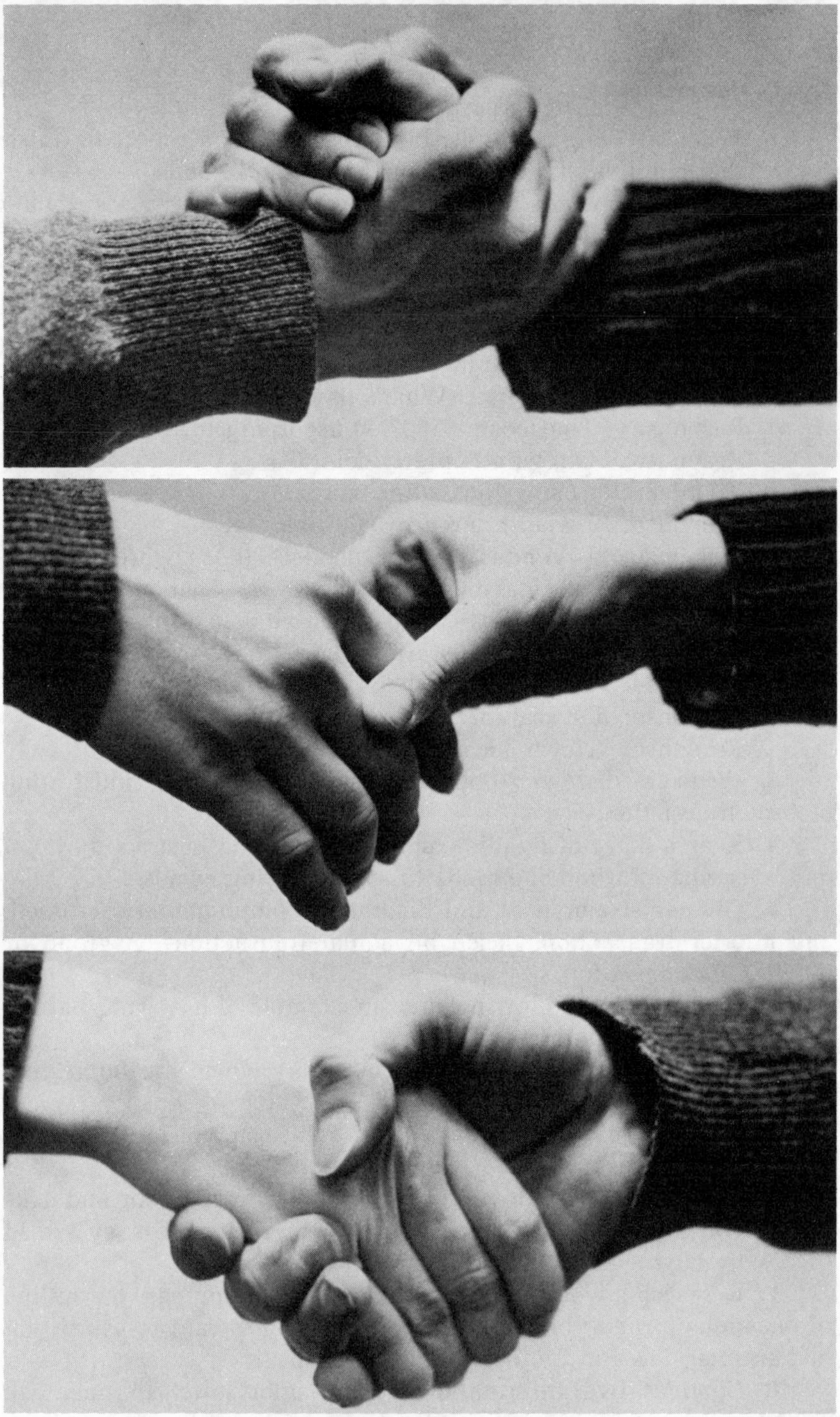

Which person would you hire? Why?

9. Select a current controversial topic and conduct two five- to ten-minute interviews with fellow students, workers, or neighbors. Use only primary questions in one interview—no probing questions into answers. In the second interview, rely mainly on secondary (probing) questions into answers obtained from a few basic primary questions. How does the information gained from these two procedures differ? How do you prepare for each interview?

10. Select a person in your planned profession who conducts employment interviews. Interview that person, asking what he or she looks for in an applicant and what interviewing techniques are used. Compare what you find out with this textbook.

11. Take an application blank from a local firm, then write an interviewing guide that will allow you to find out additional information not covered by the application blank. Consider the written versus oral methods of collecting information. Make a list of the advantages and disadvantages of each.

II

Small Group Communication

SIX

GOALS After completing this chapter you will be able to:

1. Identify the unique and common factors in small group communication in relation to other forms of oral communication.
2. Define a small group.
3. Better appreciate the role of small group communication behavior in the totality of human society.
4. Increase your understanding of the specific tasks to be performed by a small group.
5. Describe real life situations in which the elements of communication affected group action.
6. Suggest how some communication factors are more important than others to groups in your life.

Communication Process Functioning in Small Group Situations

The first segment of this text dealt with human communication in situations involving just one other person—face-to-face communication. We viewed such communication situations as our primary concern in the treatment of four communicative events.

Much of the theory discussed relative to interpersonal communication should be carried into this segment which deals with human communication in small group situations. While virtually all the material preceding is applicable to small group communication—our second communication event—this segment will develop theories relating specifically to human communication in such groups.

DEFINITION

What is a small group? First, it is a group. But that begs the question, "What is a group?" Webster says it is a "cluster" or a "division of organisms with certain characteristics." Unfortunately, this isn't too helpful. Even if we assume our inquiry is limited to human behavior, a "division of organisms with certain characteristics" could refer to something as nebulous as all of those who voted for a certain presidential candidate in a given year, or all of those who have size EEE feet, or all of those who belong to a high school club or college fraternity. Sometimes, individuals in these "clusters" have need to communicate with each other about a shared goal. Perhaps, the "cluster" intends to enter, design, and build a float for a homecoming parade. "Clusters" which have goals requiring human action need communication. Therefore, we may arbitrarily narrow our focus to "clusters" of humans with shared goals.

Those who fall into a "cluster" by accident—such as all those with size EEE feet—may not share any kind of goal; thus, they have no need to communicate. The time may come, however, when some of those individuals living in close proximity may want to take some kind of action collectively to increase the available selection of shoe styles and prices. Their "cluster" now has a shared goal. The success or failure of one person now affects everyone. Each member promotes the success of the others by supporting the group. Each one who belongs must interact with some or all of the others in the group. Most of the interaction will be oral or supportive of oral interaction.

Now it is possible to qualify our definition further by focusing on the term *small*. Research strongly suggests that groups numbering two to ten are subject to somewhat different influences than groups of twenty-five, one hundred, or several thousand.[1] Feedback is different. Reasons for response are different. The smaller groups tend to have more identifiable and specific goals than larger groups. A particular small group from a neighborhood may want street improvement for safety reasons on two or three specific streets. A community-wide group may have a broader interest for several kinds of improvements on streets in general.

In the smaller group it is possible, indeed necessary, for each person to play all roles in the communication process. Each must be a sender and a receiver. Interaction implies that a person thinks, speaks, listens. The relationship is easily perceived in the model shown in Figure 6.1. By the time the eighth step is reached, the person is thinking differently than at the second step. The person's thinking has been influenced by what he or she said, by what others said, and by the impact of those word exchanges on each other.

The focus is significantly narrowed to make a meaningful summary about what we will consider a small group. It will have the following characteristics:

1. A shared purpose in which the success of each is dependent upon the success of the total body rather than on one or more individuals.

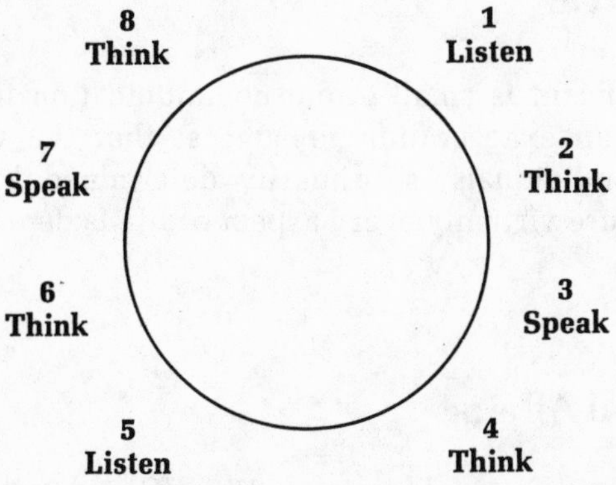

Figure 6.1 **Small Group Interaction Model**

2. Oral interaction is a predominant mode of communication.
3. Close physical proximity will exist allowing for face-to-face interaction, feedback, and trust.
4. A small number of people will constitute the "cluster" so that each will be aware of and react to others.

As a definition of small group process, consider the following: "Small group decision-making is a process that involves two to ten people with geographic proximity, interacting with one another about a problem of interest to all of them in a situation where the group has the power to make effective decisions."

The dyad—meaning two people—is a special kind of small group with unique features all its own and has been discussed elsewhere in this book.

SUMMARY PROBES

1. **Under what circumstances would each of the following be considered a small group? The United States Senate? St. Louis Cardinals baseball team? Board of Directors of U.S. Steel Corporation? Packing line workers at a cookie factory? Faculty of a junior college?**
2. **In what way do people in a small group interact?**
3. **Who should be the sender in a small group?**
4. **What is the optimum number of people for a functioning small group?**

SIGNIFICANCE

How significant is small group communication in our lives? It would not be an exaggeration to suggest that the well-being and happiness of individuals is primarily determined by small group processes because virtually every aspect of life is dependent on those processes.

Governmental Affairs

Legislative bodies could not function if the detail—the give and take of compromise—essential to legislation was not conducted first in committee. Even the committees are often too cumbersome and must be further subdivided into subcommittees. Executive functions of governmental bodies usually depend upon recommendations from advisory groups. From the Citizens Advisory Committee, to the board of a local school district, to the National Security Council advising the president of the United States, governmental bodies depend heavily upon such groups.

Nongovernmental Community Affairs

Several religious denominations are governed by themselves operating through groups at the local level. It has been said that a Methodist couldn't be a Methodist without a committee. Community service bodies, such as blood bank programs, depend upon committees to function. They must have a planning committee, a publicity committee, and a set-up work committee.

School and School-Related Experiences

Student councils and clubs make decisions and get tasks done through committees. The same is true for church youth groups, Boy Scouts, 4-H, Girls' Clubs of America. In higher education, like government, the organizations such as student senates, fraternities, sororities, Young Republicans, and Young Democrats function through committees.

Work

It is becoming common for business and industry to increase the role of junior executives in making company decisions. Those who are planning to enter professions can expect to be involved with other professionals in dealing with common tasks and problems.

Recreation

Bowling leagues, Little Leagues, and swim clubs have to organize, schedule, recruit, and have banquets. Committees wish to construct swimming pools, provide parks and park programs, and operate fairs. Again, the decisions and work fall to groups, usually committees. It is a fact of modern life that we can't even have fun without depending upon a group.

Family

Most families function to some degree with each member providing input, deciding, and assuming responsibilities for consequences of decisions.

In all group activities, the communication process is pivotal to how well, or if, the group will succeed. All four of the conditions in the definition of the small group are fundamental. Even more important are certain elements of the communication process which must be present to some degree for a small group to communicate effectively. There has been much research which suggests an important theory—that the more these elements, discussed in the next paragraphs, are present and functioning, the better the group will communicate.

SUMMARY PROBES

1. In what ways do small groups affect our lives?

2. What is pivotal to success in small groups?

ELEMENTS

What are the elements of the communication process functioning in small group communication? The elements considered here will be called factors because they are responsible for the varying success of the small group. Any discussion of these factors will be improved by grouping them according to (1) those uniquely important to communication functions of the small group, (2) those shared with all communication situations.

Communication Factors Unique to the Small Group

Group size. As the group changes from two, to three, to five, to ten, the transaction pattern of symbols changes. In the group of two, the dyad, each individual has fifty percent control over what happens to the transaction. As the group increases to three, each person has less direct control over the symbols which give meaning. A person's self is still just as important, but it appears to be more suppressed in favor of others.

Depending upon the task and the individuals, small groups—which consist of three to ten—can work effectively. If the members sense that group size of ten or more is becoming unworkable, the group will be inclined to adopt explicit rules to regulate interaction and communication patterns. It is possible that a group will become a mini-organization with a structure to inhibit openness within the group. There is no magic number, but if you want a group to have a chance to succeed, its size should not go beyond the limits imposed by task, openness desired, feelings of members toward each other. For an interview, the group is usually a dyad, two people. For an intimate conversation, it might be two or three. For a problem-solving task, three to five is usually a workable number. Investigating groups might be as large as ten to twelve.

As the group size increases, the number of lines of communication increases at a much faster rate. Figure 6.2 illustrates that a triad has three lines of communication; whereas, the number of lines of communication will increase to fifteen in a six-member group. What would happen with eight or nine members in the group? Can you imagine how the group would begin to subdivide into dyads and triads?

In the three-person group, there is a tendency for two individuals to line up together leaving out the third person. This tends to make all three overcautious. In a group of six there is still a chance that everyone will say something to each person. If the group gets larger, the communication seems to center on a few active participants, and the others are more or less left out of the discussion.

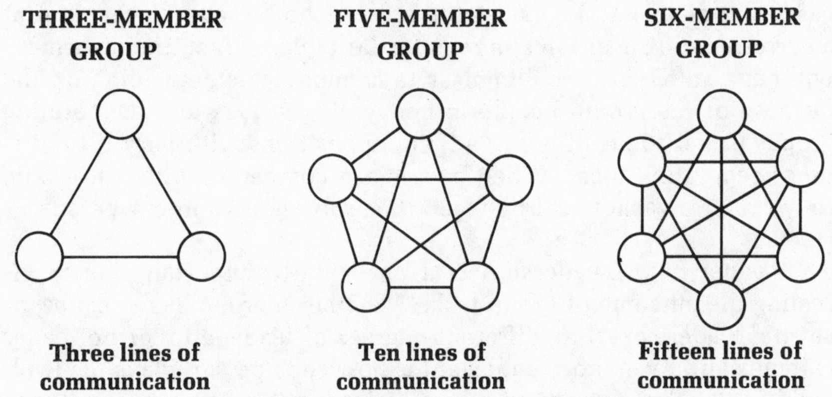

Figure 6.2 **Lines of Communication**

Information Flow. For most group tasks, it is imperative that all members contribute. An "open" communication network allows each member to contribute to the accomplishment of the task according to his or her personal capability. A communication network is "open" when some or all of the following conditions are present: (1) members will listen to any honest observation or suggestion; (2) remarks are made that are personally supporting rather than degrading; (3) trust exists; (4) individuals are honest; (5) individuals desire to share understanding; (6) individuals are willing to take risks.

Attitude of Members. The attitude of members toward the pattern of interactions is a third important factor. Within groups, a cooperative attitude will be more productive than a competitive attitude. Cooperation will facilitate satisfactory task completion.[2] A cooperative atmosphere encourages people to suggest ideas, to brainstorm, to think. A person's ego isn't threatened, and he or she will likely be willing to contribute the best they have to offer. Research has suggested that group members who cooperate interdependently in some task are friendlier and mutually more influential. A cohesion is built around a group norm. There is strong evidence to suggest that such cohesion produces more effective groups.[3]

Group Ecology. The importance of where people sit in relation to each other was dramatized by months of agonizing diplomacy regarding the seating protocol at the Geneva Conference to obtain a ceasefire in Vietnam. Resolution came after a round table was suggested as a substitute for a rectangular table. Recent research suggests that people at a round table are psychologically closer than at a corresponding position at a rectangular table. In fact, the placement will have an effect on willingness to communicate depending on the purpose of the group. People in conversing groups and cooperating groups prefer to be sitting in adjoining positions with very little distance separating them. When people are competing within a group, they prefer a vacant seat between themselves and another person.

Leadership. Leadership is a particularly important factor affecting the outcome of group tasks. Whether a group has a leader, or several leaders exerting different degrees of leadership, or no leader is important. Even more important is how each person plays his leadership role. There are many ways to lead and many different kinds of leaders, but a general statement might be that leadership consists of doing things that promote group interaction and move the group toward completion of the task.

Clearly, your groups are dependent on size, information flow, attitude toward interaction, ecology, and leadership. These are communication factors uniquely important to small group communication.

Communication Factors Shared With Other Communication Situations

It is imperative that a participant be heard. The participant must speak clearly and distinctly enough so that the message—what is being uttered—can be understood. For a group in which the task is shared exclusively by the group, it is only necessary that the members of the group be able to hear and understand each other. However, when a group is performing a task representing others or for others, such as a conference or a panel discussion, it is necessary that the listeners outside the group (audience) hear and understand. Failure to be heard and understood are clearly factors imperative to success of the small group.

All factors of nonverbal communication are important to the success of small groups attempting to use transaction to complete goals just as they are in other communication situations. One such factor is space ecology or the relationship of the physical parts to each other.

Credibility is another factor common to other communication situations, as well as to small groups. All the dimensions of credibility exist as several individuals interact to form the small group transaction.

Language is perhaps the single most important factor affecting small group communication, just as it probably is the single most important factor affecting all communication situations. Clear language depends upon the accuracy with which the words we use correspond to that thought to which they refer. The closer members of a group can come to having words correspond to reality, the better the group will function in completing its task. For a thorough discussion of problems encountered by failing to have less than maximum reality, see the discussion of verbal variables in interpersonal communication in Chapter Four.

SUMMARY PROBES

1. **What communication factors are unique to the small group?**
2. **What communication factors affecting small groups are common to all communication situations?**
3. **How does cooperation improve communication in the small group?**
4. **Why is leadership a factor in the small group communication process?**

LEARNING EXPERIENCES

1. List the groups you belong to which, at times, involve ten or less people in each of the following categories:

a. governing
b. working
c. recreational
d. educational

2. Observe several small groups. Note which ones have leaders. Note which ones demonstrate cooperation. Which of these groups were more successful in completing their goals? Can you draw any conclusions about the purpose of a group and the factors which hindered the effort of the group to complete goals?

3. For an entire day keep a log of all the dyadic communication situations in which you participate. Note especially the following:

a. What happens to your goals during the interchange?
b. What happens to your ideas as you talk back and forth?

4. Observe the chairperson of some group to which you belong. Write a short paper explaining what techniques the chairperson used and how successfully they worked.

5. Find three to five other people and form a group sitting together in a circle. Place one dollar's worth of change in front of one of the other members. Tell the person to give as much of the change to as many or as few of the other group members as desired. After five minutes discuss the following questions among the group:

a. Why was the money given to a particular group member and not another?

b. What determined how much was given?

6. How would you draw a communication model for a small group? What kind of interactions are there? Draw charts of people sitting in a circle and show these patterns:

a. A group with a leader.

b. A group that is centered around an individual.

c. A group with an emphasis on group-minded interaction.

7. What do you see as differences in communication patterns in the two following groups:

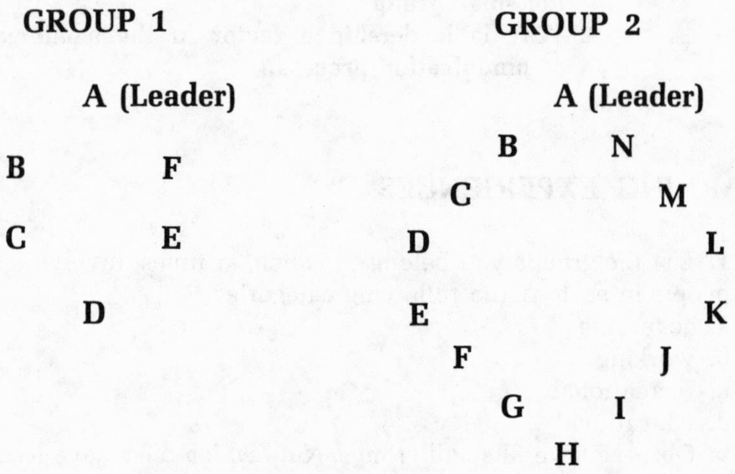

Figure 6.3 **Communication Patterns**

Which group has the most interchange among members?

Which group has the most interchange between the leader and the members?

SEVEN

GOALS **After completing this chapter you will be able to:**

1. Formulate a statement of research findings about the components of cohesion.

2. Describe the significance of each component of cohesion in the small group process.

3. List specific ways to build cohesion.

4. Relate feedback and interaction.

5. Play a positive, contructive role in small group process.

Creating Cohesion As A Participant

The preceding chapter established that, for certain tasks, group decisions are more effective than individual decisions. Such success is fundamentally dependent upon the degree of group cohesion, nature and extent of leadership, and the structure employed by the group. Cohesion is present when members of a group select common approaches to a task. When each individual moves in a separate direction, cohesion is destroyed. The extent to which one or more members of a group move in a separate direction proportionately weakens group cohesiveness. Three patterns are shown in Figure 7.1. Pattern A represents the most cohesive group—the one most likely

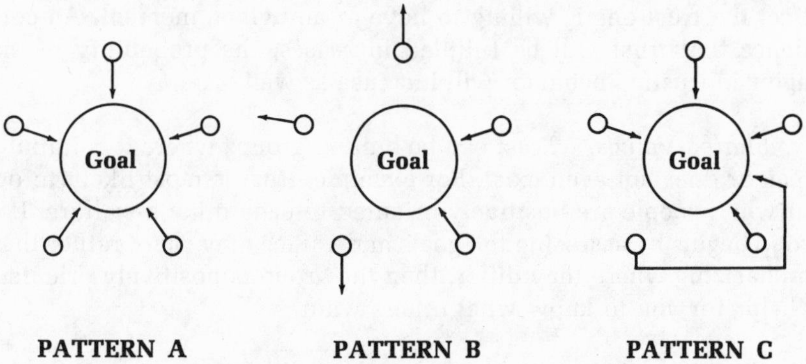

Figure 7.1 **Patterns of Group Cohesion**

to arrive at the most satisfying conclusion in the least amount of time because there is a recognized, shared goal. Pattern B represents the group where too many individuals are oriented toward independent goals. This group lacks focus. Pattern C suggests a group in which delay occurs because one or more members vacillate from one goal to another.

COMPONENTS OF COHESION

When you understand what constitutes cohesion, it will be possible to approach the group task more effectively. Several important components of cohesion are trust, cooperation, and interaction.

Trust

If you trust somone, you *expect* that certain behavior is probably going to occur. Expectation is only the logical part of trust. Inclusive in the meaning of trust is also the emotional counterpart of logic, involvement or *motivation*. If trust exists, there is a positively directed feeling about an expected behavior. Since trust involves probabilities and feelings, it is important to recognize that trust is usually not absolute but relative to the circumstances affecting probable behavior and strength of mutual feeling. Clearly, trust is a very important component of cohesion; but, perhaps even more important is accurate perception of the degree of trust warranted in a given group's approach to a task. The confidence in reciprocity will directly affect the trust one is willing to have at any given moment. As confidence that trust will be fulfilled increases, the probability of engaging in trusting behavior will increase as well.[1]

Shared Values. Trust can be built in groups where it is initially weak or does not even exist. For example, trust is most likely to occur when people are positively oriented to each other's welfare. If a group begins by assessing the goals and values they share rather than emphasizing where they differ, then the group is positively oriented. It helps for you to know what others want.

Openness. Openness is a second condition necessary for building trust. When ideas, feelings, and beliefs are expressed freely, then an open situation exists. An environment in which fear of personal devaluation, ridicule, or deceit are absent is an open environment. When the ideal situation and the environment exist together, then true openness is present. Lack of openness will be very depressing to the process of discussion. When a few people sit like statues revealing only an exterior while others are honestly trying to share something of their inner self, the whole experience will be very unrewarding.

Complete openness can be dangerous and therefore risky. There is no guarantee that another person will not take advantage of the personal openness by exploiting revealed information or feelings to his own gain. Indeed, one person's gain may be another's loss.

Constructive openness is a situation and environment during which promoting one person's gain would not be at another person's loss. It is attitudinal support rather than destructive support and actively shows assent, feeling, warmth, and concern. Constructive openness is best characterized by the following guidelines:

1. Openness must be a consequence of a desire to improve relationships with others. One must want to know the beliefs and values of others and must sincerely care that others accurately perceive his own beliefs and values.
2. Openness means taking risks. Individuals who are open thereby agree to risk rejection or even betrayal. There is also the risk that another person will respond emotionally from a strong bias. One must make some determination of how much he is willing to risk in order to facilitate realization of a group goal.
3. Openness requires an attitude of helpfulness when a person has a "mental posture" which asks "What can I do to help?" That person will be more open and in turn effect a similar "posture" from others in the group.

Creating openness requires that you know a great deal about yourself and disclose at least a significant portion of yourself to others. It is imperative that you be able to say to yourself, "I believe x, y, and z;" and then, be willing to say to someone else, "I believe x and y." This kind of self-awareness and self-disclosure is necessary to an open environment which will then contain the potential for a high degree of mutual trust by members of the group.

It is only logical that before you can be open about beliefs, values, and feelings, you must have an accurate self-awareness. The problem is that often you don't know your own self. You might want to think of yourself as a liberal-minded person on control of media;

however, upon careful self-examination of issues of controlling specific segments of the media society, you might find you aren't nearly as liberal as you thought.

Self-disclosure means that a portion of ourselves is made publicly available for others to know. Everyone has about them certain things which they know and which are known to others. This is what Luft and Ingram call our *open* area. An example might be a statement made and reported in the press regarding some issue. In addition, everyone has a group of things they are aware of but choose not to make known to others, called a *hidden* area. An example might be our unstated thoughts on an issue. Those things about a person known to others but unknown to the self constitute a *blind* area. An example may be some facial expression made unconsciously in response to a statement on an issue made by another party. Finally, there are always some things about a person unknown by anyone including the self, called the *unknown* area. This area might include biases or stereotypes. The fact that such an area exists is apparent as information from this unknown area eventually becomes known either to ourselves or to others. Then, it moves to one of the other areas.[2]

A diagram of a typical person's awareness pattern might look like the "picture" in Figure 7.2. In order to facilitate an open environment for group communication, a pattern of awareness like that in Figure 7.3 would indicate a more shared knowledge.

	Known to self	**Unknown to self**
Known to others	**Open**	**Blind**
Unknown to others	**Hidden**	**Unknown**

Figure 7.2 **Awareness Patterns**

Communication. A third factor useful to facilitate trust within a group is communication in general and feedback in particular. When

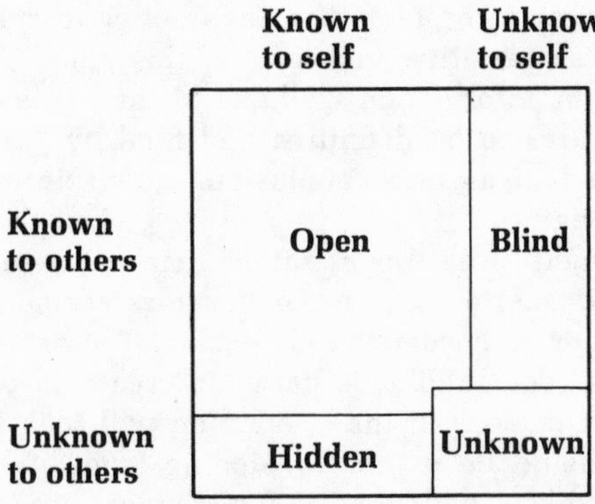

Figure 7.3 **Open Communication Awareness Pattern**

one has the opportunity to know another person's beliefs and intent, an accurate degree of trust can be determined. It has already been stressed that a desire is necessary. In addition, research indicates that if there is opportunity and ability to communicate a system of cooperation which defines procedure, trust will be increased.

Members in a group must willingly decide to accept a procedure for seeking beliefs without invoking defensiveness. Such a procedure would be giving and taking feedback. *Feedback* is the return communication, both verbal and nonverbal, provided by a receiver to a source in the communication act. By receiving feedback one is able to increase the area of known information and reduce the "blind" area. By giving feedback, one is facilitating an increase in known information.

Direct feedback will be more helpful to building trust and cohesion because the behaviors stand a greater chance of being accurately perceived. When consistent verbal and nonverbal direct feedback is supportive, accurate, and frank, it is possible for receivers to be precise in developing a realistic view of beliefs, values, and biases.

Identification of beliefs and values must occur during each stage of a group discussion. In order to facilitate feedback throughout a group discussion—and particularly during early stages—the following guidelines are suggested:

1. Feedback should be specific. A generalized response isn't very helpful since receivers may misinterpret or misunderstand. Nonverbal feedback alone cannot be a reliable means to provide explanation, exposition, or support. Verbal feedback must also be given.

2. Feedback ought to be tentative. It is better to state positions and information as tentative such as, "at this point," or "for the time being," or "the information we have so far." It is easy to fall prey to the pressures to be definitive and final by "seeming" so, even though actual ideas and conclusions about information may be tentative in nature.
3. Feedback ought to be sought rather than imposed. At times when we give feedback to someone, it becomes a kind of "pressure" to get that person to become nondefensive. The provider of feedback then "seems" dogmatic. It is better to create an open atmosphere, so that other persons in the interaction will *seek* feedback.
4. Feedback should be in nonthreatening language. Statements like "you are mistaken" and "that's a foolish idea" are certain to provoke defensiveness on the part of receivers.
5. Feedback should be concise. In order to avoid dominating, it is helpful if feedback utilizes a minimum of words and nonverbal symbols. Extraneous verbal and nonverbal feedback will clog the communication channel.

Cooperation

The second significant component of a cohesive group is cooperation. Groups which hold a common goal for all individuals within the group can be called cooperative. Groups in which each individual holds a separate goal which may be similar to others only by chance can be called competitive.

A group attempting to arrive at a consensus position on means to build a community swimming pool will be frustrated if several members of the group hold a strong private goal to obtain location of the pool in their own neighborhood. It is even conceivable that such a group may fail completely if several people let private goals create issues and arguments which distract from the question of means to build a pool.

Considerable research has focused on the question of cooperation versus competition as they relate to task completion by groups.[3] In an experimental situation Deutsch found that cooperative groups produced both qualitative and quantitative results superior to competitive groups. Subsequent research suggests that the superiority of cooperation is dependent on the degree to which members share a goal.

Cooperation in task-oriented groups can be promoted by, first, reminding members of the common goal they share, and, second, making a search for compromise positions when conflict develops. A search for compromise begins by finding minimum conditions which are acceptable to everyone, then searching for a solution to a problem which will meet these minimums. It is this condition which makes it so important that discussion groups consciously and carefully include a criteria formation stage in the systematic structure.

Interaction

Interaction is a term used to refer to the active, mutual, multidirectional, multidimensional flow of communication symbols between two or more individuals. When two people interact, the feedback of B to A will influence A's next communication. When several people interact, the communication of any person at a given point in time is influenced by several previous responses. For interaction to exist, it is necessary that *influence* through feedback exist. If each person merely speaks to others, this is not considered interaction.

Interaction begins the moment actions of others are perceived as a response or a comment on a source's message. It is then a perception of a perception and a signal that mutual agreement is reached as well as mutual influence.

Interaction continues as long as source and receiver: (1) give the receiver verbal and nonverbal feedback, (2) continue to constantly influence each other in thought and words, (3) are supportive rather than defensive.[4]

PARTICIPANT COMMUNICATION SKILLS

The following suggestions should enable individuals participating in a group to contribute in such a way as to facilitate a group's realization of goals.

Preparation

In order to have information on a subject, a group member must search and gather information. Rational opinions and even beliefs must develop from reflection on information. No matter what kind of group you are in, preparation is a must. Even when planning to participate in an informal group you must give thought to the subject or subjects and make some search for information. Before participating in a task group, the members must search thoroughly and contemplate carefully. Preparation may be completed by personal interview, library research, or experimentation. The first two methods should be planned carefully and recorded accurately. Source identification is an absolute requirement. Usually, time will preclude the last method.

Participation

A group is only as strong and successful as the aggregate of its members. In some cases, a group is only as strong as its weakest member. Information, ideas, and feelings come through participation. Groups dominated by a few are denied access to information and to that extent denied opportunity to arrive at a best conclusion. Participation should, of course, be relevant, thoughtful, and complete, including feedback.

Openness

This point was discussed earlier. The value of openness is clear: Feedback is the means by which one can give and receive information.

Control Preattitudes Sets

The effect of preconceived ideas can be minimized by recognizing they exist, that they are normal, and that they should not stand in the way of rational evaluation of data.

Listening

Since most of your time in a group will be spent hearing others, it is important that you actively listen. Active listening should be empathic in the sense that the individual receiver is trying to share a meaning with a source. Understanding through empathy is the goal of this kind of listening. You can understand what has been heard only to the extent that there is sharing of meaning, spirit, or feeling.

Avoid falling into the misconception that listening is easy or passive. It is, in fact, very active and often difficult. Several common errors in listening habits frequently create communication barriers within groups.

Listening for Facts. When you limit your attentive hearing just to a search for facts, you fail to remember the circumstances given surrounding the fact. The facts have meaning only in a context and become distorted as they get plugged into subsequent contexts. Listening to memorize specific facts in a group discussion may cause feedback to seem strange.

Criticizing Delivery and Physical Appearance. There is nothing wrong with making judgments about these two communication aspects; however to do so while someone is speaking is likely to focus your attention away from the content of a message and judgments about the content of the message. There are times when the essence of a person's message is far more important than the delivery of the message.

Faking Attention. When you just "look" as if you are listening, you may be fooling everyone including yourself. When you are using energy consciously to fake attention (i.e., sit just right, smile in a concerned way, cock the head to one side, give verbal noises of acknowledgment) you are using energy. Energy used to fake attention is energy taken away from actual attention. The end result is that you cheat yourself as well as the group.

Avoiding Difficult Listening. Too often we turn away from topics of communication because they are difficult. It is difficult to follow the economic intricacies of an explanation of tax laws or an embezzlement case. It was difficult for some to follow the legal maze of Watergate-related cases. It is necessary, however, for you to listen to the difficult economic conditions of a bond market if you are contemplating selling revenue bonds to build a new school building.

Tuning Out a Subject. Some people adopt the attitude, "interest me and entertain me." Individuals who are highly dogmatic with narrow latitudes of acceptance will tend to "tune out" a subject as soon as they hear one or two words. They may proceed to argue mentally with a speaker or they may just switch thoughts to other topics. These individuals are not listening at all. They may even cease to hear. Such a bad habit can be broken by consciously listening to a wide range of subjects. In high school your literary appreciation is broadened by consciously reading several types of literature. The same method will work to broaden your listening appreciation.

Wasting the Advantage of Thought-Speed over Speech-Speed. It has been established that the average rate of speaking is about 125 words per minute, but the brain can process words at the rate of 400–500 words per minute. Many individuals can read 1,200 words per minute. The gap between speaking time and comprehension time provides available time for the brain to become sidetracked. Competing stimuli, both internal and external, are always present. In order to avoid this bad listening habit, listening authorities suggest that we: (1) anticipate the speaker, (2) reflect on the adequacy of support for each point, (3) mentally review the communication which has been presented, (4) listen "between the lines" for additional meaning.

To be a more effective contributor to a group, it is important to cultivate good listening habits including the following:

1. Listen to the entire message.
2. Listen for main ideas.
3. Listen for details which support main ideas.
4. Listen with an open mind.
5. Listen with concentrated energy.

PARTICIPANT ROLES

Group members will engage in various roles which may promote cohesion and ultimately task completion. Some roles will promote satisfaction of strictly personal and individual needs. More useful roles are those which promote group growth and satisfaction of group needs. It is convenient to describe several prominent cohesion-building, growth-oriented roles within the framework of group task roles and group building and maintenance roles.

Group Task Roles

The roles in this classification can be expected to facilitate and coordinate the systematic problem-solving structuring of a group.

Initiator. This person will suggest ways for the group to achieve its goal or task. The person may be suggesting a structural system or a subgrouping as a means of attacking the task.

Information Giver. This person offers opinions, data, and inferences. Personal testimony and personal experience may be included in the opinions and data.

Information Seeker. This person seeks amplification or clarification of opinions, data, and inferences presented. Testing of support material is the function of a person in this role.

Elaborator. This person adds detail to generalized data and brainstorming suggestions which have originated with other individuals. Included in elaboration may be a "thinking out loud" method of speculation on the workability of some idea.

Coordinator. This person identifies relationships among ideas and the various means of support offered. Frequently, this person will play a vital role during a stage of evaluating various proposals in relation to some kind of criteria previously introduced into the group thinking. The coordinator is often asking, "how does x relate to y?"

Energizer. This person prods the group to decision making. Words of a person in this role invariably begin with, "Let's see if we can't . . .".

Group Building and Maintenance Roles

There are roles which promote group-centered attitudes as opposed to individual-centered attitudes and help to orient members to the group.

Encourager. This person readily agrees to the contribution of others even when he or she may later offer contradictory information. Encouragement may often be provided by warmth offered through verbal and nonverbal feedback. Even the simplest nod or smile when someone is explaining a point is encouragement to continue.

Harmonizer. This person functions as a mediator to resolve differences and disagreements between other members of the group.

Goal Setter. This person expresses goals as well as standards for a group to achieve in its functioning as a group.

Follower. This person is also important to a group process. It is necessary at times that someone go along with the group movement.

From a practical perspective, no one performs one single role constantly; rather, one person will likely perform several roles during a group discussion of some question. The development of skill in diagnosing role requirements is a worthy objective of anyone who will be participating in a group. Development of role flexibility is also important, so that one may easily move from role to role as the need emerges and is diagnosed. Commitment to the role-playing guidelines is an important first step but must be followed by "practice" in simulated or real situations.

SUMMARY PROBES

1. **How does openness contribute to cohesion?**
2. **How does self-disclosure contribute to cohesion?**
3. **When is self-disclosure dangerous to the self?**
4. **How can you improve the effectiveness of the feedback you give?**
5. **What is an effective participant?**
6. **How do positive participation roles contribute to effective group process?**
7. **What are the ways to build cohesion?**
8. **How valuable is cooperation to a group task?**

LEARNING EXPERIENCES

1. Observe a situation in which someone's self-esteem seems threatened. Describe the communication behaviors used by the individual to overcome the threat. Can you suggest alternate behaviors which would have reduced the threat and left the communication channel open?

2. Find a group of five to six members. Choose a problem for discussion in your group. After fifteen minutes of discussion each member should write out: (1) the problem, (2) the goals, (3) the important facts and opinion. Compare the papers. What can you conclude? Discuss among yourselves how people were trying to cooperate during the discussion.

3. Talk with a close friend about any topic of your choice. Plan to have the conversation in a location where you will have some privacy for at least twenty minutes. After the conversation, each of you should make a list of all stimuli which affected your conversation (e.g., time of day, outside noise, words, climate, culture). Which ones made you more open and trusting toward each other? Compare your lists and discuss the implications of similarities and differences on your lists.

4. Conduct your own experiment to observe the point by completing the group activity *Broken Squares.* You will need to organize two groups of five people giving Group I instructions to allow only nonverbal feedback and Group II instructions to allow verbal feedback. Complete the experiment according to the following directions.

Instructions

a. Form two or more groups of five people.
b. Have a sixth person assigned as an observer of each group. Ask each group to distribute the envelopes from the prepared packets (see below). The envelopes are to remain unopened until your signal.
c. Give whatever directions you choose to each group.
d. Read the directions aloud. It will be necessary for you to monitor each group to enforce the rules you establish.
e. When all the groups have completed the tasks, have each group discuss the experience. Discussion might focus on feelings or upon reasons why groups did what they did to solve the problem.

Preparation

A set consists of five pieces containing bits of cardboard which have been cut into different patterns, and which when properly arranged will form five squares of equal size. One set should be provided for each group of five persons. To prepare a set of squares, cut out five cardboard squares of equal size, approximately six-by-six inches as shown in Figure 7.4.

After drawing the lines on the six-by-six-inch squares and labeling them with lowercase letters, cut out each square as marked into smaller pieces to make the parts of the puzzle. Mark the five envelopes A, B, C, D, and E. Distribute the cardboard pieces in the five envelopes as follows:

Envelope A has pieces	i, h, e
B	a, a, a, c
C	a, j
D	d, f
E	g, b, f, c

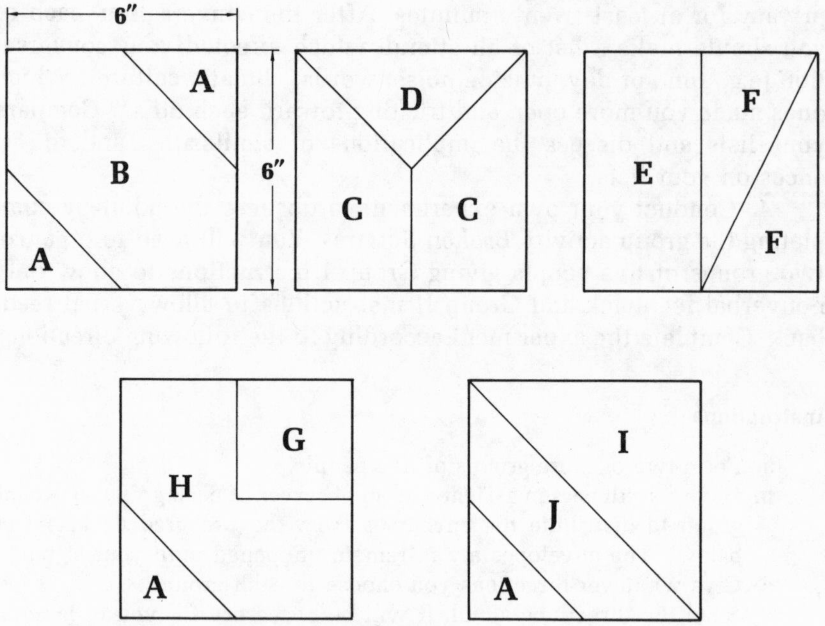

Figure 7.4 **Diagram for Broken Square Activity**

Erase the penciled letter from each piece and write, in its place, the appropriate envelope letter. This will make it possible to return the pieces to the proper envelope later.

5. Conduct another experiment with the group activity *Island.* Before beginning the activity, have one group meet separately to first review their own values about life, death, right, wrong, and then identify one point of commonality for each of the four general value areas. Proceed with the activity as described below.

> Somewhere in the middle of the uncharted Pacific Ocean there exists a beautiful, uninhabited island. Seven people have become stranded on the island: (1) a pregnant woman; (2) an internationally famous doctor; (3) a well-known American scientist; (4) a teen-age girl; (5) an elderly diabetic man; (6) a Catholic Priest; (7) vice-president of the United States. A rescue plane happens on the island and can return one person to civilization. The chances of a second trip are remote because the island is uncharted. The people left behind will not starve, but they must be able to meet necessary social and biological needs in order to survive. Problem: which of the seven should be allowed to leave?

6. List three persons with whom you expect to have significant speech communication encounters during the next week. For each person describe as best you can how that person sees the world. How does each vision of the world differ from yours?

7. On a particular day bring or wear to class an object or apparel that represents how you perceive yourself. During a class session discuss how that apparel represents you and how it is perceived by the rest of the class.

References

Cartwright, Dorwin, and Zander, Alvin. *Group Dynamics.* Evanston: Harper & Row, 1968, pp. 430–43, 461–82.

Kelly, Charles M. "Mental Ability and Personality Factors in Listening." *Quarterly Journal of Speech* 49 (1963): 152–56.

Salzinger, K. "Experimental Manipulation of Verbal Behavior: A Review." *Journal of General Psychology* 61 (1959): 65–94.

Sherif, Muzhafer, et.al. *Intergroup Conflict and Cooperation.* Norman: University of Oklahoma Book Exchange, 1961.

EIGHT

GOALS **After completing this chapter you will be able to:**

1. Explain how leadership is related to influence.

2. Define leadership.

3. Identify the characteristics of effective leadership.

4. Make a choice of leadership form by considering the advantages and disadvantages of different forms.

5. Utilize a set of guidelines to help you be a more effective leader.

Creating Cohesion As A Leader

Leadership is one of the two most important determinants of group effectiveness. It has been established by experiment and by empirical observation that groups with leaders have a better record of completion than groups without leaders.[1] This chapter will consider: (1) the definition of leadership, (2) types of leadership, (3) an identification of effective leader characteristics, (4) guidelines for leaders in small task groups.

DEFINITION

When the term *leadership* is used you usually formulate several mental images. We think of one who exerts influence on or within a group of people. Something that person does or doesn't do is partially responsible for the direction and actions of a group. The presence of some individuals is a force itself. The superb television film, "The Missiles of October," illustrated the effect of the physical presence of President Kennedy on the National Security Council meetings. In other instances, the activity of individuals itself will generate response. The capacity to generate response by presence or action is influence. The second image conjured up by the term *leadership* is usually one who exerts influence in an interpersonal manner. Finally, you think of one who is exerting interpersonal influence toward completion of some *task*. Our definition of leadership, then, would be: "A person or persons who interact with a group so as to facilitate the group to behave in a way which will lead to completion of a task."

Another similar definition is that stated by Tannenbaum: "Interpersonal influence . . . through the communication process, toward the attainment of a specified goal or goals. Leadership always involves attempts on the part of a leader to affect the behavior of a follower."[2]

TYPES OF LEADERSHIP

There are three important dimensions to be considered which give further meaning to the term leadership: function, role, and source.

Function

The functional dimension is viewed as the performance of certain acts which help the group complete its tasks. The determining factor from this perspective is the nature of the group including goal, structure, attitude, and need. The leader is one who generally verbalizes both an identification of what the group wants or needs as well as the process to be utilized in fulfilling the need. The leader is like that person who suggests that, "it seems clear the group needs to consider the criteria of cost when evaluating proposal X."

The performance of leadership as a function may be authoritarian, democratic, or laissez faire. Some of the leader behaviors viewed as a function are compared in Table 8.1.

Role

The second dimension, role, tells something about what specific things are done by the person who is the leader in a group. Major leadership role behaviors are summarized in six categories.

Structuring. The leader plays this role by directing group attention to individual members rather than on the leader.

Table 8.1 **Leadership Performance as Function**

Authoritarian	**Democratic**	**Laissez faire**
Set all policy.	Policies determined by the group with encouragement from the leader.	All policy determined by the group.
Steps dictated by the leader.	Steps to a goal sketched by the leader and technical advice given when needed. Leader often suggests alternatives.	Leader supplies materials and offers information. No other action by the leader.
Leader dictates working relations of members.	Members free to work out own division of work	Leader doesn't participate.
Leader personal in praise and criticism; aloof.	Leader tries to work with the group rather than praise or blame.	Leader doesn't participate.

Facilitating. The leader plays this role by being open and somewhat permissive toward directions the group wants to follow, thus exhibiting a high degree of trust.

Maintaining. The leader plays this role by encouraging people, by trying to mediate differences, by coordinating the information put into the group.

Directing. The leader plays this role by encouraging systematic analysis of problem and solutions. This person suggests ways to accomplish a task and keep the group functioning.

Questioner. The leader plays this role by asking questions which force members to analyze their tasks and their own ideas and information. In this role, the leader may be drawing out information from members.

Provider. The leader plays this role by arranging for materials, charts, equipment, and possibly even refreshments.

Source

The source of leadership authority is a third dimension to be considered. In some group situations, the group leader is designated. In a meeting of division sales managers of some corporation, the vice-president of sales would quite possibly be *designated* as leader of the group. In other situations, an individual or individuals will *emerge* as leader by fulfilling necessary leadership functions and roles. An "emerging" leader will usually do so through unconscious deferment from others in the group. The group with a "designated" leader may or may not have a democratic type leader depending upon the individual. It is even possible that a "designated" leader will even be authoritative or autocratic. The group with an "emerging" leader will be more likely to have a democratic type of leader.

There are valid reasons to support the existence of all three forms of leadership within a group. The validity of the autocratic leadership assumes several things about the group itself. If the members tend to be basically followers who deplore being leaders themselves, someone must do the job. There are many reasons why potentially capable group members might be reluctant to appear too forceful, this abdicating to one individual. Examples are in advisory groups composed of members who have strong trust in the character of one individual, or are all extremely involved as leaders within other groups.

The democratic leadership form assumes a desire and capacity by members to be highly involved with input of information, analysis, suggestion, and evaluation. In such a group, the leader will seek to discover the group's will and facilitate its achievement. The course of such a group can never be predetermined by anyone. All ideas are group property. Members speak when they wish. Decisions are the result of collective action.

The democratic form of leadership is based on the assumptions that (1) collective wisdom is greater than that of any single member, (2) those affected by a decision are entitled to a voice in making the decision.

Being a democratic leader may be very frustrating at times. It is difficult to watch other members trying to struggle toward completion of a task which you could easily complete; and yet, you realize that a stronger group feeling will exist if task completion is a result of the collective group action rather than leader completion. The reward to democratic leadership for patience is satisfaction seeing guidance help a group find its own direction and then succeed in completing a task.

Laissez faire leadership is in great contrast to autocratic leadership. In reality, it is nonleadership since the leader does nothing. Someone may open a discussion by saying, "Let's get started," and then exert no further influence. Such a leadership form is hard to justify with any group. Even a group of individuals skilled in discussion methods will be less productive in a laissez faire structure.

SUMMARY PROBES

1. **What is the relationship between "influence" and "leadership"?**
2. **Compare autocratic, democratic, and laissez faire leaders. Which method would you prefer to use?**
3. **What are the sources of leadership?**

LEADERSHIP CHARACTERISTICS

Considerable research has been done to identify the characteristics of those individuals deemed to be good leaders. Much early research was unsuccessful in that the traits used did not consistently separate individuals. It seems that research has failed to identify any special personal traits as characteristics, that is, I.Q., or charismatic quality. However, when viewed from a behavioral perspective, it has been possible to identify certain kinds of behavior with those in an effective leadership position. Generally, the characteristics add up to the ability to find the delicate balance between imposition upon a group and encouragement. It is also clear that effective leaders are those who are sensitive to the changing conditions of their groups and flexible in adapting their own behavior to new requirements.

When a group works toward a goal, it is usual to ascribe values to a leader, based on perceived behavior of the leader. Leaders manifest idiosyncrasies which generate degrees of trust. There seems to be direct correlation between trust and group success.

Two important characteristics of leadership identified by the Ohio State Leadership Studies are consideration and initiation of structure.[3] These two were located as characteristic of leaders in the formal small group. The considerate leader is one who expresses personal concern about members and attempts to schedule meetings at a most suitable time. Behaviors of considerate leaders include: being open to suggestions of change, being willing to explain action, giving in to others during discussion, treating everyone equally.

Initiation of structure seems to be a characteristic expected of leaders. Behaviors of leaders who initiate structure include: offering new approaches to problems, "needling" people for greater effort, emphasizing meeting deadlines.

Among educators there has been observed a high correlation between these two characteristics of leadership; that is, those perceived as considerate were also perceived as initiators of structure.[4]

Another way of describing characteristics of leaders is the reductionist approach suggested by John Geier.[5] From research, it was apparent that during the short conflict-free phase of a group process, participants with three types of personal characteristics were eliminated from leadership consideration: first, those who were misinformed; second, infrequent participants; and third, rigid or dogmatic individuals. During the second phase of a group process, participants eliminated from leadership were: first, authoritarian members, and second, incessant talkers.

Perhaps the characteristics of a good leader can be summarized by the words *balance, utilization,* and *competence.* It is characteristic of a good leader to maintain a *balance of control.* This leader uses enough control devices to maintain order within a group and to keep the group aimed at its goal, but allows enough freedom to create an open and trusting environment.

It is characteristic of a good leader to maintain a *balance of affectation.* This leader is able to use good communication skills effectively without calling attention to the communication skill itself. This leader speaks well in the sense of effective use of communication source skills. Remarks are concise, organized, pertinent, and clear.

It is characteristic of a good leader to maintain a *balance between inclusion and exclusion.* There is a delicate point of recognizing what ideas and information should be included because they are useful, and which ideas and information should be excluded because they offer little chance of productivity to the group.

It is characteristic of a good leader to make *maximal utilization of abilities and capacities* of the group. By knowing each person, the leader knows whom to encourage to participate at each point, or to whom to assign certain tasks.

It is characteristic of a good leader to be *competent.* Leaders are knowledgeable concerning the available structure by which a group may complete its task.

If a group is not functioning well, the cause may be with the group, with the leader, or with the interaction of both. Early research with group process assumed movement of a leader would solve the problem, that is, replace the leader from within the group or relocate leaders from group to group. Recent research assumes that a more useful solution is to modify the group, that is, change its operating structure or manipulate the reward system. A more contemporary view is to consider either possibility as potentially useful in order to increase group productivity.

Guidelines for Leadership in Small Task Groups

The remainder of this chapter will suggest practical guidelines for those in a designated leadership position of a group discussing policy questions. Following these guidelines should facilitate task completion.

Keep Opening Remarks Brief. It is necessary to see that all members are acquainted; however, the introduction of members and the topic for discussion should be kept brief.

Suggest Structure for the Group. If the group is to follow the Dewey reflective-thinking steps, establish that system of organization. If the group will follow an agenda, distribute the agenda. If the group is to determine what the system of organization will be, help them to a consensus on structure.

Keep the Group Goal Oriented. It is normal for a group to move into tangents from a central question. Sometimes tangent thought is productive in the sense of finding good ideas. You must sense when the tangent is no longer productive and pull the group back. The best method is to use questions like: "How does this relate to our problem?" or "What is our objective?" A less desirable, but equally effective method is a statement such as, "We have strayed from the topic and need to return to the question of . . ." The first method is a democratic communication mode; whereas the latter method is authoritarian. To do nothing at all would be a laissez faire mode.[6]

Summarize Frequently. It is necessary that internal summaries occur frequently (at least every ten minutes). The leader should provide the summary or be responsible for asking someone else to make the internal summary. The internal summary here is similar in form and function to the internal summary of a public speech. (It may be possible to complete the summary by reviewing.) The internal summary will probably begin with, "So far, we seem to have said that . . .". A final summary is the second type of summary important to the group. This should certainly be the task of the leader. The final summary might begin, "In summary, we have decided . . .".

Thoroughly Discuss All Phases of the Process of Problem Solving. It is usual that members may want to rush on from problem analysis stage after considering only one or two ideas. Even more frequently, groups tend to skip over the criteria stage.

Bring the Discussion to a Definite Conclusion. Members often rush off without clearly arriving at a consensus or even majority decision. The conclusion might be a summary of progress, a statement of how reports of the meeting will be distributed, assignments for following and implementation of the group decision, or an evaluation of the meeting.

See That All Members Have an Equal Chance to Participate. Sometimes people are just reluctant to speak out; or sometimes a person wishes to contribute but can't get a word in with several aggressive individuals present. The reluctant members can be brought out with open questions directed to them. The member trying to participate can be aided by a leader forcefully asking the others to give everyone a chance. It might even be necessary to state that, "Mr. or Ms. ——— is trying to make a point." There are also some nonverbal techniques which will be helpful. When you ask a question of the group, let your eyes meet those who are reluctant.

Listen with Interest. The leader is the one person who must be aware of all the interrelationships of ideas and information. Listening actively is just as important for a leader as it is for members of a group.

Encourage Creative Thinking. Brainstorming is an effective means to promote creative thinking. There are times when this kind of thinking is useful. The danger is that creative thinking left unchecked may lead to unproductive tangents. Watch for possible solutions and continue to ask if there are other solutions.

Leadership is not just the task of the designated individual, nor is it just one isolated act by someone. It is a function involving many acts and in some sense many individuals. Any or all of the members of a group may contribute to leadership of the group. Some will lead at one time, and others will lead at another time. Each may lead in different ways.

Commonly, someone will be designated as leader. That person, it is hoped, will know how to function in a democratic manner and will be allowed to so function. At times the person will lead serving as a guide, as a stimulator, as a challenger, as a healer. Shared leadership is what makes a group most productive.

SUMMARY PROBES

1. **How does a good leader maintain balance?**
2. **List guidelines for the leader.**
3. **Specifically, how can the leader keep a group goal oriented?**
4. **What can the leader do to equalize participation?**
5. **In what way is everyone a leader in a group?**

LEARNING EXPERIENCES

1. Attend a group discussion and locate the person who is demonstrating strongest leadership. Write down the type of leader that the person is in the discussion. List three or four specific kinds of leadership behavior which caused you to draw the conclusion that the person was the strongest leader.

2. Observe a group discussion. Keep a frequency count of the number of times each person talks. Is there a relationship between number of contributions made by each member and ability as a discussant?

3. Observe a small group involved in a problem-solving discussion. Describe the ways in which the group leader demonstrated facilitative leadership. Suggest other ways in which he or she might have utilized such leadership but did not do so.

4. Formulate a group and select some current topic of interest to discuss in an impromptu manner in the group. Take a ball and establish a rule that only the person holding the ball may speak. Allow the ball to be handed to someone or to be placed in the center when a person finishes speaking. After about fifteen minutes of discussion draw some conclusions about the "power" of leadership in a group.

5. In small groups discuss three different case problems in turn, with rotating designated leaders who move from group to group as the cases change. Each leader will role play a very different form of leadership. Discuss the impact on the group of each form of leadership.

NINE

GOALS **After completing this chapter you will be able to:**

1. **Locate information for group discussion.**
2. **Accurately record data from several sources.**
3. **Arrange a group setting to make the best environment for interaction.**
4. **Understand the structure of three organizational patterns for group discussion.**
5. **Use the best organizational pattern for discussion.**

Effective Group Action Through Preparation and Organization

Taking a stroll through a large corporate office building might provide an opportunity to observe quietly two very different groups discussing policy questions. As we enter room A, seven people are seated in a row. As each person speaks, other members crane their necks to the left or right in order to see and listen to the person speaking. The room is large enough for sixty people, so the speaker's words echo several times around the room. After several minutes, we notice that the person in the center is some kind of leader and that the person on our immediate right does most of the speaking. Soon our attention is beginning to wane as we perspire in the eighty-five degree temperature. The extremely bright lights glaring in our eyes raise the temperature even more and make us feel as if we are being interrogated by the police. Fifteen minutes have elapsed and through the heat, light, and echo, we slowly recognize that not only has the discussion been dominated totally by the three individuals in the center of the line, but nearly every utterance has been just a personal opinion. We decide to continue our stroll through the building.

Moving down the corridor, we come to Room B. Inside we are immediately aware of several differences. Soft comfortable lighting replaces the bright glare of the previous room. No echoes resound in a room twenty-by-twenty feet which nicely accommodates the seven people seated around a circular table with an outer ring of fifteen chairs for interested observers. At last we spot a person who seems to be a leader of the group because everyone in the group in turn has made comments to that person. After fifteen minutes, we are able to make three general observations: First, everyone has contributed. Second, in addition to several opinionated statements, several individuals have offered supported factual statements. Third, during the fifteen minutes most remarks have dealt with why the problem facing the group exists at all.

The two examples of group discussion are clearly in sharp contrast. We might quickly draw the conclusion that group B is going to be more effective and efficient than group A. Such an inference would not be correct since we have observed only two examples. However, based on experience and experimentation with groups over years, it is possible to make the qualified inference that group B will *probably* be more effective and efficient than group A. The two factors of preparation and organization interact with participation and leadership to determine the degree of success by group discussion of policy questions.

PREPARATION

In order to prepare for a group discussion, there are long range, as well as short-range factors to consider. We will consider preparation as a set of variables—the three factors of resources, gathering information, and arrangement of facilities as member variables in that set.

Resources

Information which becomes input into a group must originate somewhere. That input should be the result of careful search and contemplation. Good data and clear thinking are essential for everyone. Experts on a subject will readily admit that they can do a better job if they prepare *specifically*. It is even more important that the nonexpert prepare specifically. In today's organization, most problems are too complex for a casual approach. Only by dependable information from good sources, carefully tested in our minds, can we avoid a group becoming a "pooling of ignorance."

Geier made a study of how highly group members value preparation. He found that being perceived as uninformed was the greatest single reason why members of leaderless groups were quickly eliminated from any bid for influence.[1]

As you search for information, it is important that the information be relevant, accurate, valid, and complete. Where to turn for information is the question probably foremost in your mind at this time. There are essentially three sources of information—others, through interview; others, through library research; and yourself.

Interviewing Others. Information obtained from direct interview of people is worthwhile if they have some qualification as experts. Interviewing is discussed in detail in Chapter Five. Here, several suggestions will be given to aid the search for information from interview. Arrange for an interview in advance and at the convenience of the subject being interviewed. Plan carefully the topics to be considered and primary questions you will use. Consider several secondary questions which you might want to have answered. If you are looking for factual information, be certain the questions are closed and worded so that specific data or information is clearly requested. If you seek opinion, ask an open question followed by a closed question, "Why?"

In an earlier section on interviewing, it was stressed that speaking and listening are equally important. You must be an active listener to the responses as they are given and relate the responses to each other.

When gathering information through interview to be used later in group discussion, it is necessary to record information accurately. You must take notes carefully or plan to record the interview.

Library Research. The best source for information is still the library. In fact, libraries of all sizes have become so well equipped, they pose a major problem in determining what information to retrieve or select.

Books are still the basic "stuff" of any library. They may be located efficiently by consulting the card catalog where books are listed alphabetically three times: by author's name, by title, and by subject. Many books are now placed on microfilm for the sake of economical storage but gaining access may necessitate assistance from a librarian.

Magazines are the next most common source for information. Several indexes are available to help find desired articles. *The Reader's Guide to Periodical Literature* is an index of popular and common magazine articles. More specialized indexes are: *The Education Index, Agriculture Index, Engineering Index, Psychological Abstracts,* and *Monthly Catalog of the United States Government Publications.*

Newspapers and pamphlets may have timely information. Except for *The New York Times Index,* newspapers are not indexed. However, that source will be helpful in finding reports of events as well as opinions in editorials.

There are several special reference sources available. *Facts on File* will contain some useful statistical data. *Information Please Almanac* will contain statistical data of governmental regions. More sophisticated data is available from *Statistical Abstract of the United States.*

Yourself. You have experienced more than you may think. Examine yourself in terms of what you know, what you think, and how you arrive at your conclusions. Do not exclude this source from your research. On the other hand, remember two important limitations. First, you are just one source. Second, you may be biased in your perception of your experiences. Therefore, avoid the danger of relying heavily on yourself lest you contribute to a "pooling of ignorance."

SUMMARY PROBES

1. **What are two good library sources of information?**
2. **How are questions important in interviewing for information?**
3. **To what extent are you a source?**

Gathering Information

How information is retained is another important specific preparation variable. In the case of the interview, the problem is solved by carefully taking notes or using tape recording.

If you have a good memory, it is often sufficient to allow the information to remain stored in the brain until recall is necessary. If recall is often a problem, then a set of recorded notes much like those of the interview would be helpful. In the case of library research, a system of recording and filing data would be most helpful.

Step one is to develop a systematic way of classifying any information you will find. For a question of energy control you would have a category for "fuel reserves," another for "alternative fuel sources," and a third for "government and private program costs."

Step two is to record material on three-by-five cards or some other orderly card system of uniform size. Each card should contain:

1. An identification of the category of information to which this piece belongs.
2. A citation of the source giving at least author, book or article, date, and page. This should be sufficient to locate the information again.
3. An accurate quotation or careful summary. If the material is a quotation, it should have quotation marks.

Consider the sample card in Figure 9.1 for the question of providing economic assistance to bankrupt cities.

SOLUTIONS

INTERVIEW WITH WILLIAM SIMON:

Q. Can the city balance its budget and pay for essential services without defaulting on some obligations?

A. I think they should seriously look at rescheduling their short-term debt.

William Simon, "Is New York Worth Saving?" *U.S. News and World Report* (November 10, 1975), p. 33.

Figure 9.1 **Sample Note Card**

The values of using a notecard system are flexibility and accuracy. The cards can be arranged and rearranged for different interpretations and uses of the data. Cards with accurate source identification can provide locations to check the information again.

Step three is to review the material after the library research has been completed. Apply some of the tests of evidence. Consider the qualifications of some of the sources of opinion. Look for material that may be contradictory and for information which shows consistency.

SUMMARY PROBES

1. **What information should be included for accurate source identification?**
2. **What are the three steps for gathering information?**

Arrangement of Facilities

The physical arrangement of facilities will have some influence on how group participants are able to interact with each other. Control of the physical environment is to a great extent the responsibility of the leader of a group, although the task might be that of a program arranger or a conference director. At any rate, if there is a designated leader, that person can exert strong influence on what happens to the physical environment.

Research about spatial relationships should provide some helpful guidelines for arrangement of facilities. Hall has observed that space is used differently in various types of communication transactions by various people. The distance between people varies considerably by culture. Those who are of North American culture tend to prefer distances of 6-18 inches apart when engaging in intimate communication. The normal distance for people who are friendly and acquainted but not intimate is 1½ feet to 3 feet. It should be obvious to the arranger that group participants who are in an adversarial relationship rather than normal, friendly relationship should not be seated so that they are forced to "invade" another's territory or have their territory "invaded." The result of territorial invasion would be an intensification of whatever friction already existed in the group.

In the small group setting, where people sit tends to have an impact on the interaction of the group. At a rectangular table, those who sit at the head or foot of the table tend to assume more of the leadership of the group than those who sit at the sides of the table. Those at the ends also tend to dominate the participation of the group. When participants are seated in a circle, they communicate most often to those opposite them rather than those sitting beside them.

The best arrangement of tables and chairs is one which minimizes the leader position and maximizes face-to-face interaction like that shown at a round table in Figure 9.2. The square or oblong arrangement maintains face-to-face interaction but tends to emphasize strength in the head or foot position as shown in Figure 9.3. The least desirable arrangement would be seating in a row as shown in Figure 9.4. If the group is in one of the rare situations of "performing" for an audience, then a slightly curved seating pattern like that in Figure 9.5 would be most useful. The type of leadership intended

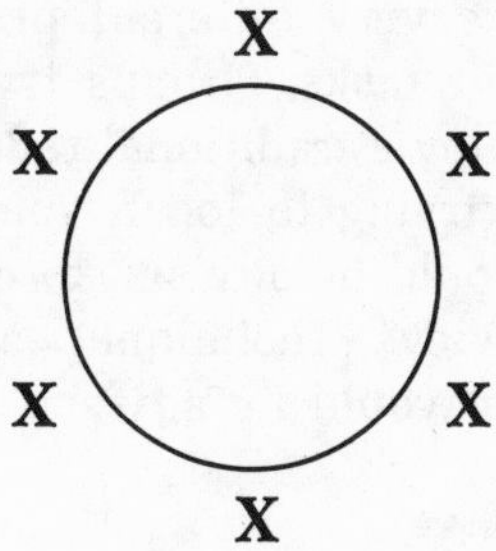

Figure 9.2.

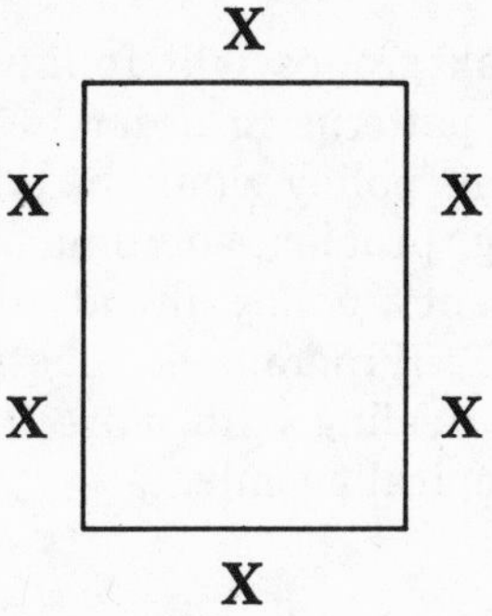

Figure 9.3.

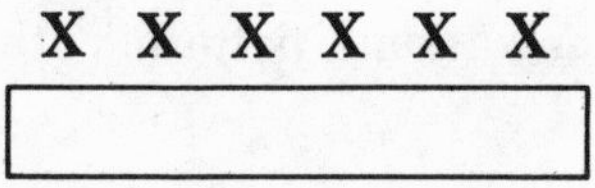

Figure 9.4.

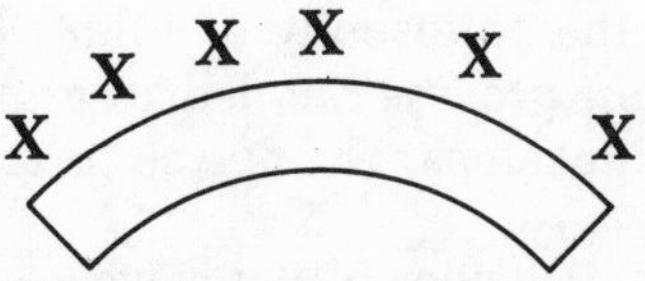

Figure 9.5

Figures 9.2—9.5 **Various Small Group Ecology Patterns**

should dictate a best pattern. For an autocratic group, a setting like that shown in Figures 9.3, 9.4, or 9.5 would be appropriate. For a democratic group, a setting like that shown in Figure 9.2 would be appropriate.

Other facilities greatly affect the comfort of members of a group and, therefore, are important to group effectiveness. Soft lighting, comfortable heat, soft carpet, and elegant furniture would usually add a feeling of comfort for members. In a classic study, Maslow and Mintz found the effects of comfortable room conditions to be noticeable on group behavior when groups were in a room briefly.[2] In a follow up study, Mintz discovered that group behavior deteriorated after the group was in an unpleasant room for an hour.[3]

SUMMARY PROBES

1. **What are the advantages of seating around a round table over seating around a square table?**
2. **What physical conditions are best for group behavior?**

PROBLEM-SOLVING PATTERNS

Task groups will follow one of three very different problem-solving patterns in order to complete their tasks. Groups trying to determine policy would be advised to employ a traditional reflective-thinking, problem-solution form. Groups trying to locate means to implement a policy already determined would be advised to employ a PERT (Program Evaluation and Review Technique) system. Groups dealing with more than one topic would be advised to follow a topical agenda.

Reflective Thinking

The reflective-thinking process has developed over four decades from the philosophy of John Dewey. Dewey's description of human thought process has led to a group organizational pattern with five essential steps. The five steps are:

1. Definition of a problem
2. Problem analysis
3. Criteria determination
4. Suggestion of possible solutions
5. Determination of best solution

Definition of a Problem. The first stage in problem-solving is identification of the problem, including consensus on definition of some important terms. This stage requires an answer to the question: "What is the problem facing the group?" It is often necessary to define the topic by limitation of the scope to be considered by a particular group. Time and interest to the group are valid reasons for limiting the scope of a problem to be considered by a group.

Problem Analysis. Analysis of the issues involved in a problem is one of the more important stages. This is a fact-finding stage in which the group searches for data to explain and illustrate the extent of the problem, and why the problem exists. During this stage the group will search for a thorough understanding of the problem. Questions are raised like, "How long has the problem existed?", "Who will be hurt as a result of the problem?", "Is the problem becoming more or less severe?", and "What are the causes of the problem?"

The importance of this stage is frequently overlooked. Hurried analysis of a problem may mean that later in evaluation of possible solutions the group will discover elements of the problem they do not understand. Then, the group will have to return to the problem-analysis stage. The result may be disorganization, irrational thinking, and considerable loss of time.

During this stage thinking should be analytic and critical. Data must be presented and tested for accuracy and relevance. Possible causal links must be critically analyzed.

This stage should be concluded with an internal summary which identifies what the group has managed to agree upon as to extent and causes of the problem.

Criteria Determination. Criteria determination is the stage most often omitted by a group. Criteria are used to judge proposed solutions to the problem. Establishing criteria means determining standards to be met by proposals. It will be possible later to make a rational choice of which proposed solution best meets the criteria. In addition to establishing criteria, it will be necessary to rank criteria in priority.

This stage may be the most critical for two reasons. First, strong differences within the group may present a challenge to members to compromise on goals. Second, omission of criteria which are subconsciously considered important by any member will make evaluation difficult and possibly incomplete.

Suggestion of Possible Solutions. Stage four, suggestion of possible solutions, is a discovery period. The stage should be rather permissive, free, and uncritical as the group brainstorms for possible solutions. Members must set aside the rigorous mental testing so important in the previous two stages and become creative thinkers instead.

It is important that more than just one or two obvious solutions are identified. Some of the less obvious ideas may become more attractive after examination; or, they may become useful additions to other ideas as larger compromise solutions.

The complete change in type of thinking required in this stage represents a special problem. Brainstorming is a particular means to solve this unique problem. There are two specific features of brainstorming: first, all critical evaluation is suspended, and second, all discussion—except for clarification—is suspended. Each member is verbalizing any possible solution which comes to mind. A list of all verbalized ideas is maintained by a group recorder.

If the group has more than five or six members, then a modification is necessary. Small subgroups of two to four persons called "buzz groups" should be formed. Each "buzz group" meets separately for a brief time and lists from the buzz groups are presented to the larger group.

Determination of Best Solution. During the fifth stage, determination of the best solution, members must return to critical analysis type of thinking and actually begin a decision-making process. Each possible solution should be considered in relation to the criteria established. It is important that each possible solution be compared with causes of the problem but also be examined for possible new problems which might be created. Pros and cons of each possible solution should be identified. Once these advantages and disadvantages are established, it is possible to do two things: (1) eliminate some solutions as clearly unacceptable, and (2) begin a system of comparative ranking. Comparative ranking is simply a means of taking two solutions at a time and ranking one above the other. The ranking is carried on through all available acceptable solutions. Assume there are four available, acceptable solutions to a problem. Solution one and two are compared and perhaps solution two is preferred. Solutions three and four are compared, and, perhaps, solution three is preferred. Solutions two and three are then compared, and, perhaps, solution two is preferred. The above system may be an oversimplification because a group may in fact decide to agree upon a compromise solution containing features from two or three original ideas.

The five stages are always essential to the reflective-thinking process with policy questions. Sometimes a group is forced to complete a sixth stage—means of action. Some task groups are charged with finding a way to implement their proposal. The concern of this stage is how something is to be done. It may be necessary to consider such matters as what communication is needed, what kinds of finances are needed, whether or not personnel will have to be hired, whether agency or governmental approval will be necessary, whether special legislation is necessary, whether outside help is required. A church group may decide to build a new parsonage and conclude during stage six that an outside money-raising group from the church conference is needed to coordinate the fund-raising drive.

SUMMARY PROBES

1. **List the five essential stages for reflective thinking.**
2. **What is one unique feature about each stage in reflective thinking?**
3. **What kind of difficulties may confront the group in each stage?**
4. **When is a sixth stage necessary?**

PERT

In his book, *Communication and the Small Group,* Gerald Phillips describes an organizational system most appropriate for groups who know fairly well what the goal is but are seeking efficient means to reach the goal.[4] In essence, this organizational system is a reverse process of the traditional Dewey reflective-thinking process.

PERT (Program Evaluation and Review Technique) is a quasi-mathematical procedure providing a workable operations plan. The process reveals the kinds of decisions which might have to be made before each stage is completed and identifies possible consequences. The PERT process is also operative in several stages as represented in the chart in Figure 9.6.

Stipulate Final Event. An event is an occurrence that takes no time but marks the start or end of a process or activity. Starting a car is not an event by this definition but the state of the car motor running is an event. A group which stipulates a final event is arriving at a predicted conclusion of the state of action likely to result from setting a procedure in motion. The state at completion time is the final event.

List Predecessor Events. During this stage the group can brainstorm on the question: "What must happen before the final event can be reached?" The focus is on determination of what must happen. Events suggested during the brainstorming must be analyzed for

Stipulate final event

List precedessor events

Determine event procedure

Diagram event relationships

List between event activities

Estimate times

Compare estimated time with necessary time.

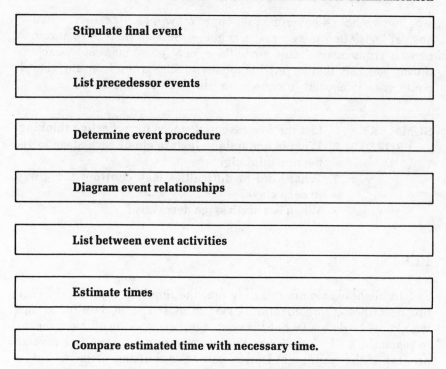

Figure 9.6. **Modified PERT Model for Decision Making**

their logic or necessity. Any events which do not meet one or the other of those two criteria need not be listed as predecessor events.

The group will not necessarily be bound by the original list of events and any event may be added or dropped.

Determine Event Procedure. The events are sorted into a rough time order. Necessity will determine what must happen before each event. Each event becomes necessary before another event. This is a rank ordering of events.

Diagram Event Relationships. A chart showing the relationship of events to each other is useful for planning. A hypothetical diagram of ten events might look like the example in Figure 9.7.

List between Event Activities. Activities are the happenings between events. It is essential to determine what activities are necessary so they may be given a realistic time allocation and so that a plan for their execution may be formulated.

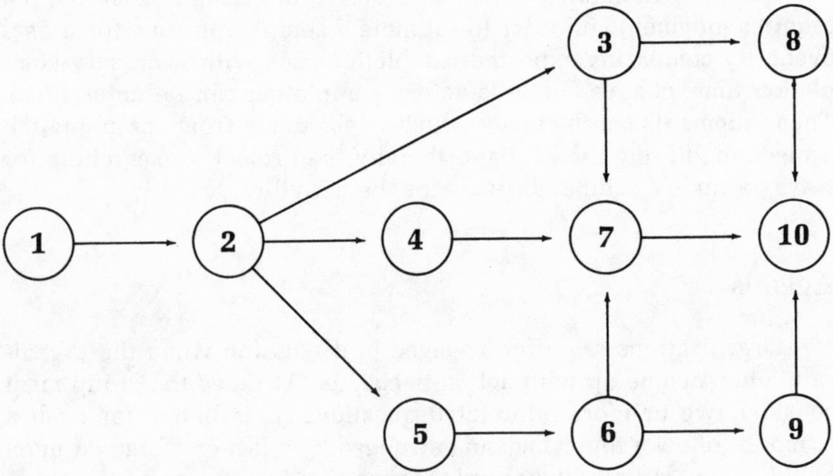

Figure 9.7 **Relationship of Events**

Estimate Times. A series of time estimates based on the activity list is made during the sixth stage of PERT. Time, in days, is estimated for activities between events (t_e). Three time estimates are made to calculate t_e. Pessimistic time (a) is an estimate of the time an activity would take if everything went wrong. Optimistic time (4m) is the fastest possible time to complete a task assuming everything went right. Probable time (b) is the time an activity is most likely to require. It assumes some things will go wrong and some will go right. Phillips suggests the following formula for estimating time of any given activity:

$$t_e = \frac{a+4m+b}{6}$$

The arithmetic mean derived is not likely to be exact in any given case but will be accurate over a large number of activities. Since any proposal considered will likely have many activities required, the overall time estimate should be fairly accurate. An example would be saving to buy a car: Pessimistic time is an estimate including allowance for illness, being laid off, inflation, et cetera. Optimistic time is the time required to save one week's pay, sign the papers, write a check. Probable time is a realistic estimate somewhere between the two extremes above.

Compare Estimated Time with Necessary Time. Stage seven requires judgments in order to estimate a completion time for a final event. By comparing expected completion time with necessary completion time, chances of satisfactory completion can be determined. Then judgments can be made which might range from scrapping the project, modifying the goal and thereby the project, to searching for ways to modify estimated times for the activities.

Agenda

Organizations are often engaged in discussion when the organization must come up with action decisions. At times the group must consider two or more nonrelated questions. It is better for such a group to follow a topical agenda arranged by a leader or agreed upon by the group. Usually the agenda is prepared in advance of the meeting.

Whatever organizational pattern a group needs or chooses to use, it is important to avoid several pitfalls. First, avoid "hidden agendas." A hidden agenda is a topic which someone brings to a group which does not appear on the organizational pattern or on the agenda. It may be an ulterior goal someone is trying to promote.

Second, avoid rushing through a pattern. Each stage is important. It needs to be completed but not necessarily exhausted.

Third, avoid the formation of "power blocs" within a group. The result may be polarization, a real barrier to trust and openness.

SUMMARY PROBES

1. **What are the stages in PERT?**
2. **What is the recommended function of PERT?**
3. **What are the effects of environment on group discussion?**
4. **When would you utilize the problem-solution, reflective-thinking process?**
5. **What is the difference between problem and solution?**
6. **Why is it important to set up criteria?**
7. **How can you apply the five-step, group problem-solution procedure to your personal decision-making?**
8. **What would you consider your three best specific sources for information on the following topics:**

federal governmental tax reform; traffic safety for school children in a given city; methods of financing campaign spending?

LEARNING EXPERIENCES

1. Attend a group meeting. Write an analysis of positive and negative features about the arrangements. Suggest two or three ways they could be improved.

2. Conduct your own research project with five people through the following steps: (1) ask two people to begin discussing any agreed-upon topic; (2) have a third person move to within two inches of either person and join the conversation; (3) ask two other people to begin discussing any agreed-upon topic; (4) have the sixth person move to a distance of three feet from the communicators—no closer—and join the conversation; (5) compare and contrast their feelings of the two sets of communicators.

3. Plan to meet with a small group for two sessions. At the first session select something to be judged and determine the standards by which this "something" could be evaluated. Be specific and try to consider all of the ramifications of the criteria. At the second session, apply these standards to something specific and make a judgment. You might set up standards for judging political speeches, television commercials, movies; then, in turn, evaluate a particular speech, a television commercial, a particular movie.

4. Interview one of your friends, questioning the person in detail on a subject on which the person feels thoroughly informed. Write a report of what you learned from his or her answers. Then, show the report to your friend and ask the person if you have reported the views accurately and fairly.

5. In a group, consider the question: "What Role Should Advertising Play in Regulating Mass Media?" List criteria, rank the criteria, and compare with another group.

6. Divide the class into two separate groups. Have one section arrive at as many "good" solutions as possible to the question, "How can an auto maker improve automobiles?" Make sure that that group only reports solutions which they feel have high merit and practicality. Have the other group discuss the same question, but have them report all possible solutions, no matter how apparently ridiculous. Compare the total number of usable solutions arrived at by each group. Were the results surprising?

7. In a group of five to seven people, select a current topic of significant national interest. State a question for a policy discussion. Gather information. Engage in forty-five minutes of discussion using five stages of the Dewey reflective-thinking process.

8. Form a group of five to seven. You are charged with raising $35,000 in a United Way drive within six months. As a group, use PERT form to determine activities necessary to the event.

9. Form a group of five to seven. Assume you are the school board of a medium-size city. It is late August and the high school must immediately replace a very fine history teacher who died suddenly. Since school starts next week, you must make a decision from among four applicants.

Applicant Number One. He has an exceptional academic record in teacher's college. He is bright and hardworking, well liked and well mannered. However, he is a very stubborn young man, a confirmed atheist, who does not hide his lack of religious belief. When asked if he intended to teach atheism to his pupils, he replied that he would teach what he believed, and no one had the right to ask him not to. The principal contends that a school owes a duty to the public not to approve a new teacher who holds a fanatical idea about atheism, which if impressed upon the minds of the young, might work to their detriment and injury. The applicant maintains that a person cannot be discriminated against for his religious belief or lack of it. He maintains that if he is qualified, he should be hired.

Applicant Number Two. He has an academic record at a small church school. His recommendations are just adequate with the clear indication that some question of competence remains in the minds of his teachers. When the principal asked how well his practice teaching had gone, the applicant replied that he did not get through all the material he was supposed to cover. The principal contends that he would be incompetent. The applicant contends that he is willing and able to learn as he teaches.

Applicant Number Three. He had an exceptional academic record at a large, well-respected, private university. His recommendations were excellent as far as academic training was concerned. Although well-liked and well-mannered, he is very uncomfortable around women and definitely prefers the company of men. He has admitted this and replies that he is a homosexual but has the situation in full control. He said that he would not teach any of his homosexual views, but if asked, would admit that he preferred the company of men to that of women. The principal contends that the school has a responsibility to protect its students from deviates and that exposure to the applicant might be a detriment and an injury. The applicant contends that this is his private life; he has his own circle of friends in a city fifty miles away and has never been in trouble with the police. He maintains that he is well qualified and that his qualifications should be the basis for employment.

Applicant Number Four. He had a sporadic record from a large public university. The principal reports that he is neat, clean, and well dressed. He was a campus radical and took part in several protests, on one occasion spending eighteen days in jail because of his activities. His record also shows that he has a strong political leaning toward Communism. Upon questioning, he admitted his association with violent factions, but assured the principal that he was now ready to settle down. He stated that he would not teach Communism, and, if necessary, would lie to the students if asked about his beliefs. The principal contends that the school cannot afford to subject its students to a Communist. The applicant maintains that his qualifications are good and that he should be considered for the position.

The Problem. Which candidate should the board select to fill the teaching position in the high school history department?

References

Felipe, N.J., and Somer, R. "Invasion of Personal Space." *Social Problems* 14 (1960): 206–14.

Hall, Edward T. *The Silent Language.* New York: Anchor Press, 1959.

Heston, Judee K. "Effects of Personal Space Invasion and Anomia and Anxiety, Nonperson Orientation and Source Credibility." *Central States Speech Journal* 25 (1974): 19–27.

III

Public Speaking

TEN

GOALS **After studying this chapter you will be able to:**

1. Understand the concept of public speaking as a continuing process, utilizing principles pertinent to both interpersonal and small group communication.

2. List points of similarity and difference between public speaking and interpersonal and small group communication.

3. Recognize public speaking as a vital human function throughout civilized history up to the present.

4. Identify four basic and major steps in speech preparation.

An Introduction To Public Speaking

The first two segments of this book dealt with communication in a one-to-one setting (interpersonal) and communication in small groups. The next logical step in communicative sequence is a concern for those situations in which the communicator transmits messages to large groups of people. Such communication is referred to as public speaking and dates back to the earliest records of human civilization.

This chapter will first view the art of public speaking as the third of four human communicative events described earlier. Public speaking will be compared and contrasted to both interpersonal and small group communication. Some attention will be given to the historical significance of public speaking, as well as its present significance. Finally, the greatest problem facing the student speaker—steps in speech preparation—will be discussed.

PUBLIC SPEAKING: THIRD OF FOUR COMMUNICATIVE EVENTS

At the outset we viewed the total communication process as it would be presented in this book as a four-step approach. First concern was the process of interpersonal communication or how the human being carries on the human function of communication in face-to-face or one-to-one situations. Our second major area of concern was human communication in small group settings. Concepts of interpersonal communication were carried over into the small group setting. Much of the material that we discovered while dealing with interpersonal communication was essential as a basic foundation to assist us in our inquiry in small group communication.

At this point in the development of the four areas, we should keep most of the concepts from the first two segments firmly in mind as a fundamental background for developing effective skills in public speaking. The first portion of the text should be viewed as necessary preliminary information in preparation for a study of speaking in public settings. It is foolhardy, at best, for a serious student to consider a study of public speaking without first gaining a knowledge of the communicative function as it occurs in interpersonal and small group settings.

PUBLIC SPEAKING COMPARED TO INTERPERSONAL AND SMALL GROUP

Public speaking has both similarities and differences when compared to interpersonal and small group communication. In some respects, the communicator will find his task easier in the public setting; however, in more respects he will find the task of completing the total communication process a much more difficult and uncertain one.

Similarities

The three basic components of any communication process—source, message, and receiver—are just as important in the public speaking situation as in a face-to-face communicative setting or in small group problem-solving. The principal similarity here is in the concept of communicative sender or source. In public speaking, just as in other forms, the source is one person who desires to transmit a message to one or more receivers.

Communication breakdowns are just as threatening in the public setting, as they are in interpersonal and small group communication. Principles of nonverbal communication play a role equally important in public speaking as in any other form. The concept of space language has important meaning in terms of separation of speaker from audience and in spatial structure and seating arrangement of the auditorium or place of speech delivery. Object language, as it relates to dress and appearance of the speaker, can affect overall communicative effect in public just as in smaller settings. The concept of paralanguage and voice manipulation loses no significance, whatsoever, when communication is shifted to the public domain.

The crucial role of feedback in interpersonal and small group communication is just as crucial in the public setting. A platform speaker who is insensitive to the needs of his listeners, regardless of how many they may be, faces the same dangers of communicative failure as the interviewee or a small group leader.

Differences

A discussion of similarities of public speaking to other forms of communication would be remiss if it led the student to believe that public speaking is no more than interpersonal communication standing before a large group. Some of the areas where similarities abound, also, contain crucial differences which the student must recognize and adapt to in order to make the effective communicative transition from one form to another.

While the component of communicative source remains basically the same in public speaking, the component of message is decidedly different. Much greater degree of preparation is involved in public messages. Normally, in public situations the opportunity for free interchange of ideas between sender and receiver is missing. The source will most likely be limited to a "one-shot" effort at transmitting his communicative intent. For that reason much more careful and detailed preparation of the message is necessitated. Clarity of meaning on the first try becomes essential in the public setting. The audience cannot stop the public speaker and ask him to repeat a point that is not easily understood.

In most public speaking settings, the source will hold much less information about the receivers than in interpersonal and small group situations. The receiver in public speaking is a collection of individual receivers. While it may be impossible to achieve the same degree of communicative success with each receiver, the source must take every step to assure success with the large majority of this collection called an audience.

You will recall that the Schramm model of communication discussed the concept of a person's field of experience. For two people to communicate effectively in an interpersonal or small group setting, their fields of experience must contain some similarity or overlap in the area of subject of message content. In the public speaking situation the communicator must multiply the problem dealing in differing fields of experience times the number of individuals making up his audience.

As we learned earlier, many of the causes of communication breakdown stem from the fact that human beings are involved in communication settings. Differing language relationships, emotional reaction to certain language symbols, and simple differences in knowledge and familiarity with language symbols can often cause breakdowns to occur in settings involving only two people. In a large audience, once again, the problem potential must be multiplied many times. Such language problems are normally receiver-oriented causes of breakdown. In the public speaking situation there is a much greater likelihood that source-oriented breakdowns will occur. Delivering a speech to five hundred people makes unique demands on the human physical mechanism. Such elements as voice qualities and control of nervous tension can cause a source insurmountable problems in a large group setting and not interfere in the least with the same person's communicative ability in one-to-one or small group settings.

External sources of communication breakdown may be increased in the public setting. Outside interference or noise may be easily compensated for when speaking to a friend on the street. You might move the friend inside a doorway to escape the noise or move closer to enhance comprehension. The same kinds of compensation are usually possible in small group situations. An entire group may consent to move the place of discussion when outside interference becomes unbearable. Such maneuvers between source and receiver are virtually impossible in an auditorium filled with people. The speaker must overcome the outside interference singlehandedly and the communication setting is rigid: the communicator would be hard pressed to move five hundred listeners away from the source of interference.

We said earlier that feedback does not lose importance in the public speaking situation. Indeed it does not; however, it does present unique problems not present in interpersonal and small group communication. Feedback from an audience to the speaker is normally much more indirect and vague in meaning than in smaller settings. An audience is usually unable to respond to the speaker: "I understand, please go on," or, "Whoa! What was that again?" At best, instant feedback in public speaking may involve a series of educated guesses by the speaker as to the degree of audience comprehension. Cues that would aid the speaker in these guesses are usually extremely indefinite. The most accurate feedback available to the public speaker is delayed feedback—or after-the-fact. But what can a speaker do if he learns after his presentation is completed that a fractional segment of his audience actually understood what he said. Most likely he will not have a second chance.

Thus, we can readily see that public speaking is basically one further step in the study of the total process of human communication. We also see, however, that differences exist in public speaking and interpersonal and small group communication in great enough proportion to warrant serious study of public speaking as an autonomous human communicative event.

SUMMARY PROBES

1. **How do communication breakdowns and feedback as part of the communication process differ in public speaking when compared to interpersonal and small group communication?**
2. **Relate similarities and differences in the sender, message, and receiver in the different forms of communication.**

SIGNIFICANCE OF PUBLIC SPEAKING

Public speaking has been a vital activity in human affairs almost since the beginning of civilization. The earliest instances of advice on public speaking on record date back to ancient Egypt. The earliest known advisers on speaking were two Egyptians named Kagemni and Ptah-Hotep.

The Greeks and Romans found speech-making to be an essential function in both governmental and private affairs. Instances of practicing orators, teachers, and theoreticians are found throughout the histories of Greece and Rome. Instances of both practice and theory in public speaking providing essential services for man are recorded throughout the history of man up to present-day textbooks on the subject.

An oft-repeated question by college students is, "Why should I take a course or unit in public speaking?" Most of us consider ourselves to be very uninteresting creatures and find it difficult to imagine that anyone else would ever be interested in hearing something that we have to say. Past human experience has shown such an assumption to be false. Most of us will at frequent intervals in life be called upon to say something to large collections of people. While most individuals fear this eventuality and approach it with extreme caution, the fact remains that each of us will most likely have to do it. Instruction in fundamental concepts and skills in public communication should be viewed as an essential preparatory step for any career or profession.

Kathleen Edgerton Kendall presented evidence collected in March 1973, that, regardless of what we may think as students, people do give speeches in life situations.[1] Surveying the blue-collar workers randomly selected, she found that almost half—46.5 percent—had given a speech to ten or more people at least one time during the preceding two years. Her conclusion was that if blue-collar workers had given speeches to that degree, that college-educated people would most likely expect to give such speeches at a more frequent rate.

We can accept the assumption that public speaking for most people may come at relatively rare intervals—certainly more rare than demands for interpersonal and small group communication. However, we can surely agree that when public speaking situations do confront us, we view them as much more threatening and demanding communicative events. So, in response to the question as to why you should take public speaking, the obvious answer is, "Because people have been speaking in public for years and will continue to do it for years to come."

OVERVIEW OF SPEECH PREPARATION

Providing the student with the basic fundamental knowledge of effective speech preparation will be our concern in the remaining chapters of this segment. Some special problems relating to classroom speaking will be separated from public situations.

Speech preparation falls into four basic steps, each of which will constitute a chapter in Part Three. Our first concern is with preliminary steps in speech preparation such as determining purpose, selecting a subject, and considering essential points of audience and occasion analysis.

Once the aspiring speaker has accomplished preliminary steps, he must, then, begin to collect materials and forms of support for the points he intends to emphasize in the speech. After the speaker has assembled the necessary material, he then must organize that material, transferring it from a collection of information to an organized communicative message.

After these three steps, the speaker is ready to consider specific points in delivering the speech. Providing the student speaker with enough basic information to enable him to prepare an effective public message designed for ten or more people will be the aim of the final chapters of Part Three.

SUMMARY PROBES

1. **What evidence exists that public speaking has been a vital human function throughout the history of man?**
2. **Relate the four basic and major steps in speech preparation.**

LEARNING EXPERIENCES

1. After listening to a speaker in a public setting, carry on a face-to-face conversation with the speaker. What differences did you note in the speaker in the two differing situations?

2. Investigate for yourself to determine how frequently people you know speak in public. Interview several people in various types of jobs and careers. Based on your information, how important is public speaking today?

References

Kendall, Kathleen Edgerton. "Do Real People Ever Give Speeches?" *Central States Speech Journal* 25 (1974): 233–35.

Wilson, John F., and Arnold, Carroll C. *Public Speaking as a Liberal Art*, 2nd ed. Boston: Allyn and Bacon, 1968, chapter 2.

ELEVEN

GOALS **After completing this chapter you will be able to:**

1. Identify the three most common general purposes of public speeches.

2. Distinguish the three types of persuasive speeches.

3. Recognize the significance of audience and occasion analysis to the public speaker.

4. List three areas of concern to the speaker in selecting a subject.

5. Understand the importance of phrasing a specific statement of purpose for every speech.

Preparing The Speech Preliminary Steps

The key to delivering a credible public speech whether for a public audience or the academic classroom lies in the accuracy and completeness of the preparation involved. Speech preparation does not consist of simply putting ideas down on paper and restating those ideas aloud on cue. Speech preparation involves many steps of mental activity which, for maximum results, should be completed in chronological fashion.

This chapter develops the preliminary steps involved in speech preparation. First, the speaker must determine the purpose of the speech to be presented; he must formulate a general purpose which is usually determined at the time of invitation or assignment. The second step in preparation is to engage in some form of audience and occasion analysis. Third, the speaker must select a subject and, finally, he must develop a purpose statement before he starts to collect materials for the speech.

DETERMINING GENERAL PURPOSES OF SPEECH

You will recall in the opening chapter of the book that the utilitarian function of communication was discussed. Many communication theorists hold that all communication is utilitarian in nature.

A simple, "Hello, how are you?" is uttered by a communicator with a purposeful intent of making the receiver respond favorably toward the sender. The communicator may not really be concerned with the physical well-being of the person addressed, but is more concerned that the receiver knows that the communicator cares about the person as an individual and is seeking a favorable attitudinal response from the receiver.

Many would say that based on the utilitarian nature of communication, all public speaking is persuasive in nature. To some extent this is true—an informative speech may have a persuasive intent if only in the selection of topic and material. The speaker, in essence, is saying, "I feel this topic is important for you, and I have selected those points that I feel are most important for you to know." In this respect, we can agree that there is some degree of persuasive purpose in a speech to inform.

If a speaker's general purpose is to entertain, he seldom delivers a speech in which the sole purpose is to entertain an audience. Such entertainment speeches or monologues are normally found in nightclub settings, on televised variety shows, or on records. A speech to entertain will usually contain secondary general purposes. While an after-dinner speaker's primary intent is to entertain the listener, he very often may have a serious point or thesis to communicate.

While at the outset we will accept the thesis that all public speaking may contain some elements of persuasion, we can identify sufficient differences in speaking situations to warrant discussion of three general purposes of public speaking. We will now discuss the speech to entertain, to inform, and to persuade.

The Speech to Entertain

A great deal of the speaking done in public settings is entertaining in nature. A speech to entertain does not imply that success require uproarious laughter on the part of the audience. The most common form of speeches to entertain delivered today are probably referred to as after-dinner speeches. Most organizations, groups, or affiliations use the traditional after-dinner speaker for formal banquets or luncheons. Such a speech must be light in nature; however, most successful after-dinner speeches have some significant point combined with the lighter approach.

The speech to entertain, then, is a speech usually delivered in a setting which finds audience members relaxed and comfortable.

The speaker presenting such a speech should strive to reinforce relaxation and comfort. This does not imply, however, that a successful speech to entertain should be a comedy monologue or a series of unrelated jokes. Most "in-the-flesh" speakers cannot compete with television as a source of comic relief for the public. The successful speech to entertain should stress an informative or perhaps persuasive point but do so in such a way that audience members "enjoy" the presentation.

The Speech to Inform

The speech to inform attempts to pass along information from a speaker to a group of listeners—information which the speaker assumes the listeners do not have at this time. A speech to inform may take on several different formats; however, the speech will usually define, clarify, or demonstrate a concept or process.

Defining and Clarifying. The most common vehicle for the speech which defines or clarifies is the common lecture. As students you are exposed constantly to this form of speaking in the classroom. Most job-related demands for speaking to large groups of workers require informative speaking of this nature. The speech to inform which defines or clarifies a concept may be enhanced greatly with the use of visual aids; however, a speech using visuals should not be confused with the speech to demonstrate.

Demonstrating a Process. The speech to demonstrate a process is a specialized form of informative speech. The demonstration speech goes further than just defining or clarifying; the process under discussion is actually demonstrated with the use of an object or scale drawing of the object. While any informative speech may utilize visual aids for maximum effect, the demonstration speech requires that a visual aid—usually the physical object under discussion—be used.

Determining the Nature of the Informative Speech. The decision to use the demonstration method in informative speaking must rest with the complexity of the topic. Normally, a demonstration speech should only be presented when the subject requires a demonstration to achieve the purpose of the message. If the speaker feels that the purpose can be achieved without demonstration, the presence of a physical object may actually hinder the outcome of the speech.

For example, if you choose to deliver an informative speech on varying national traditions in celebrating Christmas throughout the world, you could perhaps explain the different customs with no visual aids and certainly no demonstrations. If, however, you choose to inform the audience on the artistic excellence of German Christmas decorations, it would no doubt be helpful to your purpose to have examples of the decorations to display and perhaps to demonstrate their nature at varying stages of construction.

The essential question to be answered in terms of what kind of informative speech you should deliver is, "What do I need to do to assure getting my point across to my listeners?" As a speaker you are obligated to do no less and use as many techniques of clarification as necessary; however, a speaker can be guilty of over informing. Do not explain a simple point into a state of complex confusion.

The Speech to Persuade

Volumes of literature exist in many academic fields treating the subject of attitude change in human beings. The persuasive speech is a communicative attempt to change attitudes and behavior in the listener. A persuasive presentation may well have informative elements within it, and for maximum effect, the persuasive speech may also entertain. The distinguishing factor, however, is that the primary purpose of the speech to persuade is to alter the attitudinal structure of the listener in some way and, in some instances, to effect a modification of behavior.

Persuasive speeches can normally be categorized into three types. As a speaker facing the task of constructing a persuasive speech, you will probably be trying to convince, stimulate, or actuate —to incite into action—your audience.

The Speech to Convince. A common form of persuasive speaking is found in the speech to convince which is an effort on the part of the speaker to get his listeners to agree with him. The speech to convince may be reinforcement of an already existing view. If such reinforcement is the speaker's goal, accomplishment of his desired response will be greatly facilitated. A speaker who addresses a group of public school teachers and attempts to convince his listeners that they are underpaid faces the task of reinforcing an already existing view.

The speech to convince may pose a more difficult problem for the speaker if the listeners are predisposed against his view. Delivering the same speech on teacher pay scales to an organized group of concerned taxpayers would most likely provoke an entirely different audience response.

Whether or not the audience is predisposed toward or against the speaker's view, or whether or not an audience has no identifiable attitude, the speech to convince is a persuasive speech in which the speaker's goal is to achieve listener agreement at the conclusion of the speech.

The Speech to Stimulate. The speech to stimulate attempts to arouse an emotional reaction in the listener. In most cases the listener is either favorable or neutral to the particular view being expressed; however, he is not emotionally or ego involved.

Examples of speeches to stimulate can be found in holiday commemorative addresses such as patriotic Independence Day speeches. The pregame speech delivered by the college football coach to the players in the locker room has one major purpose in mind: to stimulate, to arouse team spirit, and to win the game.

The Speech to Actuate. The speech to actuate may be the most difficult of all persuasive speeches to deliver. The speaker must not only alter attitudinal structure, but some observable behavioral expression of that change must occur. Messages meant to actuate bombard the American public in many forms. Advertising messages seek to actuate the receiver to make a purchase. Political messages seek to actuate the receiver to cast a vote in a particular manner. Charitable organizations seek to actuate receivers of their messages to donate time, money, or materials. Regardless of who is doing the speaking, if the purpose of the message is to actuate the listener, the listener must do more than just agree with the speaker—he must demonstrate that agreement via some form of behavior.

Combination of Persuasive Purposes

The three subpurposes of a persuasive speech may appear as specific speeches. It is possible to deliver a speech meant solely to convince, to stimulate, or to actuate. A more common form of persuasive communication, however, is the speech which strives to effect all three responses from the listeners. The following hypothetical situation will demonstrate a message which strives to stimulate, convince, and actuate in that order.

Assume that a speaker representing a teacher's union is permitted to address a group of nonunion teachers. Such a speaker's ultimate purpose is to actuate his listeners to sign membership cards and pay the first month's dues. Before the speaker can actuate his listeners, it is very likely that he first must stimulate and convince. The speaker's first effort may be to arouse emotional responses in his listeners to lead them to believe that problems in their status do exist. He may choose to do so through arousal of a feeling of professional and personal pride. Once accomplished, the speaker then must convince the listeners that a strong union membership is the most viable solution to the problems facing the teachers as a group. Having aroused pride in the listeners and having convinced them that the union is the answer, the speaker, then, must actuate them into "signing up." Once a significant number of the audience have joined the union, the speaker has successfully actuated the audience; however, he first had to stimulate and convince them.

Purposes Related to the Public Situation and the Classroom

A speaker normally does not have to deliberate as to what the general purpose of his speech should be. In the public setting, the purpose of the speech normally emerges within the invitation or request to speak. If you are invited to a luncheon as guest speaker, the expectation will most likely be an entertaining speech with some substantial base. If you are invited to speak to a group to explain a job-related concept, you may assume that the purpose intended is informative. If you are invited to address a monthly meeting of the County Republican Club, the assumption exists that the speech should be primarily persuasive in nature. The point remains that in most instances the general purpose of the speech is determined at the time of the invitation.

In the classroom setting you will most likely be assigned to prepare and deliver a particular type of speech. Again, determining general purpose will not likely be a deliberative task of the speaker.

SUMMARY PROBES

1. **How does the utilitarian nature of communication lead some to believe that all public speaking is essentially persuasive?**
2. **What are the most common forms of speeches to entertain? What is meant by the multiplicity of purpose in most speeches to entertain?**

3. **What are some considerations to be made by a speaker in determining whether an informative speech should be a demonstration?**
4. **Why is the speech to actuate considered to be the most difficult of persuasive speeches?**
5. **How can one persuasive speech combine all three types of persuasion?**

AUDIENCE AND OCCASION ANALYSIS

Once the general purpose of your speech has been determined, you must begin to consider specific topics and your specific purpose for the message. Preliminary to settling the issue of topic and specific purpose is the need for the speaker to have some degree of knowledge about that group of people who will be his listeners and some knowledge about the nature of the occasion.

Audience Analysis

Two categories of information about audiences exist that may be of interest to the speaker preparing a message. Certain items of knowledge about people are factual in nature and others are inferential. The two categories of knowledge are distinguished by the varying ability to observe physically certain features of audiences.

In some instances, all knowledge about a specific audience may be inferential. Before a speaker can possess any factual information about his audience, he must either know the audience personally or have an opportunity to observe them. If this is not possible, he must depend greatly on a program chairman or another informed individual to answer questions about audience members.

Factual Audience Data. Eight questions representing bits of factual information about audiences may be of special importance to the speaker before selecting a topic and preparing the speech.

1. How large will the audience be? Audience size may prove a very significant factor in speech preparation. Planned use of visual aids and audience interaction can be severely hampered if the speaker does not know in advance how many listeners to expect.
2. What will be the general age range of the audience? Attention span differs greatly with audiences of different age groups. Speech prep-

aration and planning can be altered greatly by such questions as "Will children be present? Will the audience be similar in age range or will a variety of ages be present?" If audience age range is similar, meaningful points of illustration from relevant events of the past can be utilized effectively.

3. Will the audience be of the same sex? Needless to say use of humor, illustrative material, and emotional appeals can differ greatly depending upon the sexual composition of the audience. A speaker who is invited to address a local men's group such as Kiwanis might discover that one-half of his speech is inappropriate if he arrives on the scene to discover that it is Ladies' Night.
4. What occupations will be represented in your audience? If all or most members of your audience have the same occupation, you, as the speaker, need to know that. Regardless of the general purpose of the speech, one of the most effective ways to appeal to listeners is to relate communicative messages to the interests and backgrounds of listeners.
5. What religious beliefs will be represented in your audience? Most people who hold even moderately strong religious convictions are very sensitive concerning those views. Appealing to religious concepts either favorably or unfavorably can be a great asset to a speaker's purpose; on the other hand, it can be devastating. You, as a speaker, need to discover as much information as possible concerning your audience's religious beliefs.
6. Is your audience politically oriented? The speaker should discover the political nature of his audience. Will a wide spectrum of political beliefs be represented, or will your audience most likely be sharing general political views and beliefs?
7. What affiliations will be represented within your audience? An audience, assembled to hear a speech, may well be a meeting of a particular group of people accustomed to meeting together. The speaker needs to know. A supposed "general audience" may be composed of several smaller groups of people who are affiliated in respects other than the assemblage of people to hear your speech.
8. What degree of homogeneity exists in your audience? A "general" audience is one normally assumed to have no particular common bond resulting in their assembling. An open-air meeting at a county fairgrounds on Independence Day with no admission charge may indicate that little, if any, homogeneity exists in the audience. Some may be present because they are tired of walking and want to sit down. Others may be using the speaking location as a meeting site with friends. Degree of homogeneity can be of special importance to the speaker and can usually be determined with a minimum amount of inquiry on his part.

Inferred Audience Data. A great deal of information a speaker may collect about a specific audience must be inferred. Inferences may be made on the basis of factual data as described above, or, in some cases, the speaker may have little or nothing on which to base inferences.

1. What attitudes and beliefs does the audience share? It is impossible for a speaker to be sure how his audience feels about certain issues. It is essential, however, that the speaker at least try to make some guesses as to how his listeners feel. Careful research on questions such as politics and religion may lend the speaker valuable attitudinal information about his audience.
2. What is the audience's attitude toward the speaker? Many audiences possess fixed attitudes about speakers prior to the speaking occasion. If such attitudes exist, it is essential that the speaker know as much about them as possible. If a speaker faces an audience which will grant him a high degree of credibility, his task is significantly less difficult than the speaker who faces a hostile or unfavorably inclined audience.
3. What personality traits are likely to exist in the audience? It can be of great importance for the speaker to discover any distinguishing personality traits the audience possesses either as individuals or collectively. How has the same audience treated past speakers? Are audience members favorably inclined toward assembling together for the purpose of your message?

Occasion Analysis

The primary question to be determined in occasion analysis is why is the audience assembled? The speaker's selection of topic and purpose may need to have no relationship to the purpose of the gathering; however, the answer to the question, "Why is the audience assembled?" may dictate specific considerations in topic selection. If a speaker is invited to address an industrial banquet honoring retirees, he doesn't want to deliver a speech on the harms of alcohol to society.

Most questions of vital importance to the speaker in occasion analysis focus on the physical aspects of the speaking situation. As a speaker, you may want to consider some or all of the following questions:

1. What time of day is my speech scheduled?
2. Am I the only speaker on the program or one of several?
3. If others will speak, will they speak before me or after me?
4. Will the speech be given in a hall or room which will lend itself to good acoustical effects?

5. Will physical objects needed for the speech such as a speaker's stand be provided?
6. How will my listeners be arranged? Will the setting be informal or formal thus creating an atmosphere for the speaker?

Audience and Occasion Analysis in Public and in the Classroom

If you are to speak in public, you may expect difficulties in answering all questions posed above relating to audience and occasion. If you are fortunate, the program chairman or individual responsible for acquiring the speaker will be willing and able to provide you with many of the answers you need. Don't expect such treatment, however. Many times an invitation to speak includes nothing of import to the speaker in terms of audience and occasion analysis, and efforts to acquire such information often fail. Be prepared to infer a great deal, and, by all means, proceed with extra caution.

The speaker's task in audience and occasion analysis in the classroom is greatly simplified by the fact that the speaker knows his audience. Most of the factual data can be answered with a significant degree of certainty by the speaker. Using the factual data, the speaker may infer even more accurately. If time permits, the speaker may have the opportunity to pretest his classroom audience to determine attitudes and beliefs relating to the topic and the speaker.

The simplest task of all for the student speaker is to analyze the occasion for the classroom speech. The tremendous advantage that the student speaker enjoys in the classroom is that all audience and occasion factors are shared by all others in the same class.

SUMMARY PROBES

1. **What is the most significant distinguishing characteristic between factual audience data and inferential audience data?**
2. **State as many of the eight factual audience factors as you can.**
3. **In what ways is audience and occasion analysis more difficult for public speeches than for classroom speeches?**

CHOOSING THE SUBJECT

The most often-heard question by this writer in many years of teaching at various levels of education is, "What am I going to talk about?" Most of us feel that we are the most boring creatures on the face of the earth; we couldn't possibly deliver an original speech interesting enough to captivate even the most willing and cooperative listener. Such is not the case, and the beginning speaker should face that reality before he begins to select a topic.

When we discussed interpersonal communication you will recall the Schramm model of communication. In it we found that every human being has a field of experience slightly different from every other human being. No two human beings have had identical experiences and learning conditions. Even identical twins who have been reared alike, dressed alike, and treated alike in virtually every respect have some experiences that distingiush them one from the other.

Many individuals, when faced with the task of selecting a subject for a speech, mistakenly assume that the first place to go is the library or some form of reference work to search for a topic. No doubt, the process of speech preparation will likely take the speaker to the library at some stage; however, topic selection is not usually the proper time for a library visit.

If a speaker finds it necessary to go to the library to discover a subject, he probably shouldn't use that subject, for he has admitted that he doesn't know a great deal about it. The first place to search for a topic is within the self. If done thoroughly and in the correct frame of mind, the search need go no further.

We will analyze three areas of concern to the speaker in selecting a subject. The first of the three—the speaker—is of great importance to both public speaking and classroom speaking. Areas two and three—the audience and the occasion—may be of limited concern to the classroom situation, however, very important to the public speech setting.

The Speaker

Before a speaker decides finally on a speech subject, he should consider two essential questions: (1) Do I have the knowledge necessary to deliver a speech on this subject? and, (2) Do I have enough interest and enthusiasm about the subject to create the same feeling in my listeners? Answers to both questions should be affirmative whether the speech is designed for the classroom or public setting.

Speaker's Knowledge of Subject. Certainly, no one expects a student speaker to be an authority on any given topic; however, some basic knowledge should exist. If the assignment is an informative speech, the speaker should search his past hobbies, job experiences, travels, et cetera, to discover a subject on which his scope of knowledge may be a bit greater than most of his audience. A necessary step in topic selection at this point is some kind of self-inventory. Don't make the common mistake of assuming that you know nothing worthwhile to say. It may take a while for you to discover your subject within yourself, but it is there.

The nature of a persuasive speech may produce more difficulty in finding a subject from within the speaker's personal knowledge. Every human being has a well-defined set of attitudes and beliefs about most controversial subjects. Select a persuasive speech topic on which you have some feeling at the present time. Most assuredly your speech preparation will take you to many other sources to refine and support your beliefs on the issue; however, the initial topic selection should come from your own beliefs and attitudes, not the editorial columns of daily or weekly news publications.

Speaker Interest and Enthusiasm. If you hope to arouse any degree of interest or enthusiasm with your listeners for your subject, that interest and enthusiasm must be present within yourself when you deliver the speech. Nothing dampens audience enthusiasm more than a speaker's obvious lack of enthusiasm for his subject. If your reaction to a subject when you select it is, "This is boring, but I have to have something," your work is just beginning. Throw that topic out and keep searching.

The Audience

If you have selected a topic about which you have a significant degree of knowledge and about which you are interested, you have probably selected a good topic for the speaking occasion. You must, however, consider some items concerning your audience in addition to your self-analysis. You must make an effort to assess the degree of audience interest in your speech, audience knowledge of your subject, and the extent to which your audience cares about your topic.

Audience Interest. Will your audience be immediately interested when they hear your subject? If so, you have overcome a major obstacle. If initial audience interest is not there, you as the speaker face two alternatives. First, you must create the interest within the audience. If it is not possible, then perhaps you need to select another topic.

Audience Knowledge. You as speaker must also make an effort to assess the degree of knowledge held by the audience on the subject. Preparation ease will be facilitated if the audience has some preliminary knowledge of the subject; however, if the audience has too much information, the subject may fail the test of uniqueness. If you find yourself unable to tell the audience anything they didn't already know, another subject should be selected.

Does the Audience Care? Time is important to most human beings. As a speaker, you are asking your audience members to give you a specified amount of their time to listen to what you have to say. The ultimate question of an audience member is, "Why should I give you, the speaker, X amount of time to hear this speech?" They may ask, "Is what you have to say worth five, ten, or more minutes of my time?" The subject selected by the speaker may appear obviously vital to the listeners; if so, the speaker will receive a positive initial response from his audience. If the response of the audience, however, upon hearing the statement of the topic is, "You've got to be kidding," the speaker must be prepared to demonstrate audience need for the information. If such need cannot be demonstrated, the speaker needs a new subject.

The Occasion

Points of occasion analysis have been discussed previously. Only one item needs special attention here: how much time do you have to deliver your speech? Time limit can be a factor in both public and classroom settings. If an audience is expecting a twenty-minute speech and they get a forty-five-minute speech, they won't like it. When selecting a topic for a public speech, you must consider the time allotted for your presentation and plan accordingly. Most problems involving time limit for speakers are caused by the speaker selecting a topic that he cannot develop in the time allotted. One of two things occurs: either the speech is poorly developed, or it is woefully overtime—either extreme is bad for the speaker and worse for the audience.

Special problems with time exist in the classroom setting. Class size, semester or quarter length, and course expectations normally result in class speeches being significantly shorter than public speeches. It is not uncommon for a student to be assigned a four- to six-minute speech in class; however, it is most uncommon for a speaker on a public platform to speak for only four to six minutes.

Most classroom speech topics could be narrowed much more than they are when presented. Do not try to do too much in the time allotted in class for your presentation. It is reasonably safe to assume that your first subject selection will have to be narrowed one or more times to make it appropriate for your class assignment.

PHRASING THE SPECIFIC PURPOSE

By this time you have undergone several steps of speech preparation. You have been assigned a general purpose for your presentation; you have completed steps in audience and occasion analysis; you have selected a subject for your speech. Now you must answer the question, "What response or reaction do I want from my listeners?" The answer to this question should provide you with a statement of specific purpose.

It may sound unbelievable that many speakers complete their presentations without knowing themselves what their specific purpose is in the speech. If the speaker doesn't know the purpose, it is impossible to expect that the audience will understand and accept the purpose. Before the speaker proceeds any further beyond topic selection, he must formulate a purpose statement and keep it constantly in mind throughout preparation and delivery of the speech.

Listed below are sample purpose statements for speeches. Each sample shows a well-narrowed and defined specific purpose with a broader and unacceptable purpose assumption.

Not this: Today I'm going to talk about bowling scores.
But this: My purpose is to teach each of you how to keep score in bowling.

Not this: Today I'm going to talk about Christmas decorations.
But this: My purpose is to demonstrate to you how to make an attractive Christmas decoration out of a plastic bag.

Not this: Today I'm going to talk about the metric system.
But this: My purpose is to explain the differences in the metric system and the unit system.

Not this: I'm going to talk about school spirit.
But this: My purpose is to arouse school spirit in each of you for tonight's ball game.

Not this: I'm going to talk about the financial problems that our schools face.
But this: My purpose is to convince you to support the school referendum.

Not this: Today I'm going to tell you advantages and disadvantages of legalized abortion.
But this: My purpose is to convince you that abortion is a legal issue and not a moral issue.

We have examined what are considered to be the preliminary steps in speech preparation. Let us now create a hypothetical situation which will direct us through all the preliminary steps.

Assume that you are a student in a beginning public speaking class, and you have been assigned a six- to eight-minute persuasive speech to deliver in two weeks. The general purpose of the speech has been determined by the instructor. You must make an effort to persuade your listeners; however, you must choose from the subcategories whether you will attempt to convince, stimulate, or actuate. Not trusting your prowess as a beginning speaker, you choose to convince rather than stimulate or actuate.

Audience and occasion analysis will be a rather simple matter. First, you know over one-half of your class personally. Factual data concerning your audience leaves little question in your mind. Since you know many of them personally and factual data for all is essentially the same, you are in much better position to make inferences about other types of data.

Selection of subject becomes your first major problem. You aren't overly interested in politics; you have never debated issues. What can you choose as a persuasive subject? You have just returned to campus from a weekend at home where your parents were emotionally upset because an elderly grandparent on a fixed income was being forced to dissolve personal belongings and properties in order to receive state aid. You, too, became emotionally aroused—your topic is born. Why can't social security benefits increase automatically with inflation with cost-of-living increases to alleviate hardships on those with fixed incomes?

You have some first-hand knowledge based on personal experience; you have interest and enthusiasm because it is a personally based problem. What about the audience? Will a roomful of students ranging in ages from eighteen to twenty be concerned automatically with your topic?—hardly. Can you make them interested in your topic?—you answer, certainly. Every person in the room probably has at least one relative surviving on a fixed income; if it can happen to your family, it can happen to his.

After the preceding steps your purpose statement emerges: "My purpose is to convince each of you that social security benefits and other sources of fixed incomes should increase automatically with inflation and cost-of-living increases." From there you collect materials, organize your thoughts, and deliver the speech.

SUMMARY PROBES

1. **Where is the first place one should go in searching for a speech topic?**
2. **What audience factors should be considered in selecting a topic?**
3. **What are some of the special problems a speaker faces in selecting a subject for a classroom speech?**
4. **Why is it crucial for a speaker to formulate a specific purpose statement early in the process of speech preparation?**

LEARNING EXPERIENCES

1. When listening to informative speeches, such as classroom lectures, make an effort to determine how other general purposes such as persuasion and entertainment overlap.

2. Listen to an after-dinner, or some other form of speech to entertain. Identify the more serious message other than straight entertainment.

3. Prepare an audience analysis for the members of your class answering all factual and inferential factors. Select several potential speech topics to fit the information you discover.

4. Prepare a self-analysis inventory or biographical sketch of yourself. Have a friend or class member read the sketch and compile a list of speech topics taken from your personal knowledge and experience.

References

Crocker, Lionel. *Public Speaking for College Students,* 3rd ed. New York: American Book, 1956, chapter 11.

Eisenson, Jon, and Boase, Paul H. *Basic Speech,* 3rd ed. New York: Macmillan, 1975, pp. 321–30, 328–32, 341–47.

Gray, Giles Wilkerson, and Braden, Waldo W. *Public Speaking: Principles and Practice.* New York: Harper & Brothers, 1951, chapter 6.

Hance, Kenneth G.; Ralph, David C.; and Wiksell, Milton J. *Principles of Speaking,* 2nd ed. Belmont: Wadsworth, 1969, chapters 4 and 8.

Hughey, Jim D., and Johnson, Arlee W. *Speech Communication: Foundations and Challenges.* New York: Macmillan, 1975, Unit 6.

McCabe, Bernard P., and Bender, Coleman C. *Speaking is a Practical Matter,* 2nd ed. Boston: Holbrook Press, 1973, Parts IV, V; pp. 127–30, 77–83.

Monroe, Alan H., and Ehninger, Douglas. *Principles and Types of Speech Communication,* 7th ed. Glenview: Scott, Foresman, 1974, chapters 7, 8.

TWELVE

GOALS **After completing this chapter you will be able to:**

1. Identify and distinguish three classical appeals available to the student in a speaking situation.

2. Understand the importance of source credibility to informative speaking.

3. List advantages and disadvantages to the use of both testimony and statistics as persuasive appeals.

4. Distinguish reasoned materials from factual material in persuasion.

5. Identify the problems involved in the use of humor in entertaining speeches.

Preparing The Speech: Collecting Materials And Supporting Points

Once the speaker has formulated a specific statement of purpose for his speech based on general purpose, audience and occasion analysis, and careful selection of subject, the next step in speech preparation lies in collecting materials and adequately supporting points. The degree of difficulty experienced at this stage of preparation is dependent on many factors such as type of speech, knowledge of speaker and audience concerning the subject, and predisposition of the audience toward the speaker's subject.

This chapter will examine the three general purposes of forms of support that have survived since classical Greek times. Then, the reader will be exposed to kinds of materials and forms of support pertinent to each of the three general purposes of speaking.

ETHOS, LOGOS, AND PATHOS

Classical Greek rhetoricians formulated the three basic appeals available to the speaker as ethos (ethical appeal), logos (logical appeal), and pathos (emotional appeal). We will attempt no discussion as to which of the three is most effective, but most assuredly the best speech will include bits of all three methods of appealing to listeners.

The degree to which one of the three appeals should outweigh the other two is heavily dependent on variables within each speaking situation.

Ethos

Ethical appeal refers to the predisposition of the audience toward the speaker. Contemporary communication theorists may refer to the concept as source credibility, speaker image, speaker prestige, charisma, et cetera. Regardless of what we call the concept, the concern is with the same basic questions: Does the speaker know what he is talking about? Is the speaker a trustworthy person? Is the speaker honest? Do I like the speaker?

Logos

Logical appeal refers to those methods of supporting points which come from outside the speaker. The use of logical appeal by a speaker, usually, will result in a higher credibility rating for him by the listeners. The basic question for which the speaker provides an answer via logical appeal is, "Why should I do or believe what the speaker proposes?" If an audience perceives the speaker as an expert in the field on which he speaks, they may need no logical appeal. The high credibility rating given the speaker may be enough for him to carry the day.

Pathos

Emotional appeal refers to the practice of a speaker appealing to one of the many basic human emotions for acceptance of points. The human being is an emotional animal, and the best thing to be said about appealing to human emotions for effect is that those appeals very often work. Emotional appeal usually must be tempered with both ethical and logical appeals. While a speech void of any emotional appeal may appear boring and dry, a speech appealing to nothing but emotion usually produces a negative credibility rating for the speaker, and, hence, does not serve his purpose.

MATERIALS AND FORMS OF SUPPORT FOR THE INFORMATIVE SPEECH

There are four basic methods of supporting points in an informative speech. The first, source credibility, if it exists at all, is found within the speaker. External methods of support are explanation, illustration, and specific instance.

Source Credibility

Ethos plays a major role in the presentation of an informative speech. Since the informative speech seeks to impart new or unique information to a group of listeners, those listeners will very often accept the speaker as a so-called "expert" on his subject. If a representative from the Peace Corps is invited to address a group of high school students, the initial assumption is that the speaker knows enough about the subject to present a meaningful speech. An invitation to an individual to give an informative speech in a public setting will usually include the assumption that those extending the invitation have already awarded the speaker a high credibility rating on the specific topic. The speaker in such a situation must be sure that he does nothing in his speech to destroy that initial credibility rating.

If high ethical appeal is awarded the speaker, he may need very little in terms of supporting material in addition to the inherent ethical appeal. The audience will be satisfied to "take the speaker's word" for what he is saying, without demands for logical and emotional appeal.

In some instances the speaker's relationship to his topic may be unknown by the listeners. In such a situation the speaker must build a favorable ethical appeal among his audience. This point can best be demonstrated by considering the classroom speaker. As a student in a speech class, you will probably not be accepted by other classmates as an expert on any given topic. This does not mean that delivering an informative speech need be any more difficult than if you were viewed as an expert. It simply means that as a speaker you must, at the outset of your presentation, establish yourself as possessing adequate knowledge and experience on the topic to enable your listeners to accept your word.

For example, having practiced the hobby of breeding tropical fish since you were twelve years old will likely make you the most qualified person in almost any classrooms to present information on breeding tropical fish. If your audience is to accept your expertise, however, they *must* be told of your past knowledge and experience. Consider the following opening of a classroom informative speech:

> Different people have lots of different hobbies to occupy spare time. Since I was twelve years old, I have taken an active interest in breeding tropical fish, and after having been responsible for over 20,000 healthy baby fish, I have found that hobbies can sometimes be very financially attractive as well as enjoyable. This morning I would like to explain to you some advantages and disadvantages to raising tropical fish as a hobby.

Prior to the above introduction, it is highly possible that not one person in the class including the instructor would have considered the speaker an expert in tropical fish. After a very simple statement, however, most would sit back and anticipate some accurate, first-hand information.

Explanation

Explanation refers to the process of clarifying a concept or procedure through the use of amplification, definition, or restatement. Explanation may be descriptive in nature, or it can occur by simply giving instructions. The essential purpose of explanation on the part of the speaker is simply to make a point or idea more clear to the audience than it appears as stated.

The use of an object or diagram to demonstrate a process is a form of explanation. The use of any form of visual aid in speaking implies that the concept under discussion does not possess clarity adequate for audience comprehension as it is stated. Explanation can be in various forms both verbal and nonverbal; however, the presence of explanation in any form implies a need for further clarification.

Illustration

Like explanation, the use of illustration in speaking may be either verbal or nonverbal. An illustration, unlike specific instance, may or may not be true. Technically, an illustration is the use of an example to make a point more clear than it is as stated. Illustrations may come from a variety of sources available to the speaker such as literature, other people, history books, and so on.

The use of the hypothetical illustration can be effective at making the illustration particularly relevant to the listeners in a given situation. A hypothetical illustration is an example that is not necessarily true but very well could be. If a speaker is unsuccessful at finding an actual illustration involving school teachers for a speech to be delivered to a group of teachers, he may effectively develop a point by creating a hypothetical illustration involving teachers. Audiences will accept the fictitious nature of the hypothetical illustration as long as the illustration is feasible.

Specific Instance

A specific instance is similar to illustration; however, it is a method of supporting a point drawn from reality—preferably the speaker's reality. Ideally the speaker will be able to draw on his own past experiences to cite specific instances to demonstrate points desired. The use of specific instance is, perhaps, more effective than illustration because the speaker is attesting to the authenticity of the happening or event.

Samples of Explanation, Illustration, Specific Instance

Listed below are samples of the three external forms of support for informative speaking. The topic formulated in Chapter Eleven on fixed income and inflation is the one presumed to be under discussion.

Explanation. Point to be clarified is a definition of fixed income:

> By fixed income I mean that a person has an income established by an external agency such as social security or a pension fund, with no anticipation of regular future increases.

Illustration. Point to be clarified is that a fixed income can make it impossible for a person to meet living expenses:

> Assume that when you enter college you are given $1000. per year for living expenses. During your freshman year the amount is adequate;

however, at the start of your sophomore year dormitory expenses increase by 25 percent, 35 percent at the beginning of your junior year, and 45 percent at the beginning of your senior year. If your income is truly fixed like millions of elderly Americans you will very quickly face financial crisis.

Specific Instance. Point to be clarified is that a fixed income can make it impossible for a person to meet living expenses:

In order to impress this point on you I would like to tell you of the situation my great-grandfather has found himself in for the past two years . . .

SUMMARY PROBES

1. **Name and characterize the three speech appeals that have survived since classical Greek times.**
2. **How can a speaker "make" himself credible on a topic?**
3. **What is meant by a hypothetical illustration?**
4. **How does a specific instance differ from both an explanation and an illustration?**

MATERIALS AND FORMS OF SUPPORT FOR THE PERSUASIVE SPEECH

As with the informative speech, it is highly important that the audience have a positive credibility image of the speaker. Unlike the informative speech, however, source credibility will not usually be found with the student speaker in sufficient quality or quantity for an audience to alter attitudinal structure and, perhaps, change behavior. Audience members will expect a speaker to be knowledgeable about a persuasive speech topic; however, they are likely to raise additional questions when they are asked to agree with the speaker and, perhaps, change their own stand.

Source Credibility

A credible speaker in a persuasive situation will be expected to establish arguments to accompany his points. For our purposes, argument will be defined as a *reason* for belief or acceptance of a proposition. A persuasive speaker asks an audience to agree with him; the audience will, in turn, ask the speaker, "Why should we agree with you?" The speaker's credibility is important, but not usually enough in a persuasive effort.

Forms of support external to the speaker for persuasive speech efforts can be categorized into two general types: factual material and reasoned material.

Factual Material

Debate has existed for years as to what is fact and what is not. Some philosophers contend that nothing is factual just as academicians have traditionally defined fact. We will not begin to engage in a debate as to the existence or nonexistence of fact. However, for our purposes we will define factual matter in speech development as material which a speaker uses which can be authenticated as true. For instance, it is a fact that the president of the United States made a speech on March 30, 1968, in which he withdrew from the presidential race. It is also a fact that the price of gasoline is higher today than it was twenty-five years ago. For speaking purposes, we should identify two kinds of factual materials.

Testimony. The use of testimony to support points in a persuasive speech refers to the practice of quoting another person or organization either for or against a proposition which the speaker is trying to get the audience to accept. Testimony in a persuasive speech can be the result of the speaker's trying to plug existing holes in speaker credibility. For instance, if a student speaker delivers a speech in a classroom to convince the audience that shale oil is the panacea for our energy problems, that student speaker will no doubt be forced to use testimony of experts to fill the credibility gap created by his status as a freshman student. A typical audience response to such a topic might be, "Why should we accept your proposition—you're just a freshman student like us?"

Expert testimony, then, is one major form of testimonial available to the public speaker. The major problem facing the speaker in the use of such supporting material is in verifying the expert as a true authority on the subject under discussion. If an audience will not accept the speaker as an expert, the audience probably won't accept

Sam Smith either unless the speaker informs his audience of Sam Smith's credentials which make him an authority.

The speaker should be especially aware of the problem arising from using popular and well-known figures as experts on subjects outside their field. Advertising strategists have found that the public is susceptible to testimonials as to whether the person giving the testimony is an expert in the specific field or not. Joe Namath may truly qualify as an expert on the best offensive play with a third down and four yards to go; however, it is doubtful that he is any more of an authority than a student speaker on the quality of different brands of panty hose.

Statistics. The use of statistics in public speaking can take various forms; however, the two most common are the average and the percentage. We are constantly hit with average rates of inflation, average salaries, average ages, and so on. Percentage appeals competing for our attention are almost as numerous. The use of meaningful statistics can do a great deal to enhance the credibility of both the speaker and the speech. We cannot overemphasize, however, the term *meaningful* as a modifier to statistics. Very often we are too impressed with statistics and fail to examine them critically.

The average. Simply defined, an *average* is the sum of the parts divided by the number of parts. Averages can be very meaningful as a form of persuasive support; they can also be practically meaningless. As a general rule, though, the speaker should attempt to discover more about the statistic being used than just the printed number. An essential question involved in the average is how many parts were added to produce the average. When the number of individual parts included is small, the final statistic can be distorted by parts extremely high or extremely low. A large number of parts will normally neutralize the distortive effect of extremes when figuring averages. The point important to the speaker is that if the average used is meaningful you must know more about the statistic than the final statement of average.

The following example will demonstrate how an average can be practically meaningless. The proprietor of a local drug store has boasted for years that his store pays the best wages in the downtown area. The average salary of people working for him is $9680. per year. Now let us examine to determine how the average was figured:

Employee	Annual Income
Proprietor	$28,000
First clerk	6,000
Second clerk	6,000
Third clerk	6,000
Custodian	2,400
	$48,400 divided by 5 people

Average salary of those working in the store: $9680.

The average salary figure is accurate in every respect. Because we have conditioned ourselves to expect that an average statement means that most people are near the average, an audience might assume that most people who work in the drug store make at or near $9680. Actually, no one makes a salary even close to the average figure.

The percentage. Like the average, the percentage can be a very meaningful and supportive statistic to use in developing persuasive points. Percentages are normally used as measure of rate or increase or decrease. While both averages and percentages can be strong benefits to the speech, the percentage can be distorted just like the average. Just as it is dangerous to pick up a statement of average for use in a speech without seeking more information as to how the average was figured, the conscientious speaker must raise questions about the statement of any percentage before using it as supportive material. The basic question concerning percentage is "percentage of what?" The following example demonstrates a percentage which could be distorted by listeners attempting to interpret the statistic.

In a speech opposed to national health insurance, the speaker desires to show that the increase in cost of food in the past 40 years has been greater than the increase in medical care. The statement of support in the speech is as follows: "The cost of medical care in the United States since 1935 has risen 150 percent while the cost of food during the same period of time has increased 600 percent. Certainly I agree that we have a problem, today, with increasing cost of living, but perhaps the greatest problem is not in the area of medical care."

Again, let us examine the method used by the speaker in arriving at his percentage figures:

	1935	1975	Percent increase
Appendectomy	$100	$250	150
Loaf of Bread	$ .10	$ .60	600

The calculation of the percentage of increase for the specific items is undeniably accurate. Only when the listener extends the percentages to the totality of all food and all medical care does the statistic become distorted.

The student speaker should strive to find supporting materials in the form of statistics for persuasive speeches. The student speaker does, however, have an ethical obligation to his listeners to examine published statistics for complete meaning before using them in a persuasive effort.

Reasoned Material

If the amount of factual material available to the speaker is plentiful, the persuasive task will be simplified. In the absence of factual material, however, the speaker must rely on various forms of reasoning as supporting material to strengthen his arguments. *Reasoning* refers to the process of collecting available nonfactual materials in the form of observations and drawing substantive conclusions from them after engaging in one of four established and organized mental processes. The four forms of reasoning to be discussed are inductive, deductive, causal, and analogous.

Inductive Reasoning. The process of reasoning by induction refers to drawing conclusions based on examination of one or more specific instances or singular observations. Supporting persuasive arguments through induction can be a sound procedure; however, the greatest limitation of the process is that often a speaker examines too few specific instances to warrant the sweeping nature of the conclusion. Following are four examples of reasoning by the process of induction; the first two, while not 100 percent certain, are acceptable, and the last two are very weak. Explanations follow each.

> I have interviewed 1000 of the 8000 students enrolled at this university using a randomly selected sample. I discovered that 150 of those interviewed are left-handed. Therefore, I conclude

> that approximately 15 percent of the college students in the country are left-handed.

One might safely draw this conclusion if the students were truly randomly selected. Accompanying acceptance of the conclusion, however, is a necessary assumption that college students on the campus where the interviews took place are characteristic of all college students.

> Half of the people in this classroom feel that it is much too cold in here. We need to turn up the thermostat.

To accept the inductive reasoning above one would have to assume that all people in the classroom are exposed to the same climatic conditions. If half are sitting by an open window and those are the ones who say it is too cold, perhaps, the window should be closed.

> Dr. Smith in the Economics department is a liberal; so is Dr. Jones in English. Almost all college professors are liberals.

The political beliefs of two selected individuals on one campus is not sufficient grounds to conclude anything about "almost all" college professors.

> Look at that lady in the Buick driving in the wrong lane. Women are lousy drivers.

Need we say more?

From the examples cited above, we can conclude inductively that reasoning by induction can be sound and effective for use in supporting points in public speaking. The primary point of criteria, however, determining soundness is the number of specific instances examined or observed before drawing a conclusion.

Deductive Reasoning. Deductive reasoning generally follows the reverse pattern of induction. In deduction the speaker begins with a general statement, and after deduction the result is a conclusion consisting of a specific statement. Again deductive reasoning can be sound in supporting points in persuasive speeches.

The most effective method of demonstrating the process of deduction is by casting arguments in syllogistic form. Syllogism refers to a piece of reasoning consisting of a major premise (broad, general), a minor premise (specifying, singling out), and a conclusion (end result of the process). You will recall that the syllogistic form of deductive reasoning was discussed in the segment on interpersonal communication.

For deductive reasoning to be judged sound, both the major and minor premises must be accepted by the listener as probably true. Below are four examples of syllogisms depicting the deductive process. Again, the first two are sound due to the probable acceptability of the first two premises. The final two are in question.

Major premise: All dogs have four legs.
Minor premise: Daisy is our family pet dog.
Conclusion: Therefore, Daisy has four legs.

Both major and minor premises are probably acceptable to an audience, therefore the conclusion is sound and valid.

Major premise: All college students should respect library materials.
Minor premise: Jim is a college student.
Conclusion: Therefore, Jim should respect library materials.

The major premise in the above syllogism may not be as universally acceptable as in the first; however, assuming a significant degree of universal acceptance, the conclusion would be valid.

Major premise: All children like chocolate ice cream.
Minor premise: Jeff is a child.
Conclusion: Therefore, Jeff likes chocolate ice cream.

Validity of this reasoning is questionable due to the major premise. It is doubtful that enough children in the world could be observed to make such a generalization.

Major premise: All dogs have four legs.
Minor premise: Daisy has four legs.
Conclusion: Therefore, Daisy is a dog.

This syllogism is invalid, however, not because either the major or minor premise is false. It is similar to the first example with one major exception. The minor premise extracts the wrong factor from the major premise as the "allness" factor. The major premise does not say that all animals with four legs are dogs. Daisy might be a cow, horse, goat, or cat. A syllogism such as the one above is said to be internally invalid.

Two major limitations of deductive reasoning can be drawn from the preceding examples. First, both the major and minor premises must be accepted as probably true by the listener. Second, the process of deduction must be internally correct in that when specifying statements from generalizations, the proper factor must be extracted.

The student of public speaking should recognize that seldom does the syllogistic format find use in speaking or thinking. Casting deductive reasoning in syllogistic form simply demonstrates the process. In speaking, writing, or thinking, we usually omit the major premise and many times the minor premise. Rather than state all three components, in public speaking or interpersonal communication one might state the first example as follows: "Of course Daisy has four legs. She's a dog, isn't she?"

Causal. Using causal relationships in reasoning implies that the speaker assumes something that isn't known based on something that is known. Accepting one point as true, we may in turn accept as true that something else caused what we know to be true. This procedure is called reasoning from a known effect to a presumed cause. On the other hand, if we assume something else will be true as a result of what we know is true, we are reasoning from cause to effect. We are in actuality saying first, that what is true now was caused by ——— . In the second method of reasoning we are saying that what is true now will cause ———.

An example of valid causal reasoning can be demonstrated when we look out the window and observe that the streets and sidewalks are wet. From that observation, we reason that it has rained recently. Most would consider this to be valid reasoning since the choice of possible causes for making the street and sidewalks wet is very limited. It probably, in fact, did rain.

An example of invalid causal reasoning follows: "Our basketball team only won three games this year; we need a new coach." When we examine the possible causes for a basketball team losing games, we discover several, of which coaching is only one. Assuming that the coach has had successful years in the past, the differing variable this year was not the coach, but the players. Perhaps, we need new players to produce a successful basketball season.

An example of acceptable cause to effect reasoning follows: "The furnace is broken; it's going to be too cold to sleep in here tonight." Most would accept this reasoning simply because we are conditioned to expect cold temperatures as an effect of lack of heat.

An example of unacceptable cause to effect reasoning follows: "A Democrat was elected president; the country will be in financial ruin in one year." Most would not accept this as valid reasoning simply because the effect produced would most likely be judged to be too far reaching to be brought about by one man.

Thus, we can see that causal reasoning can be an effective method of supporting points in a speech. Any piece of reasoning, however, using either effect to cause or cause to effect analysis must be examined thoroughly for other possible variables producing effect or cause. A very significant factor in validating causal reasoning is found in what we have learned to expect from certain events based on past experiences.

Analogy. Reasoning from analogy is the process of comparing two objects that are similar in some respects and concluding that they are or should be similar in additional respects. The primary validation test for an analogy is the determination if the two objects being compared are similar enough to warrant comparison.

An example of a valid analogy can be found in comparing two university towns to determine what one of the towns needs that it doesn't have. Let us assume that a speaker is trying to support a proposal for a community theater group in a university town of 15,000 population with no major industry. The location of the town is remote in that no other communities of significant size are nearby. To use analogy as support for his project, the speaker would have to find a university town close in population with no major industry, also remote, which has a thriving community theater group. If such a community could be located, it would serve as a strong analogous argument for his cause. The speaker could not use a larger city, industrial center, or a suburb of a metropolitan area as a valid comparison.

One of the oldest examples of analogous reasoning is the comparison made between the United States government with its three branches—legislative, executive, and judicial—and a three-legged stool. The argument follows that if one of the three branches of government were eliminated, it would be unstable and topple just as the stool would do if one leg was removed. Validity of the analogy is questionable, however, for a massive government function composed of thousands of human beings is hardly comparable to a three-legged inanimate object totally incapable of making any internal compensation for deficiencies.

SUMMARY PROBES

1. **What major problem faces the speaker in using expert testimony to support a point?**
2. **Before either an average or a percentage can be truly meaningful to the speaker certain facts must be known. What are they?**
3. **What is the major difference between factual and reasoned material in persuasive speaking?**
4. **State one example of each of the following types of reasoning: inductive, deductive, causal, analogous.**

MATERIALS AND FORMS OF SUPPORT FOR THE SPEECH TO ENTERTAIN

Much of the material contained in a speech to entertain and the method of supporting points in such a speech parallel those outlined in both informative and persuasive speaking. The speaker's purpose will be aided significantly if he has a high ethos rating with the listeners. A speech to entertain might well make effective use of statistics and methods of reasoning. The speech to entertain normally makes use of emotional appeal to the listener in the sense that the speaker seeks to provide pleasure for his audience.

One aspect of speech-making deserves special attention when discussing entertaining speech-making. Humor, while not a necessary item, usually is considered an important part of a speech to entertain. Humor, however, need not be restricted to speeches to entertain. Both informative and persuasive speeches can be aided by inserting humor.

The Use of Humor in Public Speaking

The student speaker will find entries in the References section directing him to sources with full discussions of theories and types of humor in public speaking. The primary point to be made here concerning humor in any public speaking situation is that *humor should always contribute to the purpose of the speech.* The after-dinner speaker who begins a speech with ten to fifteen minutes of unrelated jokes and stories, and proceeds to deliver a twenty-minute nonsmiling message has not made effective use of humor.

The student of public speaking should remember three fundamental rules regarding the use of humor in presentations.

Humor Should be Used Sparingly. As a beginning speaker, if you are in doubt as to whether to attempt humor or not—*don't.* Nothing is more somber and sad than a person *trying* to be funny.

Humor Should Be Inserted Throughout the Speech. There is no proper time in the sequence of the delivery of the speech that is appropriate for humor and other times that are inappropriate. Humor is an excellent device for gaining attention in a speech introduction; however, it is also an excellent device for regaining attention in the body of a speech or to use in the closing words of the speech.

Humor Should Be Related to the Speech. The relationship of humor to a point in the speech should be made obvious to the listeners. Humor is complementary to the entire speech situation. If an audience can only remember your jokes after a presentation, you have not achieved your purpose as an effective public speaker.

SUMMARY PROBES **1. What are three fundamental rules regarding the use of humor?**

LEARNING EXPERIENCES

1. Prepare at least three opening statements of speeches on three different topics which would establish you as an expert on each.

2. Develop an explanation, illustration, and specific instance as forms of support for a point in an informative speech.

3. Find or develop two sets of figures; one for which the average is meaningful, and the other for which the average is meaningless.

4. Find examples of both inductive and deductive reasoning in a newspaper editorial, magazine article, or speech.

5. Bring examples of both causal reasoning and analogy to class from some form of mass media.

6. Watch for and record good and bad examples of humor in speech.

References

Bradley, Bert E. *Fundamentals of Speech Communication: The Credibility of Ideas.* Dubuque: Wm. C. Brown, 1974, chapters 2, 8.

Hance, Kenneth G.; Ralph, David C.; and Wiksell, Milton J. *Principles of Speaking,* 2nd ed. Belmont: Wadsworth, 1969, chapters 15, 16, 17.

Hughey, Jim D., and Johnson, Arlee W. *Speech Communication: Foundations and Challenges.* New York: Macmillan, 1975, pp. 116–24.

McCabe, Bernard P., Jr., and Bender, Coleman C. *Speaking is a Practical Matter,* 2nd ed. Boston: Holbrook Press, 1974, Part IV, V.

Monroe, Alan H., and Ehninger, Douglas. *Principles and Types of Speech Communication,* 7th ed. Glenview: Scott, Foresman, 1974, chapters 18, 20, 21.

Thonssen, Lester, and Baird, A. Craig. *Speech Criticism.* New York: Ronald Press, 1948, chapters 11, 12, 13.

THIRTEEN

GOALS **After completing this chapter you will be able to:**

1. Identify the three major organizational components of a speech.

2. List five prominent factors of attention important to the public speaker.

3. Identify four of the most effective motive appeals available to the public speaker.

4. Distinguish between three of the most widely used organizational patterns for public speaking.

5. Identify several methods of ending the speech.

Preparing The Speech
Organizing And Outlining

We discussed methods of collecting materials and supporting points for public speaking situations in Chapter Twelve. The next logical step in speech preparation is in organizing the collected material and developing an outline for the speech presentation.

Various authors have developed several alternative methods of organizing ideas and material for public speaking. For our purposes we will utilize one of the simplest and most common. Our speech organization will fall into three parts: introduction, body, and conclusion. Before the speaker even begins to develop an outline, we assume that he has a clear and concise purpose statement.

THE SPEECH INTRODUCTION

Study of communication of any type recognizes the importance of a favorable initial impression on the part of the receiver toward the message to be communicated. The public speaking situation is no different. The success or failure of a speech is often determined within the first minute of presentation. The speaker must create a reaction from the listeners favorable to the remainder of the speech.

A good speech introduction should serve three purposes for the speaker. First, it should gain the attention of the audience. Second, the introduction should appeal to motives of the audience; and, finally, the introduction should provide the audience with a general overview of the purpose of the speech.

Gaining Attention Through Attention Factors

Attention is crucial in the introduction to a speech. If the audience's attention is not captured at the outset, it is doubtful that the speaker will be able to gain it later in the speech; even if he does, it will be a much more difficult task than at the outset. Before a speaker utters his first words, most audience members have made no value judgment as to the worth of the speech. We use the first few sentences of a speech to answer the question, "Will the audience listen further?" A highly favorable response to that question based on the speaker's opening can give the speaker a healthy start on the road to a successful speech.

One should not mistakenly assume that attention is only a concern for the introduction of a speech. Getting initial attention is a simple factor—it can be done by firing a gun; holding attention by relating points of attention to speech purpose is a more difficult task. Attention factors should be of concern to the speaker throughout the speech; however, they play an especially significant role in the introduction.

We could list great numbers of factors that can be utilized by the speaker to gain the attention of audiences. For our purposes, however, we will concern ourselves with five of the more important and prominent factors of attention.

Uniqueness. The human being is attracted to situations that are different from the ordinary. The speaker who can open his speech with a statement that presents a unique or different concept to the listeners is likely to receive their attention at least momentarily.

The following speech introduction and commentary provides an example of a different approach to the speech introduction. The speaker in this particular situation faced a difficult task in that her audience was predisposed against her position on the topic. She began, "I have some candy to give you today." (At this point the speaker took her hand from behind her back and threw a handful of wrapped candy in the air. Most members of the class scrambled to the floor like animals to retrieve the candy.) Continuing, she admonished, "Please get back in your seats and give me your attention. Today I'm going to persuade you that high school students act in a childish manner most of the time. I want to thank you all for demonstrating my point."

The preceding introduction is a clear example of uniqueness. Most audiences are not accustomed to having speakers throw candy at them. It is also an excellent example of effective use of introduction to promote the purpose of the speech. Through her introduction, the speaker was able to "trap" her listeners into proving her point.

Activity. Our attention is attracted much more effectively to moving objects than inanimate ones. If possible, the speaker should strive for some kind of movement during the opening stages of the speech. Through movement, attention is drawn to the speaker and consequently, to what the speaker will say later. Of course activity should not be too gross or prolonged, or the audience members will continue to look at the movement rather than listen to what the speaker says.

Movement used in introductions need not be movement on the part of the speaker's body. Flashing a picture or chart momentarily can provide enough activity to get the attention of the auditors focused on the speaker.

Suspense. Most human beings have difficulties coping with suspenseful situations. We don't like television programs or movies to have endings which fail to tie up all loose ends of the plot. We don't like things to remain unsettled in our minds. With this human trait in mind, the speaker has an effective attention-getting device at his disposal if he can arouse a suspenseful reaction in the minds of the listeners.

Opening a speech with a statement like, "Wouldn't you like to know . . ." acts as a tease in the minds of the listeners. The implication exists that the speaker is going to tell the listener what he would like to know; first, he must listen attentively to what the speaker has to say.

Conflict. Normal human beings don't like conflict. We take great pains to avoid conflict with those around us; if conflict does arise, we normally seek to resolve it as quickly as possible. The task of the public speaker rests with presenting a conflict in the minds of the listeners. Accompanying the conflict, however, must come an expectation on the part of the listener that the speaker will, through his speech, resolve the conflict and restore his mental state to an atmosphere of balance.

Vital. If the speaker can convince his listener that what he has to say to him is vital to his welfare or well-being, he can be assured that the listener will award him his initial attention. An example of an opening statement stressing a vital concept to college students could be, "Would you like to be assured of raising your cumulative grade point average by a full .5 this semester?" Rest assured that with such an opening, even the sleepiest and most docile student will snap to attention—at least temporarily.

Using one of the preceding factors of attention will assure the speaker the initial attention of his listeners. The speaker cannot stop at this point, however. Attention must be maintained throughout the speech which means that the effective speaker may have to reinsert attention factors during the speech. The speaker should keep in mind that attention factors producing longevity in attention are those that are directly related to the topic. Anyone can get the attention of a group of people—you can crash two cymbals together, fire a gun, or scream just before you begin to speak. Your audience will be at attention. However, longevity in audience attention is provided by that factor which is directly related to the purpose of your speech.

Appeal to Audience Motives

Regardless of what kind of activity in which human beings engage, we must be motivated to do so. Motivation provides a reason for doing something. Appealing to an audience's motives provides those audience members with a reason for listening to your speech. The speaker who overlooks this step in preparation may find that his listeners would prefer to daydream or doodle than listen to the words of the speaker. Audiences ask, "Why should I give you, the speaker, five minutes or more of my valuable time?" As a speaker, you must always remember that your listeners deserve an answer to that question.

Four motive appeals will be discussed here. The four cited do not constitute an exhaustive list of human motives; however, as with attention factors, they are considered to be most effective.

Curiosity. Human beings are very curious animals. A speaker who appeals to the curiosity of his audience, in a sense, taunts the audience at the outset with the expectation of more information to come later in the speech. If the device is used effectively, the audience has reason for listening: to get the rest of the story.

The best example of curiosity as a motive appeal in practice can be seen on commercial television. Most crime shows begin with a scene of the crime being committed—a scene of high activity and perhaps violence. Of course, the expectation on the part of the audience is that more will follow. We will even learn who committed the crime later in the show. The need for watching is present, just as the need for listening is present when a speaker uses this device effectively in the introduction to a speech.

Security. We all like to feel secure in all that we do. Security can come in many forms: financial, personal, health, interpersonal relations, and so on. When our security in any sense becomes threatened, we immediately seek ways to restore it. The speaker who can appeal to the human need for security is assured that he will have a group of motivated listeners.

A speaker who opens his speech, "Have you been wondering how you will cope with an 11 percent cost of living increase next year on this year's salary? Perhaps, what I have to say today will help you," has motivated his listeners. He has provided you with a *need* to hear what he has to say.

Fear. Of all human emotions, fear is probably the most dramatic in its effect. If we put a gun to a man's head, we can make him do things he would never do under any other circumstances. People will jump out of windows five floors above ground if a fire is approaching them from the rear. Fear used in moderation as a motive appeal will normally deliver an audience ready to listen. The audience members, however, must be convinced that you can do something to alleviate their fear.

We cannot stress too heavily that the use of fear as a motive appeal must be used in moderation and without dramatics. Sometimes, attempts to "scare" people into listening can backfire and build a wall of resistance between speaker and listener. Tread softly!

Sex. Whether we will admit it or not, we all like to consider ourselves attractive as sexual objects to others. Pick up any magazine or look at the commercials on television today, and you will see a mélange of products advertised based on sex appeal for the user.

Using sex as a motive appeal in a public speaking situation may be more difficult than other types of appeal, but if it can be utilized effectively, it will produce results. Difficult as it may be, it is extremely effective.

Overview of Speech

After the speaker is reasonably confident that he has accomplished the first two purposes of the introduction—that he has gained the attention of the audience and provided them with a reason to listen—he must quickly convince the listeners that the speech to follow will fulfill the needs aroused. A quick overview of the main points to be covered in the speech should be provided as a final segment of the introduction. At this point in the speech, the purpose statement should be made perfectly clear: The audience should have no doubt beyond this point what the speaker intends to do.

SUMMARY PROBES

1. **What three purposes should be served by a good introduction to a speech?**
2. **Give an example of each of the five attention factors cited.**
3. **What necessary question do effective motive appeals answer for the listener in a public speaking situation?**
4. **Which motive appeal is probably the most effective?**

THE SPEECH BODY

Once the speech has been properly introduced, the speaker is ready to present the main points previewed in the introduction and develop each main point with the forms of support and other materials collected earlier. Development of main points occurs in the segment of the speech referred to as the *body*.

The time of phrasing the main points for the speech is, perhaps, the most important period for the speaker to keep his time limit in mind. If the time allotted for the speech is short, the speaker will not be able to include very many main points. A six-minute speech with eight main points will most likely result in a shallow approach to most topics. Main points imply that subpoints and materials of development will follow each one.

While no rigid restrictions as to number of main points should be established, a general rule for most speeches under ten minutes would be from two to five main points. A longer message might contain more main points. More than five main points in the body of a short speech will most likely result in insufficient and inadequate support for some or all of the main points. If the speaker feels that he cannot possibly treat his topic with five or less main points, he should probably "go back to the drawing board," and either narrow the topic further or select a new one.

The speaker should select one of several possible organizational patterns for the body of the speech. (An organizational pattern is simply a systematic method of arranging the main points of a speech.) Several organizational patterns are available for the speaker's use: three of the most often used are time or chronological order, categorical order, and problem-solution order. A discussion of each and a sample outline utilizing each follows.

Time or Chronological Order

As the name implies, time or chronological order follows a step-by-step sequence, such as first step through to last step or earliest to latest. Time order is especially appropriate for informative speeches describing processes or relating events in the past. Demonstration speeches often utilize time or chronological patterns of organization.

The following speech outline demonstrates the time or chronological pattern for an informative speech. The subject area in the speech is historical development of the motion-picture industry.

I. Introduction
  A. Did you ever realize that you are part of a group of people who buy two of every three tickets purchased at motion picture theaters?
    1. Sixty-five percent of all movie admissions are individuals between the ages of twelve and thirty.
    2. I would assume that very few, you possibly included, know anything at all about the historical growth of the motion picture.
  B. My purpose today is to explain three significant periods in the development of a form of media which induces Americans to spend $1.5 billion per year.

II. Body
   A. The first period of film production in the United States was one of individual expression.
      1. Individual expression in motion pictures refers to the film in which the content is the result of one person's ideas.
      2. Two early pioneers produced examples of such films.
         a) George Méliès was responsible for *A Trip to the Moon*.
         b) Edwin S. Porter made two significant contributions to early filmmaking.
            (1) His first was *The Life of an American Fireman*.
            (2) The second was *The Great Train Robbery*.
   B. Commercialism brought about the middle period of film as a media form appealing to the masses.
      1. Silent films created a habitual audience in the late teens and twenties.
      2. Sound had great effect on the movie industry.
         a) Sound ruined many movie careers.
         b) Sound introduced the musical to the film industry.
         c) Sound confirmed movies as a mass media form capable of successful competition with radio.
   C. The immediate popularity of television started the movie industry on a slow trail back to individual expression.
      1. Early efforts of filmmakers to combat television were unsuccessful.
         a) The practice of withholding recent movies from television failed.
         b) New "gimmicks" proved to be passing fads.
      2. Underground movies of the late sixties were similar to early films of Mèliés and Porter in concept.
      3. Movies today appeal to specialized audiences and are normally the products of the mind of one individual.

III. Conclusion
   A. Thus, we have seen that the motion-picture industry has moved in a full circle from individual expression to mass entertainment and back to individual expression.
   B. The next time you pay your two dollars plus to gain admittance into a theater, remember that you may be paying to see the results of one person's expression.

Categorical Order

Categorical order refers to the divisions of points to be covered in a speech into distinguishable groupings which can be labeled or categorized. The categorical order can be used effectively in both informative and persuasive speeches. In an informative speech, categories might include kinds of objects or concepts to be described, while a persuasive speech could effectively categorize kinds of arguments supporting or denying a stand on a controversial subject.

The following speech outline demonstrates the use of categorical order in a persuasive speech opposing abortion.

I. Introduction
   A. Regardless of how you stand on the issue of abortion, you probably base your position on either a legal argument or a moral argument.
   B. To grasp a topic as complex and important as abortion, everyone should realize that legal issues and moral issues involving abortion are very separate and distinct categories.
   C. My purpose today is to present both legal and moral arguments in opposition to the legalization of abortion.

II. Body
   A. Two very significant legal issues exist.
      1. At the time of conception is the fetus a person by law, or not until actual birth?
         a) Court decisions and interpretations in this area have traditionally been vague and in some cases conflicting.
         b) Since growth and physical development begin at the time of conception, the fetus is a person at that point.
      2. What are the lawful rights of the father of the child in determining whether or not to abort?
         a) The father shares the responsibility for a child after birth; therefore, he should share the responsibility and concern for the child before birth.
         b) A recent court decision upheld the father's legal right to share in the decision-making process concerning abortion.
   B. There are also two significant moral issues.
      1. Does any mortal being have the right to determine whether or not another mortal being should be allowed to exist?
         a) If conception is an act of God, as I believe it is, man should not intervene.
         b) There are numerous Biblical passages supporting this point of view.
      2. If a mother does not want a child, shouldn't she offer the child for adoption?
         a) There are hundreds of adoption agencies in the country which do not have enough children to meet demands.
         b) Thousands of childless couples are eagerly awaiting the time when they can adopt an unwanted child.

III. Conclusion
   A. Keep in mind that the abortion issue has two distinct categories of argument.
   B. I urge you to do all in your power to oppose legalized abortion based on both legal and moral issues.

Problem-Solution Order

The problem-solution order is a two-step process which states and analyzes an existing problem in the first main point. The second main point in the body of the speech proposes a solution to the stated problem and offers development and support for that solution. Organization according to problem solution is most effective for persuasive speaking.

The following speech outline demonstrates the use of problem-solution order in a persuasive speech on eliminating victimless crimes as a means of reducing the crime rate.

I. Introduction
   A. If you spend more than one year in a major city in the United States, your chances of being the victim of a crime are at least 50–50.
      1. Two out of four inhabitants of major cities will be crime victims.
      2. The crime rate in smaller cities is increasing although not as dramatically as in major cities.
   B. Americans should be able to walk the streets of cities relatively free of fear.
   C. In this speech I will present what I consider to be the problem primarily responsible for increased crime rates and convince you that my solution will best solve that problem.

II. Body
   A. Overcrowded jails and court dockets cause increases in crime rates.
      1. Overcrowded jails result in law-enforcement officials overlooking some crimes.
      2. Overcrowded jails result in a lenient approach to setting bond for alleged offenders.
      3. Overcrowded court dockets encourage plea bargaining.
      4. Overcrowded court dockets contribute to instances of dismissed charges before trial.
   B. Eliminating victimless crimes would eliminate overcrowded jails and court dockets.

1. Victimless crimes are defined as charges resulting from gambling, prostitution, homosexuality, marijuana offenses, and violation of pornography and obscenity standards.
2. Approximately 50 percent of the criminal cases in the courts are offenders of the above victimless crimes.
3. Eliminating 50 percent of arrests and subsequent court cases would alleviate the pressure now felt by our judicial system.

III. Conclusion

A. In conclusion, eliminating victimless crimes is by far the most sensible solution to rising crime rates.
   1. When walking on a city street, we should fear the mugger, rapist, murderer, or thief.
   2. We need not fear being the victim of a prostitute, a poker player, blue movie producer, or homosexual.

B. I appeal to each of you to urge our government at all levels to concentrate on those criminals who want to hurt us, and leave offenders of victimless crimes alone.

The body of the speech, then, should contain a limited number of main points depending primarily on the time limit allowed for the presentation of the speech. Some systematic form of organization of main points should be selected, and all subpoints and materials of development and forms of support should fall within that chosen format.

The speaker should keep in mind throughout delivery of the body of the speech that factors of attention and appeals to audience motives continue to play an important role. Assuming that the speaker did an effective job of gaining attention at the outset, the body of the speech must effectively retain the attention.

Also, assuming that the speaker effectively aroused motive appeals within his listeners, the body of the speech must make it evident to the listeners that the speaker's message is sufficient to satisfy the needs aroused. Audience attention and motivation are not matters solely for concern in the speech introduction.

SUMMARY PROBES

1. **Why is the existence of too many points in a speech potentially harmful to its overall effect?**
2. **For what kind of speeches is time or chronological order most appropriate?**
3. **Why do attention factors and motive appeals continue to play an important role in the body of the speech?**

THE SPEECH CONCLUSION

The precise content of the conclusion of a speech is greatly dependent on the purpose of the speech. Whatever the intent, however, the conclusion is a vital part of the speech in that it serves as the speaker's final chance to achieve his purpose. Audience attention is normally at a high level during the conclusion of the speech if the listeners are made aware that the end of the speech is at hand. Regardless of how bored listeners may be during the body of the speech, hearing the speaker utter the words, "and, in conclusion," will usually snap them to attention, ready to listen to the final words.

We can generalize that all conclusions, regardless of specific purpose of the speech, should include some form of summarization of main points. The summary should be concise and phrased in such a way to enhance audience retention as much as possible. The conclusion may end with the summary; however, the speaker may find it beneficial to his purpose to employ one of three devices in addition to the summary.

Summary Plus Application

In an informative speech, the speaker may find it useful to conclude with a direct application of the speech content to the needs of the listener. The use of application in the conclusion assumes that the speaker made a strong appeal to audience motives or need for receiving the information being offered. Application informs the audience as to what they should do with the information, or how they should utilize it.

Summary Plus Appeal

In a speech to stimulate or convince, the speaker should conclude the speech with a final appeal to the listeners to accept the arguments he has offered. The speaker may refer to an appeal made in the introduction to the speech, or he may initiate another in the closing statement of the speech. When a speaker wishes to make a final appeal to his listeners in concluding the speech, he may find an attempt to arouse emotion effective.

Summary Plus Actuation

If the purpose of the speech has been to actuate the listeners, some reference to the specific action requested of the audience is needed in the conclusion. Actuating an audience is normally the most difficult of all tasks for a speaker. If an audience is expected to perform some physical action as a result of the speech, they must never lose sight of the specific act being requested of them.

Any effort to identify one of the three parts of a speech as more important than the other two should be carefully avoided. Certainly, a poor introduction will decrease the potential effectiveness of the overall speech. A carefully planned introduction with good attention devices, however, followed by an unorganized mishmash of verbiage will not lead to fulfillment of the speaker's goal. An abrupt conclusion, or, worse yet, no conclusion at all can destroy all the gains made by an effective introduction and carefully planned body. The best speech is one that receives careful planning and development throughout all three parts with each of three parts being critical to full understanding and appreciation of the other two.

SUMMARY PROBES

1. **Why is the conclusion of a speech a vital part in the speaker's effort to accomplish his purpose? Why is attention normally at a high level during the conclusion of a speech?**
2. **Why is it impossible to label the conclusion the most important part of a speech?**

THE SPEECH OUTLINE

A speech outline is meant to serve one and only one purpose: to assist the speaker in delivering the speech. Outlining is a method of organizing thoughts and setting them down in logical and sequential order. As a student speaker, you should prepare an outline carefully; doing so will make your task of delivering the speech much easier.

There are two basic kinds of outlines: a topic outline and a sentence outline. A sentence outline organizes all parts of the speech into complete sentences with all necessary grammatical components.

A topic outline need not use complete sentences; however, points included in the outline should be complete enough for speaker comprehension. As a speaker, you many find it beneficial to prepare both kinds of outlines.

The Assigned Outline

If your instructor assigns a speech outline to be turned in, it should most likely be a sentence outline following precise outline style specifications. Preparation of such an outline, even if it is not the one you use when delivering the speech, will give the speaker a much better understanding of the relationship of his main points to each other and to their specific subpoints. Keep in mind that an assigned outline to be handed in to your instructor is one meant to be read and understood by someone other than yourself. Topic outlines may suffice well for the speaking situation; however, to another reader a topic outline can be virtually meaningless.

The Speaking Outline

You may find it to your advantage to use the same outline that you submit to your instructor for delivering the speech. Normally, however, a speaker should take no more notes with him to the lectern than he feels absolutely necessary for effective presentation. The amount of notes needed or desired in delivering the speech will depend on several factors, such as the specific assignment as outlined by the instructor and the mode of delivery chosen for the speech.

SUMMARY PROBES

1. **What is the major difference between a sentence outline and a topic outline?**
2. **In what ways does the assigned outline differ from the speaking outline?**

LEARNING EXPERIENCES

1. Watch television programs to record methods used by programmers of gaining viewer attention at the outset of the program.

2. Look through several current magazines to identify as many uses of motive appeals in advertising as possible.

3. Write two speech outlines for the same informative speech topic. In one use a time or chronological order of organization and in the other use the categorical order of organization.

4. Write three conclusions for the same persuasive speech using summary plus application in one, summary plus appeal in another, and summary plus actuation in the third.

5. Prepare a sentence outline for either an informative or persuasive speech to be turned in to your instructor and a topic outline on the same speech topic to be used as a speaking outline.

References

Bradley, Bert E. *Fundamentals of Speech Communication: The Credibility of Ideas.* Dubuque: Wm. C. Brown, 1974, chapters 6, 7.

Eisenson, Jon, and Boase, Paul H. *Basic Speech,* 3rd ed. New York: Macmillan, 1975, pp. 367–70, 392–97, chapter 17.

Hance, Kenneth G.; Ralph, David C.; and Wiksell, Milton J. *Principles of Speaking,* 2nd ed. Belmont: Wadsworth, 1969, chapters 7, 10, 11.

McCabe, Bernard P., Jr., and Bender, Coleman C. *Speaking is a Practical Matter,* 2nd ed. Boston: Holbrook Press, 1968, pp. 100–112; 196–206; 228–32.

Monroe, Alan H., and Ehninger, Douglas. *Principles and Types of Speech Communication,* 7th ed. Glenview: Scott, Foresman, 1974, chapters 9, 12, 14, 15.

FOURTEEN

GOALS **After completing this chapter you will be able to:**

1. **Recognize the nature of stage fright and its implications in the speaking situation.**
2. **Identify two fundamental concepts important to all aspects of speech delivery.**
3. **Distinguish four methods or modes of delivering speeches and be aware of both advantages and disadvantages to each.**
4. **List five vocal aspects of delivery significant to the public speaker.**
5. **Understand the importance of each of the five bodily aspects of effective speech delivery.**

Delivering The Speech

After completing the steps outlined in Chapters Eleven, Twelve, and Thirteen, we will assume that the speaker is now ready to concentrate on the actual physical presentation of the speech. For most inexperienced speakers the fears and apprehensions associated with actual delivery of the speech pervade the entire preparation process. Few individuals have self-confidence concerning speech-making; your lack of such does not indicate that you are different or deviant from the norm.

This chapter will include a brief discussion of stage fright, followed by the statement of explanation of the two most crucial principles concerning physical delivery of speeches. The modes of delivery will be discussed, followed by a presentation of both vocal and bodily aspects.

STAGE FRIGHT

Most individuals who face the task of delivering a speech to a group of listeners cannot give an exact definition of the term *stage fright;* however, most know how it feels. *Stage fright* refers to the tensions experienced by the speaker in anticipation of and during actual delivery of the speech. The inevitable presence of stage fright in the speaker can have both physical and mental effects on the individual's composure. Two points concerning stage fright should be kept firmly in mind by all speakers.

Stage Fright Is a Normal Phenomenon

Many speakers feel that they should not be tense at the prospect of giving a speech. We often assume that experienced speakers never suffer from stage fright, and the presence of such feelings within us is a negative evaluation or indicator of our speaking prowess. Such thoughts should be expelled from the mind at once. *Stage fright, audience tension, speech fear,* or whatever term one chooses to attach to the "funny feeling" in your stomach and your cold, clammy hands is a perfectly normal human reaction to the speech situation.

A speaker who is approaching the date of speech delivery should not give any thought to trying to "get rid of" stage fright. It just isn't possible. Even a teacher with several years of experience, a minister, or anyone else who speaks before groups as part of normal everyday life will often attest to feelings of tension before facing a new group. If you as a beginning speaker can face the fact that stage fright is a normal feeling and—in many cases—a healthy one, you will be in a much better position to learn to control the physical and mental reactions that accompany severe stage fright.

The only time stage fright interferes with the communicative effectiveness of a speech is when reaction is so severe that it affects the audience's ability to maintain attention to the subject matter. In other words, when stage fright becomes the predominant factor noticed by audience members, it is a negative factor in the speaking situation. As long as the audience doesn't know you are terrified, go right ahead and be terrified; such a feeling on your part will not affect the outcome of your speech.

Determine Precisely What Makes You Afraid

The term *stage fright* implies fear of something. What is it that the speaker fears? He doesn't fear physical harm or danger in any form; he doesn't fear financial failure or loss of security in some other form. The fear involved in the speaking situation involves one horrifying thought on the part of the speaker: he is afraid of making a drastic mistake in front of a group of people, or—to put it more bluntly—he is afraid of making a fool of himself in front of others.

Various authors have presented a wide array of helpful hints, physical exercises, and other gimmicks to alleviate stage fright. Many of these are useful; however, the greatest benefit to the speaker in a speaking situation is confidence in his topic and his ability to deliver the speech adequately. The most superior method of developing self-confidence is through the development of a thorough and confident knowledge of the subject. Thus, it would appear that the most effective method of alleviating stage fright would be twofold: (1) careful selection of a subject that the speaker can be interested in and knowledgeable about, and (2) the speaker should engage in systematic preparation until he knows his speech as part of his person. If rules concerning alleviation of stage fright could be summarized into one word, it would be *preparation*.

SUMMARY PROBES

1. **Why should student speakers not be concerned with feelings of anxiety and fear as they approach a speaking situation?**
2. **Precisely what are speakers afraid of when they are experiencing stage fright?**

TWO FUNDAMENTAL CONCEPTS REGULATING DELIVERY

Before any detailed discussion of principles of delivery transpires, the speaker should keep in mind two basic and fundamental concepts regarding physical delivery of speeches. These concepts should be foremost in the speaker's mind as he considers himself and his physical delivery.

Delivery Must Be Natural

Observe people around you as they engage in everyday informal conversation. Have a friend observe you for a few days and tell you how you behave physically during natural communicative intercourse. When conversing and speaking in informal, nontense situations, we do all the physical things that we are unable to do when we stand before an audience. We use good vocal variety, we look at the people to whom we are speaking, we use fluent and meaningful hand gestures, and we communicate with our body. In short, we practice delivery in speaking that is effective for us and that blends with our individual personality.

The ideal delivery in the public speaking situation would be one that duplicates our physical mannerisms in conversational and informal situations. When preparing for the presentation of the speech it can be a drastic mistake to rehearse gestures and movement. If you are relaxed in a speaking situation, movement and gestures will come naturally. Rather than strive for rehearsed, canned movement in public speaking, make an effort to render yourself so comfortable with your topic and your audience that you aren't even aware of the movement that will certainly occur.

Delivery Should Not Call Attention to Itself

Delivery that calls attention to itself is harmful to the speaking situation. When specific mannerisms of delivery are perceived as being dominant over the content of the message by members of a speaker's audience, the result is harmful to the outcome of the communicative intent. How often have you heard an audience member comment, "My, what a beautiful voice the speaker had." If the beauty of the speaker's voice is the dominant factor in the mind of the listener after a speech, such a comment should actually be considered a negative observation rather than a compliment. The next time you hear someone make such a comment, respond with, "Yes, what did you think of what the speaker had to say?" If that question cannot be answered, then the delivery of the speech—even though it might be considered "good" by performance standards—obstructed communication rather than enhanced it.

Delivery must always be viewed as an aid to the communicative purpose of the speaker. When delivery becomes the end goal of a speech rather than one of many means to attain the goal, it is not "good" delivery. Thus, the speaker who rehearses movement, vocal inflections, and gestures may be just as guilty of inadequate delivery as the tense speaker who trembles, whose voice breaks, and who never looks at his listeners.

MODES OF DELIVERY

As the speaker surveys the speaking situation, he realizes one of the first questions to be resolved is the method to be utilized in delivering the speech. Should he memorize the speech, read it, rely on notes to varying degrees, or "cuff" it? The speaker, preparing a presentation for the classroom, will most likely have this question resolved for him via the assignment by the instructor. However, for a public situation, the speaker has at least four modes or methods of delivery available to him.

Impromptu

An impromptu speech refers to one that has extremely little or no preparation at all. In an impromptu situation the speaker may be called upon suddenly and without advance warning in a group of people to give a report or react to a concept. When an individual finds himself in such a situation, he must think and speak almost simultaneously. Students in academic settings often find themselves in impromptu situations when an instructor calls on them for recitation without advance warning.

One obvious advantage to the impromptu method is that it will insure an unrehearsed and nonartificial delivery. Disadvantages far outweigh advantages, however, in that the speaker in an impromptu setting is very likely to lack clear organization of ideas and may well forget significant points.

While the impromptu method of delivering communication messages is one that individuals often have to face, in most public speaking situations the impromptu method is not appropriate. The aspiring speaker, who decides to wait for the inspiration of the moment, may find the moment arrive without the inspiration.

Manuscript

Manuscript speaking refers to the practice of reading from a complete text of the speech content. For most public speaking situations manuscript speaking is not appropriate. The primary disadvantage of this mode of speaking is that most speakers lose personal contact with audience members when they read from manuscript. It is difficult to read a manuscript well. Ideal manuscript reading would occur in a situation in which the speaker relies on a manuscript; however, the listeners are not aware that he is reading the speech. Many experienced, professional speakers can accomplish this task; however, most student and beginning speakers forfeit most of the personal touch of the speaking situation for the "security blanket" of the manuscript.

In certain situations manuscript speaking may be the preferred method of delivery. When extreme importance rests in the audience hearing every word of a very important message, the speaker may choose to read the message. An example of such a situation would occur in the case of the president of the United States commenting to a television audience on a situation of world crisis. A slip of the tongue or a "wrong" word by the president could result in international crisis. For purposes of clarity and exactness the president very often chooses to read important messages.

Memorized

Memorized delivery refers to the practice of first preparing a manuscript, then committing that manuscript to memory, and reciting the speech. One advantage to such a method is that it can enable the speaker to concentrate fully on personal contact with the audience. Having no manuscript or notes to refer to, the speaker is more likely to establish and maintain effective eye contact with his listeners. To be effective at delivering a speech from memory the speaker must, as in manuscript speaking, deliver the memorized message in such a way that attention of the audience is not drawn to the fact that the speech has been memorized. The task of delivering a message from memory without audience awareness is a difficult one; many actors study for years to be able to do so on stage.

As with impromptu and manuscript speaking, the disadvantages of memorized delivery outweigh the advantages to the extent that the student speaker should probably not utilize the method. Memorizing a speech results in placing the speaker's mental emphasis in the wrong place. When a speaker must depend on word-for-word recall, a mental block involving one word can completely disrupt the speech and cause a total memory breakdown within the speaker. The public speaker should be primarily concerned with communicating *ideas* to his audience—not *words*. Many speakers have abruptly had to end their presentation because they were unable to remember the first word of a new paragraph. The word itself may be totally unimportant or trivial to the total speech message; however, until the trivial words appear in the speaker's memory the ideas to follow are permanently blocked from his cognitive field.

Extemporaneous

The extemporaneous method of delivering a speech is by far the most acceptable for most public speaking situations whether they be in the classroom or in life situations. When a speech is delivered extemporaneously an outline of ideas may be committed to memory, but specific words in expressing ideas are not memorized. The speaker may choose to use notes or not to use them. He should do what he feels comfortable in doing. An extemporaneous speech delivered three times by the same speaker should develop the same main points in each instance and present the same materials of support and development; however, if transcriptions were made of all three presentations none would be exactly like any of the others. Specific words chosen to communicate the main points and their development might change slightly each time of presentation.

Several advantages result to the speaker who uses the extemporaneous method of delivery. If he uses notes, he enjoys the advantage of being able to have some assistance in keeping main points and subpoints in proper order in the speech. The speaker, then, is able to rely on notes; however, he does not have to follow each word of a manuscript or depend on rote recall of the proper word order to establish the message intent.

If notes are used there are certain points for consideration by the speaker which, if followed, will increase his effectiveness. First, the speaker should use no more notes than he needs. Don't write the entire speech out with the intent of only referring to your notes occasionally. The temptation is far too great when the whole speech is included in your notes. Different speakers will find different amounts of notes appropriate for them. Some speakers may wish to use their entire sentence outline as an aid at the time of presentation. Others may find that a small index card with key words or phrases is sufficient for their purposes. Experiment to discover what works for you; use no more than you need.

Second, be sure your notes are easy to read. Print, type, or write large enough that you can see what you need to see with a glance. Trying to squeeze too much on note cards may result in the speaker having to squint and search for the point in question. Such searching will serve as an obstacle to audience comprehension of the message.

Finally, don't try to hide your notes. No matter how hard you try to fool the audience, if you are looking at note cards audience members will know it. If a lectern is available, place your notes on the lectern where you can refer to them easily and with little travail. If you must hold the note cards in your hand, don't try to hide them in the palm of your hand and cast fleeting glances at the cards. Notes will be much less disruptive to both speaker and listener if the speaker simply holds the note cards at his side until need arises to use them.

SUMMARY PROBES

1. **What is an obvious advantage to the impromptu method of delivering a speech?**
2. **In what kind of situation can a manuscript speech be the most appropirate of the modes of delivery?**
3. **What is meant when it is said that a memorized speech results in putting the speaker's emphasis in the wrong place?**
4. **What are the three points a speaker should keep in mind if he chooses to use notes?**

PHYSICAL ASPECTS OF SPEECH DELIVERY

The physical aspects of speech delivery, are normally divided into two distinct categories. The speaker's use of his voice for communicative effect and the use of his body represent the two most available and effective aspects of delivery available to him.

Vocal Aspects of Delivery

The speaker's use of his voice can serve as a complementary factor to the overall comprehension of the speech. Five areas are of special concern to the student speaker: breathing pause; loudness projection; vocal variety; articulation; and emphasis.

Breathing Pause. We are normally very much unaware of our breathing during speaking situations. Normal breathing, however, often does not serve the speaker well for public situations. The use of pause at the proper time (or at the improper time) can greatly enhance or detract from message content. Effective use of pause normally requires methods of breathing different from normal breathing.

Public speakers should generally consider diaphragmatic breathing as the most effective in delivery. Diaphragmatic breathing results from taking deep breaths from the stomach. The diaphragm is a muscle below the rib cage which for maximum breath control should move downward and force the stomach out when inhaling and move upward forcing air out of the lungs when exhaling. Many times when an individual takes a deep breath, he sucks his stomach in and throws his chest out; such breathing, sometimes referred to as chest breathing, will not contribute to good breath control and effective use of pause in public speaking.

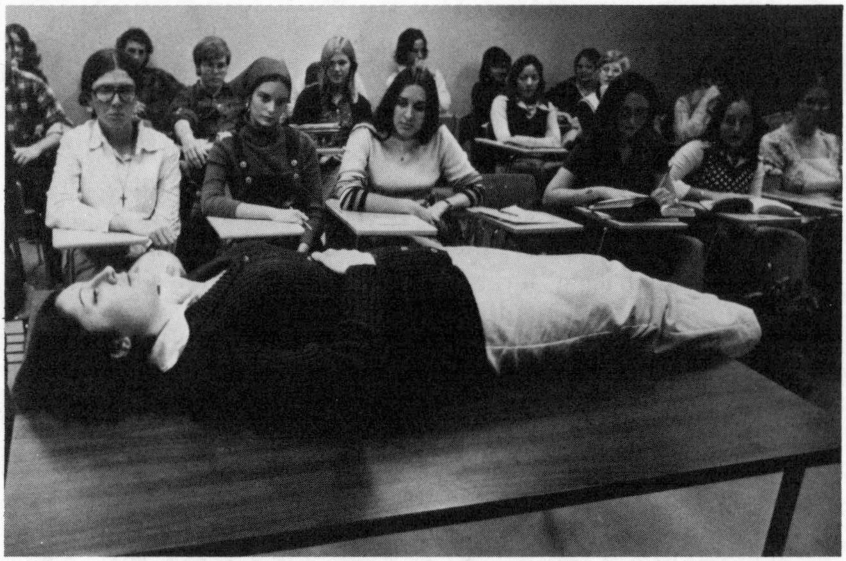

This student is demonstrating diaphragmatic breathing to her classmates. Try it yourself: lie on your back and place your hand on your stomach and "feel" the diaphragm at work.

The most effective way to practice diaphragmatic breathing is to lie down on your back and feel the movement of your stomach when you breathe. When a person is lying down the normal body function is for diaphragmatic breathing. Strive for the same kind of muscular control and movement when standing and speaking before a group.

A problem for many speakers closely related to the concept of pause is the too frequent utterance of a mental filler like "Uhh" (referred to as "trough noises" in an earlier section of this book). Most of the time when a speaker says, "Uhh," he does not realize he is saying it. When we communicate in writing, we can lay our pen or pencil down and pause for thought. When the need to pause momentarily for thought occurs in speaking, our normal tendency is to fill the dead air with some kind of sound. That sound normally appears in the form of "Uhh." Keep in mind that the use of the mental filler is a natural phenomenon, and that all speakers do it to some extent. It becomes a problem in public speaking only when used to excess and to the point of distraction.

Loudness Projection. Perhaps the most frequent complaint leveled at beginning speakers is that they can't be heard. All your preparation, hard work, your nervous tension and practice will be for naught if you stand before a group and fail to speak loudly enough to be heard by everyone in the room.

Don't be afraid of your own voice. Project your voice to the farthest member of your audience. If you are sensitive to the needs of your listeners, you will be able to tell whether or not they can hear you by looking at them during your speech. If their feedback indicates that they are having difficulty hearing your speech, you have an obligation as a speaker to speak loudly enough to permit them hear you.

Be constantly aware of outside disruptions during your speech. Such disruptions will necessitate varying your level of loudness and projection. Be ready to adapt any way necessary to assure that your listeners will hear every word.

Vocal Variety. Different points in your speech will no doubt require different variations in voice. The speaker who uses the same rate, pitch, and tone will quickly put an audience to sleep. Again, listen to friends in conversation; notice how their voices "talk" in addition to their words when the emotional content of their message varies. A natural public speaking delivery requires the same essence of vocal variety as conversation.

Vocal variety is enhanced by the use of either the impromptu or extemporaneous methods of delivery. Reading a speech can often result in a monotonous vocal delivery. Memorizing a speech can often result in voice mannerisms that are completely separated from the meaning of the message being communicated.

Articulation. Articulation refers to the modification of vocal tones to produce clear and intelligible words. The teeth, tongue, and lips are the principal articulators. Clear articulation is a must to a successful speech in that the audience in a public situation does not have the opportunity to ask the speaker to repeat something. In an interpersonal situation if one doesn't understand something a person says, he may indicate lack of understanding and ask for the word or phrase again. Such opportunity does not exist in the public speaking situation.

Negative results of poor articulation usually exist in "sloppy speech." Words being run together, consonants not sounded out one by one within a word, and final sounds in words dropped, and thus unheard, are probably the most bothersome problems resulting from poor articulation to most listeners.

Below is a tongue twister which effectively demonstrates the importance of clear articulation. Read the selection aloud twice. First, read it rapidly and with no attention to consonant sounds. The tendency will be for all the *t*'s in the statement to sound like *d*'s. Read it through a second time stressing the *t* sound in each appearance. While the result will obviously be exaggerated and artificial in sound, at times in public speaking, articulation must be exaggerated for clear understanding on the part of the audience.

> Betty Botter bought a bit of butter. But, she said, this butter's bitter. If I put it in my batter it will make my batter bitter. But a bit of better butter will make my batter better. So Betty Botter bought a bit of better butter and it made her batter better.

Emphasis Paralanguage. In our discussion of nonverbal communication relating to interpersonal communication we developed the concept of paralanguage as it affects the communication process. Paralanguage is equally important in public speaking in the area of meaningful emphasis that the speaker places on words to change or alter meaning.

It is possible to take one sentence and change the meaning in as many ways as there are words in that sentence. Oral communication has a distinct advantage over written communication in this respect. When writing a message, one must rely on inanimate markings to change or emphasize meanings of words. For instance, a word *underlined* implies that additional emphasis should be placed on that word. If we place two lines under a word, the anticipation is that a great deal of additional emphasis be accorded the word. Our voice is much more flexible and capable of implying many more meanings of identical words and word combinations.

Below is a very simple sentence which can have meaning changed in various ways by emphasizing different words. By reading the sentence aloud and emphasizing the word indicated, extra components of meaning can be inserted.

> "I want you to go?" (the question mark used as a punctuation mark and a sharp rise in inflection for the last word will render the meaning of the sentence as a question)
>
> "*I* want you to go." (meaning me—not anyone else present)
>
> "I *want* you to go." (why should you go? because I want you to)
>
> "I want *you* to go." (I mean you—not the guy behind you)

SUMMARY PROBES

1. **How does diaphragmatic breathing differ from chest breathing?**
2. **How can a speaker be sensitive to the needs of his listeners in terms of loudness and projection?**
3. **What is meant by "sloppy speech?" What causes it?**
4. **Compare and contrast methods of emphasizing words for meaning in written and oral communication.**

Bodily Aspects of Speech Delivery

We learned earlier that a great deal of our bodily communication is unintentional. No matter how hard we may try not to communicate, we constantly communicate as long as we are in the physical presence of others. The five aspects of bodily delivery discussed here occur in the speaking situation both intentionally and unintentionally.

Posture. The public speaker should demonstrate a concern for effective communicative posture before he begins to speak. If you are called to the front of the classroom to give a speech and you shuffle and "lumber" to the front of the room, your posture and approach to the speaking situation will already have communicated possible negative messages to your listeners.

Speaking posture can be either too relaxed or too rigid. A speaker who drapes himself over a lectern, or wraps himself around a post, or sits in a chalk ledge may be exhibiting physical mannerisms that will distract the audience from the message content. On the other hand, a speaker who stands at military attention with arms rigidly fixed on the lectern, a straight neck, and rigid back may exhibit mannerisms equally distracting.

There are no fixed rules for posture. The best approach is to stand as you normally stand. To do otherwise may affect your delivery in that you will be aware of your artificial posture, thus, very likely making your listeners aware of it.

Movement. Some movement during a speech is a natural phenomenon for most people. The amount and degree of movement utilized by a speaker in a given situation should be adapted to his need for relaxation. Don't force yourself to move. The old oratorical

Both speakers in the illustrations above demonstrate very different and very relaxed postures. Neither speaker appears to be too relaxed or too rigid.

tradition of carefully plotted steps at strategic points in a speech does not lend itself to clear communication in a public speaking situation.

If you are using a lectern, and you feel like moving out from behind it—do so. If you feel that moving away from the lectern will increase your self-consciouness or reduce your security—don't do it.

Natural, spontaneous movement during the course of a speech normally results in more spontaneous communication on the part of speaker and reception of content by the listener. Movement should, however, be used in moderation. We do move in natural, conversationl settings; however, we don't jump around or pace back and forth before those to whom we are talking. The key to speaker development of effective movement during a speech lies in the speaker's ability to bring himself to a relaxed and comfortable mental state in front of his audience group.

Gesture. A relaxed, natural public speaker will automatically make frequent use of meaningful gestures. He probably will not have an awareness of every gesture. Audiences like naturally appearing hand, arm, and body gestures. In conversational settings, we talk constantly with our hands and many other parts of our body. A relaxed public speaker will make effective use of the same kinds of movement.

Timing of gestures can be a crucial factor in their meaning. Natural gestures are normally perfectly timed to coincide with verbal message content. One grave danger of rehearsing gestures is that they will appear to be off in timing. Such ill-timed movements usually result in more distraction from message content than additional meaning.

Facial Expression. The face, particularly the eyes, is the most expressive part of the body. In conversational settings, we communicate constantly with facial expressions complementing the emotions and feelings we are communicating. In a large public situation with an audience separated from the speaker by a great distance, the effect of facial expression is diminished almost to the point of no effect. In the classroom situation, however, facial expression can be the greatest asset with which a speaker has to work.

Facial expression should always be consistent with message content. Audiences can become extremely disconcerted with a speaker who is discussing the tragic illness of a small child and smiling at the same time. Such inconsistencies in verbal and physical

These gestures are examples of relaxed and natural movement in the public speaking situation.

communication can cause an audience to lose confidence in a speaker's sincerity.

The speaker should not allow facial expression to give away errors in speech delivery. Most mistakes made by speakers in the course of delivery of a speech go unnoticed by audiences. A grimace or pained expression on the part of the speaker can tell the world of a previously unnoticed mistake.

Eye Contact. Audiences like to be looked at. One of the most crucial components of physical delivery is the establishment of good eye contact with audience members. Again, in a large public auditorium with great distances separating speaker and listeners, the effect of eye contact may be diminished or eliminated. In the classroom or in the smaller public setting, the speaker must maintain eye contact with the audience.

Eye contact can be an effective device at holding the attention of the audience. If audience members know that you, the speaker, are going to be looking directly at them periodically, they will feel some obligation to return the contact. It is difficult to go to sleep while a speaker is looking at you.

Severe stage fright can result in making eye contact a difficult component for a speaker to develop. Many times we are afraid to look at audiences, for we are afraid they will communicate some kind of disfavor to us. Many speakers prefer to look at the wall, their feet, or out a door or window. Such speakers will quickly lose audience contact. Audiences are generally sympathetic to the plight of the public speaker, especially the student speaker. Look at them; they may even try to help you.

Special Points on the Effective Use of Visual Aids

Using visual aids in the presentation of a speech can sometimes cause special problems for the student speaker. One should always keep in mind that visual aids are complementary to the message of the communicator. Visual aids should only be used when the speaker determines that they are needed to assure message comprehension.

One of the biggest dangers in the use of visual aids is that they may interfere with the speaker's eye contact with his audience. If the speaker uses a chart or an object, he should be especially aware of the tendency to look at the object or chart rather than the listeners. Monroe and Ehninger offer five pieces of advice to the speaker for the effective utilization of visual aids:

1. Choose only objects and materials that are relevant.
2. Prepare all display materials before giving the speech.
3. Keep charts, graphs, and diagrams simple and clear.
4. Place visual materials where they can be seen easily.
5. Use nonverbal supporting materials at the proper psychological moment in the speech.
6. Keep visual supporting material visible only when it is in use.[1]

Many problems can result from the student not adhering to these guidelines. Of special importance is the necessity for visuals to be large enough and clear enough for all audience members to see. Nothing can be more disconcerting to listeners than for a speaker to use a chart or diagram which only those on the front row can see well enough to comprehend.

SUMMARY PROBES

1. **Why is it not a good idea to force yourself to move during a speech?**
2. **How is timing important to the effective use of gestures?**
3. **What special problems should the speaker be aware of in using facial expression?**
4. **How does stage fright contribute to a speaker's problem in establishing and maintaining eye contact?**
5. **What are some of the special delivery problems the speaker may face if he chooses to use visual aids?**

LEARNING EXPERIENCES

1. Interview several individuals who regularly speak before groups of people such as ministers, lawyers, or teachers concerning their experiences with stage fright both as beginners and later after a great deal of experience.

2. Watch a television speech of a prominent figure such as the president or a governor who reads a statement. Evaluate the speaker's ability in reading. Could you tell the speech was being read? Why or how?

3. Lie on your back and place your hand on your diaphragm. Feel the muscular movement and, then, attempt to breathe in the same manner on your feet.

4. Find several tongue twisters and practice reading them aloud until you can do so with no errors in articulation.

5. Observe the posture and movement of others when they are in nonthreatening, informal conversation groups. Strive for the same degree of posture and movement in public speaking.

6. To demonstrate the effectiveness of facial expression and eye contact, the next time you talk to a group of friends deliberately use facial expression lacking consistency with message content and avoid looking directly at anyone. What is the reaction of the listeners?

References

Bradley, Bert E. *Fundamentals of Speech Communication: The Credibility of Ideas.* Dubuque: Wm. C. Brown, 1974, pp. 225–49; Appendix B.

Crocker, Lionel. *Public Speaking for College Students,* 3rd ed. New York: American Book, 1956, chapter 5.

Eisenson, Jon, and Boase, Paul H. *Basic Speech,* 3rd ed. New York: Macmillan, 1975, chapter 14.

Gray, Giles Wilkerson, and Braden, Waldo W. *Public Speaking: Principles and Practice.* New York: Harper & Brothers, 1951, chapter 19.

Hance, Kenneth G.; Ralph, David C.; and Wiksell, Milton J. *Principles of Speaking,* 2nd ed. Belmont: Wadsworth, 1969, pp. 268–72, chapter 14.

McCabe, Bernard P., Jr., and Bender, Coleman C. *Speaking is a Practical Matter,* 2nd ed. Boston: Holbrook Press, 1974, pp. 27–47.

Monroe, Alan H., and Ehninger, Douglas. *Principles and Types of Speech Communication,* 7th ed. Glenview: Scott, Foresman, 1974, pp. 318–19, chapter 6.

IV

Mass Media

FIFTEEN

GOALS **After completing this chapter you will be able to:**

1. Discuss the present impact of broadcasting on society.

2. Identify seven significant events in broadcast history which have resulted in the present impact on society.

Historical Development Of A Broadcasting System

We have now progressed through the first three of our four major human communicative events described in the Introduction to this book. We have given our attention to essential concepts involved in interpersonal communication settings. From interpersonal we progressed to the small group setting taking with us a great many of the concepts studied in one-to-one communicative events. We have just completed a study of communicating in public situations.

All of the first three human communicative events dealt with people facing people in live situations. Our fourth communicative event introduces the use of electronic media in human communication. Principles and concepts studied earlier still apply to communication behavior when electronic media is introduced. The three essential components—source, message, and receiver—prevalent in all three previous communicative events play a role just as essential in the world of mass media.

While the history and development of our previous three forms of communication date back to earliest recorded civilization, the history of the human being communicating via electronic mass media is much shorter.

Electronic means of communication was a nineteenth-century achievement. The year was 1894; a young Italian named Guglielmo Marconi was experimenting in an elaborate villa in Italy with self-made equipment called "wireless." In the midst of his experimentation, he succeeded in sending an electronic impulse across a villa courtyard to a receiver in an upstairs window.

More than eighty years later that simple experiment has resulted in an American system of broadcasting like none other in the world. The influence of mass media on society has been recognized for years but that influence has created numerous controversies. Presidential commissions have been appointed, speeches have been heard on the floor of the United States Senate, and civic groups have stood in protest to what we hear and see on radio and television. It is difficult, if not impossible, to read any newspaper or periodical today that fails to include some reference to or discussion of controversy in broadcasting.

This chapter will establish the impact of the broadcast media on society today and identify significant historical events leading to our national system of broadcasting. The terms *mass media* and *mass communication* will be used interchangeably in this segment. Even though the term *mass* can apply to many forms of communication, our primary concern lies in the area of media utilizing spoken communication: radio and television.

IMPACT OF MASS MEDIA ON SOCIETY

In a paper presented for the Media Task Force of the National Commission on the Causes and Prevention of Violence, Otto N. Larsen presented three factors upon which the individual and social effects of mass communication must depend: (1) the pattern of content offered by the mass media; (2) the opportunities for access to the media; and, (3) the credibility attributed by audiences to media content.[1]

While many theories have been advanced in an effort to explain the pattern of content in the media in our society, perhaps the most palatable is Lee Loevinger's reflective-projective theory.[2] Loevinger postulates that "mass communications are best understood as mirrors of society that reflect an ambiguous image in which each observer projects or sees his own vision of himself and society."[3] The apparent conclusion is that media, especially television, serves as a mirror of society. What we see is what we are.

The content of programming in the media, especially recent television trends, has received criticism from all strata of society. Whether media content molds society image or whether one subscribes to the reflective-projective theory of mass communication, the impact of program content on society is evident to the American public on a daily basis.

Opportunities for American access to media, Larsen's second concern, has steadily increased since the history of broadcasting. The media saturation point is nearly total among the noninstitutionalized population of America. Most American households currently have a television set. Further, many of the small number of homes without television sets have access to television indirectly through relatives, neighbors, or the corner bar. Voelker and Voelker report that 372 million radios receive programming from 7,430 radio stations in the United States, and 108 million television sets are tuned in to 931 television stations.[4] The average amount of time each individual in the United States spent watching television in November 1974 was 3 hours and 2 minutes per day.[5] The daily exposure figure has shown a slow but steady increase from 1961–74.

Now that we have established that the pattern of media content is influenced by society, and that the American public has unprecedented access to media, the third question arises as to how much credibility media audiences are willing to attribute to its content.

The Roper organization has made regular, periodic measurement of the relative credibility the public ascribes to four of the mass media: television, radio, newspapers, and magazines. Credibility ratings given to television in preference to the other three have steadily increased until November 1974, when more than 50 percent of the American public preferred to believe television over radio, newspapers, or magazines.[6]

In summary, one can see that in a short period of slightly more than eighty years, our system of broadcasting has moved from a hobby that nurtured experimentation in Italy to one that is reflective of our society. It is a system that is at least indirectly accessible to virtually every member of our society, and, finally, one that has been given unprecedented credibility by the average American.

SUMMARY PROBES

1. **What daily evidence exists to confirm widespread controversies involving broadcasting?**
2. **What are the three factors upon which individual and social effects of mass communication must depend?**
3. **How is television similar to a mirror?**
4. **What is meant by the conclusion that the media**

saturation point is nearly total among the non-institutionalized population of America?

5. **How does the credibility of television compare to that of radio, newspapers, and magazines?**

DEVELOPMENT OF RADIO AND TELEVISION AS MAJOR FORMS OF MASS MEDIA

The most significant events in the history of our system of broadcasting can all be attributed to the medium of radio rather than television. This is not to say that radio was or is a more significant force in society than television. The wireless paved the way for television in that it was the first instance of bringing live entertainment into the home via electricity. Since the American people had learned to depend on radio as a major force in family life, television was sure to succeed simply because acceptance and habit patterns were already established.

We will examine seven events in the history of radio that have followed that simple home experiment in 1894 to develop into a system of mass entertainment and information like none other in the world. The seven events are (1) the Marconi experiments; (2) the tragedy of the Titanic in 1912; (3) the first commercial broadcast on station KDKA in Pittsburgh, Pa. in 1920; (4) the first paid commercial broadcast in 1922; (5) the development of the National Broadcasting Company in 1926; (6) the Great Depression programming; and finally, (7) World War II news programming.

The Marconi Experiments

The young Italian, Guglielmo Marconi, was encouraged to experiment with electromagnetic energy as a result of scientific hypotheses of two other gentlemen. In 1873 James Clerk Maxwell developed a theory of electromagnetic energy supported primarily by mathematical proofs. A paper confirming Maxwell's theory based on experimental research was published in 1888 by Heinrich Hertz. All that remained at this point was for some innovator to apply the theories of Maxwell and Hertz. Marconi came on the scene in the early 1890s. Fortunately for the future of broadcasting in the world, Marconi had the spare time and the wealth to experiment freely. Following Marconi's 1894 experiment, he further tested his new-found gadget, and in 1896 he applied for a British patent. Three years later the American Marconi Company was founded, which was the initial introduction of the wireless to America.

Even though Marconi modeled his experiments after the theorizing of Maxwell and Hertz, he is generally credited as being the first person to put the theory of wireless into practical application. Thus, he earns the title, "Father of Radio."

The Titanic

Development of the wireless was slow during the first decade of the twentieth century. Very few people in the world had heard of the new phenomenon, and many of those who had heard about transmitting electrical impulses through space without the use of wires didn't believe it.

One of the earliest uses envisioned for wireless was for emergency situations for ships at sea. In 1910 the United States Congress passed the Wireless Ship Act which required that all ocean-going vessels have wireless equipment on board. Two years later a disaster demonstrated graphically the potential value of radio if taken seriously.

The unsinkable Titanic left on its maiden voyage and struck an iceberg, whereupon the "unsinkable" sank. The radio operator on board the afflicted vessel sent frantic SOS signals to any ship within hearing distance. A ship near enough to the Titanic to save most—if not all—the lives eventually lost, did not hear the signal because their radio operator was not on duty at the time. A ship several hundred miles away did pick up the SOS signal and arrived in time only to save those who had escaped in life boats. The end result was that the 1,517 died because the world had not taken the proper use of radio on board ships seriously. Rescue for the 1,517 was only fifteen miles away; however, the distress signals went unheard because no one manned the radio equipment.

The news of the tragedy of the Titanic and the needless deaths of its victims rocked the entire world into an awareness of the new gimmick called "wireless."

Station KDKA-Pittsburgh

All the early services of radio were telegraphic in nature. Consequently, most early development of radio was in terms of point-to-point communication rather than any form of communication to a mass audience. Before the system of commercial broadcasting common to us today could be envisioned, some method for transmitting sound and voice over air waves had to be developed. In 1916 Lee de Forest was one of the first to successfully transmit voice via wireless.

Dr. Frank Conrad of the Westinghouse Corporation set up a homemade radio transmitter on top of the Westinghouse factory in Pittsburgh, Pennsylvania in 1920. At that time, the only receivers were those owned by amateur radio operators; Dr. Conrad began transmitting music and election returns to operators within range of his station. Newspaper accounts of his experiments followed, and the first significant public interest in radio emerged.

A department store in Pittsburgh sensed some commercial value and began to sell radio receivers to the public so that they could listen to Dr. Conrad's broadcasts. What has been generally accepted as the first commercial broadcast occurred on November 2, 1920, when Dr. Conrad and a small group of associates broadcast recorded music and banjo numbers, interspersed with election returns of the Harding-Cox presidential race. Dr. Conrad's station was named KDKA and is recorded in broadcasting history as the first commercially licensed station in America.

Immediate reactions from the public hearing the first broadcast were shock and intense interest. While, perhaps, only a few hundred people heard the first election night broadcast, news spread rapidly and within just a few months broadcast stations became prolific.

First Paid Commercial in 1922

While early radio stations were prolific, they also experienced an unusually high mortality rate. As public interest grew in the new "sound box" for the home, so did listener expectation of program quality. Most broadcasters at this time were private individuals who had limited financial backing for their efforts in radio transmission.

Securing talent became an increasing problem for radio stations. No one had devised a means for radio to make money other than through the sales of receiver sets for home use. Obviously if you couldn't pay talent, you couldn't get talent. Most early radio stations would air anyone or anything that breathed. If an enterprising mother wanted her cherub to sing on radio, all she had to do was drop by the local station, and the station management was happy to put the child on the air simply to fill the broadcast time. Such amateur, and sometimes rank, talent was accepted by the public as long as the concept of radio was new. However as the newness wore off, the expectations of the public for quality programming increased dramatically.

Radio station WEAF in New York was the first station to experiment with selling broadcast time to private concerns in exchange for use of the airwaves. On August 28, 1922, a Long Island apartment complex called Hawthorne Courts presented a ten-minute, soft-sell program for which they paid WEAF a fee. This was the first commercial in broadcast history.

Even though the practice of selling broadcast time grew during the 1920s, severe restrictions were placed on advertisers. Many early commercials consisted of a five- or ten-minute informative program about a product or business concern. At no point in the program could the sponsor employ the hard-sell tactic of suggesting that the listener should actually buy the product. No personal items such as toothpaste, deodorant, et cetera, could be the subject of a paid program during these initial years of commercials.

While the practice of selling air time to generate revenue to support programming provided temporary relief from the talent drought, it was not until our present system of broadcasting networks came about that program quality began to reach the proportions of the contemporary era.

Founding of NBC in 1926

The practice of selling air time to generate revenue was a first major step in improving quality of entertainment on airwaves. As the numbers of local stations increased, however, it was evident that the thousands of local communities supporting commercial radio stations could not provide the quality of programming necessary to prevent radio from becoming a passing fad.

In 1926 three major electrical manufacturing corporations joined together to form the National Broadcasting Company (NBC). RCA had 50 percent interest in the new venture; Westinghouse 30 percent; and General Electric 20 percent. The concept advanced by the newly formed corporation was that better programming could be provided for the public if production was done in talent centers such as New York and Los Angeles, and the resultant programming relayed to subscribing stations all over the country.

The success of the first major programming network was phenomenal. The public liked the better program quality; local stations were relieved to find that the task of daily program scheduling was reduced to simply pressing a network feed button.

One year later two events confirmed the popularity of network programming: NBC divided into a blue network and a Red network. (Sixteen years later the Blue network became what is now the American Broadcasting Company (ABC).) Also in 1927 a group calling themselves the United Independent Broadcasters received financing from the Columbia Phonograph System and founded the Columbia Broadcasting System (CBS).

In a brief period of two years what eventually became the three major networks in competition today emerged to provide American radio listeners with the highest quality programming available. Had the concept of network programming not been developed, it is doubtful that radio or television would have ever served more than a local informative function.

The Great Depression

The concepts of selling air time to generate revenue and establishing entertainment networks assured local station managers of quality programming. Even in the late 1920s, however, the American public had not become en masse followers of the new entertainment box called radio. Americans still preferred the moving picture theaters over staying home and listening to radio.

Perhaps the greatest tragedy ever experienced by the American people became the single historical event that made Americans faithful followers of broadcasting. With the coming of the depression in the late twenties and early thirties, many people discovered that they could no longer afford an evening at the theater. Radio became ever more attractive as an amazingly economical form of entertainment. In return for the initial investment in a radio receiver and the small cost of electrical current required to operate the equipment, a family of any size could have free entertainment of high quality in the home seven days and nights a week.

Radio stars, also feeling the stress of the collapsed economy, began to play to the mass public and made every effort possible to raise the sinking spirits of Americans. Many comedians, who themselves had suffered severe financial losses, led the depressed American people through the traumatic period with singing and joking.

The near total dependence Americans felt toward radio during the depression created a home audience. The concept of entertainment in the home was here to stay. Television simply capitalized on a public already conditioned to low cost and high quality entertainment.

World War II

The final event in history that significantly affected the public acceptance of broadcasting was World War II. Up to December 7, 1941, Americans had learned to rely heavily on radio for entertainment. The famous news bulletin read on Sunday afternoon in December 1941 shook the public to its foundation. More Americans probably heard of the bombing of Pearl Harbor via radio than any other of the forms of communication.

Throughout World War II, Americans depended on their radios for daily newscasts of military events in Europe and Asia. Some of the most gripping moments in broadcast history can be heard in live transmissions of wartime scenes. For example, preserved by radio news are the Iwo Jima Invasion, the last broadcast from Corregidor, and the D-Day Invasion.

Once again the radio entertainers played to the American public by aiming their entertainment content toward one goal: to ease the tragic strain being felt by virtually every American family as a result of the war.

Most Americans learned of the end of the war just as they had learned of its beginning. In August 1945, millions of people were tuned to the radio networks to hear the first news bulletin declaring an end to the war with Japan.

SUMMARY PROBES

1. **What theory, developed by Maxwell and Hertz, did Marconi's experiments test in the 1890s?**
2. **Of what significance was the sinking of the Titanic to the history of radio in America?**
3. **Describe the nature of the first entertainment program in Pittsburgh in 1920.**
4. **Why was the advent of paying for broadcast time necessary for quality programming?**
5. **Explain the rationale for national program networks such as NBC and CBS.**

6. **Describe the effects of the Great Depression and World War II on Americans and their dependence on radio as entertainment.**

LEARNING EXPERIENCES

1. Keep a media diary for yourself for a period of three days. Record in the diary every exposure to radio or television. Specify what program you watched or listened to, and how long your attention was given to the media. Be prepared to discuss your diaries in class.

2. Interview an older friend or relative who has first-hand memory of some or all the seven significant events in the development of broadcasting. Be prepared to discuss your interviews in class.

References

Emery, Michael C., and Smythe, Ted Curtis. *Readings in Mass Communication: Concepts and Issues in the Media.* Dubuque: Wm. C. Brown, 1974.

Head, Sydney W. *Broadcasting in America: A Survey of Television and Radio.* New York: Houghton Mifflin, 1972.

Hiebert, Ray Eldon; Unguriat, Donald F.; and Bohn, Thomas W. *Mass Media: An Introduction to Modern Communicaiton.* New York: David McKay, 1974, chapter 4.

Schramm, Wilbur, and Alexander, Janet. "Survey of Broadcasting: Structure, Control, Audience." In *Issues in Broadcasting,* edited by Ted C. Smythe and George A. Mastroianni. Palo Alto: Mayfield, 1975.

"Trends in Public Attitudes Toward Television and Other Mass Media." A report by the Roper Organization, April 1975.

Voelker, Francis H., and Voelker, Ludmilla A. *Mass Media: Forces in Our Society.* New York: Harcourt Brace Jovanovich, 1975.

SIXTEEN

GOALS **After completing this chapter you will be able to:**

1. List at least five stages in the development of radio programming.

2. Identify three characteristics in contemporary radio programming.

3. Comprehend the similarity of early radio program trends to those of early television.

4. Identify four concepts resulting in significant contributions to contemporary television programming.

5. Comprehend the progression of a television series from an idea to a successful program.

6. Recognize at least three types of nonentertainment television programming.

Development Of Broadcasting Content

Premiere broadcasting audiences have traditionally been similar to a small child with a new toy at Christmas: early fascination with the newness of the item and a rapid loss of interest unless some additional newness appears very soon. The very first programs on both radio in the early twenties and on television in the late forties were not of sufficient quality to sustain interest for a very long period of time.

When Americans first heard voices floating over airwaves into their living rooms via radio, they cared very little about what the voices said. The novelty of the new invention was enough entertainment; consequently the voice transmitting to the living room needed to do little more than recite nursery rhymes to hold the listening audience entranced. (Earlier we stated that the first commercial broadcast featured music interspersed with a man reading election returns.) Later radio programming did little more than provide noise to fascinate the listeners at home. Very soon, however, the novelty of the new invention began to wear off, and the home listener demanded "quality" entertainment in return for time spent with the radio receiver.

Television programming began in a similar fashion. The anticipation of Americans at seeing moving pictures in a box in their living rooms prepared them to accept almost anything that appeared on the screen. A typical scene in a small midwestern town in 1949 would reveal several families gathered in the living room of the fortunate family who owned a television set. Programming beginning with sign-on time—usually early in the evening—often consisted of a brief children's show followed by a newsreel and a few brief drama or variety shows with sign-off ending the evening around 10:00 p.m. Families fortunate enough to be invited to see the new "picture box" were not about to criticize the quality of programming. The novelty of new inventions wore off quickly, however, and public demands for better programming in both broadcast media were imminent. The object of the game was entertainment; the pressure was on for programmers to provide the best entertainment available.

EARLY DEVELOPMENT OF RADIO PROGRAMMING

Prior to the development of program networks in 1926, station managers faced a monumental task of feeding a growing public hunger for entertainment on the airwaves. Since no networks or syndication outlets existed, managers had to depend on talent they could coax, beg, or coerce into the studio for live transmission. Top quality talent remained untouchable due to the absence of dollars to pay such talent. Amateur singers appearing in the studio and remote coverage of scheduled events such as concerts and sports attractions constituted the bulk of programming. The program listing in Table 16.1 for station WEAF in New York in 1924 provides an example of what audiences had to look forward to before the national network.

Table 16.1 **Program Schedule for Radio Station WEAF In New York on Wednesday, November 12, 1924**

11:00 a.m.	Minnie Weil, Soprano
11:10	Talk: Are You An Example to Your Children
11:30	Minnie Weil, Soprano
11:40	Children's Religious Problems
12:00	Columbia University Chapel Services
12:20 p.m.	Market and Weather Reports
4:00	Katya Romanovsky, Soprano
4:20	Musical Program
6:00	Waldorf Astoria Dinner Music
7:00	United Synagogue of America Service
7:30	Winifred Bauer, Soprano Albert Weiderhold, baritone
8:20	Philharmonic Concert direct from Carnegie Hall
10:00	Sign-off

Failure of talent to appear as scheduled and other similar emergencies made the life of a station manager nearly unbearable—not to mention the lives of the listeners at home. Charles Popenoe, manager of station WJZ in New York in 1924, spoke of the problems encountered in obtaining free talent.[1] Regular announcers, employed by the station, frequently had to stand in as singers for the station whether the announcer had a singing voice or not. Popenoe recalled that, "when a listener tunes in to be entertained, the station manager may be wondering what he will do to keep the station on the air."[2]

Less than one month after Popenoe's assessment of the plight of the radio station manager, Secretary of Commerce Herbert Hoover began to sense a feeling of discontent in the American public. The Radio Act of 1912 had placed broadcast licensing under the control of the Secretary of Commerce; Herbert Hoover was appointed to that post in 1921 by President Warren G. Harding. Consequently, Hoover became one of the first government officials to take a sincere interest in radio. Hoover proclaimed in December 1924 that the main concern of radio should no longer be growth of the medium, but that the material being aired be really worthwhile.[3]

Throughout the next two years public demands on the quality of programming grew more intense, and pressure from the Secretary of Commerce increased. The problem facing those responsible for providing program content for the new medium was immense: station managers had to produce newer and more talent with extremely limited financial resources.

The Emergence of Networks

With hundreds of small, medium, and large radio stations scattered across the country competing for talent, it became evident that a system had to be developed whereby program content could be fed to several stations simultaneously. Events necessitated some system of program sharing if the new medium expected to face the challenge of public demands.

In 1926 the Radio Corporation of America (RCA) founded a program network called National Broadcasting Company (NBC). The concept of the program network was that radio programs would be produced in talent centers such as New York or Hollywood and the results relayed to all stations in the country subscribing to the network service for simultaneous broadcasting. Thus, top name stars could be relayed into the living rooms of America via "wireless."

The concept of commercial advertising—as we know it in media today—jelled in the late twenties and early thirties, thus providing the needed revenue to pay salaries demanded by top stars. As we shall discover later, the accomplishment of broadcast advertising was not an easy feat. Programmers and advertisers had one major point of disagreement: when to broadcast the commercials. Programmers contended that advertisements should be placed either at the beginning or at the end of a radio show—to interrupt program continuity would destroy the medium as an entertainment device.

Advertisers countered that if they were to provide large sums of money to produce programs in return for commercial announcements, they must be assured that the listening would be at its numerical peak when commercials were broadcast. What appeared to be a hopeless deadlock eased quickly when radio programmers capitulated and agreed to work program material around commercial announcements. Had this deadlock not been resolved, radio might never have become the nation's number one source of entertainment a few years later.

The tremendous success of NBC's first year made it apparent that the nation needed another network. Cities large enough to have more than one major radio station were faced with having two stations competing with the same network programming or only one station providing quality entertainment, while those stations not affiliated with NBC retained a prenetwork program quality.

After only a year's time, the Columbia Broadcasting System was developed followed quickly by a second network from NBC. In 1927, then, the American public had three major networks providing program material: CBS, NBC-Blue; and NBC-Red.

The "Golden Age of Radio"

By the very late twenties and early thirties the status of radio in the United States was such to make it the constant home companion of millions of Americans. The Great Depression was a grim reality; Americans had no money to seek entertainment outside the home. The quality of radio programming had been perfected to the extent that fixed audiences awaited favorite programs on a weekly, and sometimes daily, basis.

The thirties became the "Golden Age of Radio": Prime-time evening entertainment similar to that provided today by the three major networks in television programming originated in those years.

Evening programming appealed to family listening with situation comedies, dramas, and variety shows flooding the airwaves. The loyalty of Americans to programs such as "Amos 'n' Andy," "Fibber McGee and Molly," "Edgar Bergen" and a score of others has never been surpassed in later years of radio and television entertainment. The loyalty of the public was so great to the "Amos 'n' Andy Show" that motion-picture theaters advertised that they would stop the movie and turn on the radio when America's favorite program came on.

In 1934 a third company, the Mutual Broadcasting System, joined in competition with NBC and CBS. By the time the decade ended, the networks competed for prime-time audiences with program content similar to prime-time television in the 1970s. The following schematic of evening offerings by three network-affiliate stations in New York typified program material offered across the country. A quick comparison of the 1940 program schedule, as shown in Table 16.2, with Table 16.1 which details 1924 programming reveals a drastic revision of program concepts made possible by the advent of the program networks and full acceptance of commercial advertising.

Evening hours were not the only focus of the new networks. Network officials sensed an available daytime audience in the American housewife and during the Golden Age of Radio the "soap opera"

Table 16.2 **Radio Programming—Network Style on Sunday, October 13, 1940**

	WABC (CBS)	WEAF (NBC)	WOR (MBS)
6:30 p.m.	Gene Autry Melody Ranch	Beat the Band Quiz	Lopez Orchestra
7:00	News of the World	Jack Benny/Dennis Day	Ramona
7:30	Screen Guild Theatre	Band Wagon Music	News
8:00	Farewell to Arms (Drama)	Edgar Bergen Variety	Forum
8:30	Drama: Crime Doctor	One Man's Family	Forum
9:00	Symphony Orchestra	Manhattan Merry Go Round	War News: Berlin
9:30	Symphony Orchestra	Album of Famliy Music	Battle of the Boroughs: Quiz

came into existence as a staple in program content. Housewives across America soon became a faithful following of "Ma Perkins," "Helen Trent," "Backstage Wife," and several others. Twenty years later the networks would again copy the radio daytime format for television just as they duplicated evening prime-time programming.

World War II intensified the public reliance on radio as a near-constant companion. In addition to using the radio for an entertainment escape from the everyday traumas of a nation at war, the public looked to the radio networks for the most up-to-date war news. All the major networks and news services offered live coverage from the battlefront.

Post World War II Radio

The end of World War II saw technical advances begin anew in broadcast areas, which had been temporarily frozen during the war. The coming of television as a new form of entertainment for Americans was imminent. In addition, a new radio broadcast service called FM, which would be free of interference and designed for shorter range transmission, was being readied for the public market.

Radio, after 1950, was to undergo a slow transition in emphasis and purpose as a result of America's new fascination with the radio with "pictures." Some predicted that radio would suffer a slow, lingering demise from public attention after television became a household word. Had radio programmers attempted to compete with the new medium of sight, perhaps doomsayers would have been correct. One must remember, however, that the same networks that were involved in pioneering television programming had brought radio from a novelty to a necessity in American life. Rather than scrap radio as obsolete, programmers began to develop new services to be offered by the "talk box." Reliance on radio is as great—if not greater today—than it ever was in the past.

The change in America's use of radio has produced three characteristics of radio evident today.

Radio is a Local Medium. The vast majority of radio stations in America today serve a small, local geographic area without the benefit of network entertainment programming. Most stations are not affiliated with a network, and the majority of those that are affiliated rely on network sources for little more than national newscasts.

Radio is a primary source of information concerning local news and events. Most radio advertising revenue comes from local merchants serving the immediate area of the station.

Radio is a Secondary Medium. Rarely do you find anyone today sitting down in a chair to do nothing but listen to radio. Americans have learned to rely on radio as a complementary background while doing something else. Prime time in radio has shifted from the evening hours to traffic rush hours when thousands of people drive to and from work with their car radios turned on. Millions of Americans wake up to radio every morning via clock radios. Housework is done to music supplied by radio. Houses are painted, garages cleaned, and cars washed with a radio background.

It is likely that if you are reading this chapter at home in your bedroom, you are doing so with a musical background supplied by radio. If radio served a primary function you could not study and listen at the same time. Try to imagine reading and comprehending material from a textbook while trying to follow the story line in a suspense-filled, sixty-minute, private investigator television show.

Radio in the 1930s required full attention just as television does today. Families now sit together in living rooms and watch television as a source of primary entertainment. Radio program content has adapted successfully to allow people to do something else while taking advantage of an entirely new program format. We rely on radio just as much today as our parents did; however, our dependence is for very different reasons.

Radio is a Portable Medium. Until the early 1950s most families owned radio sets housed in attractive wood cabinets comparable to television sets today. Because radio required full attention, families stayed home to listen. In 1975 most radios manufactured are small, portable, and transistorized in order to make them as mobile as possible.

Radio has become our traveling companion. We can take a radio with us to school, to the office, to work in the garden, and to sunbathe in the back yard. A transistor radio may serve as a camper's only contact with the outside world in the woods or in the mountains.

Making radio a portable medium was necessary if the medium was to survive in a broadcast era with television. If we had to stay home to listen to radio, most of us would choose to watch television instead.

SUMMARY PROBES

1. **How were radio in 1920 and television in 1949 similar to a new toy at Christmas?**
2. **Why was the life of a radio station manager nerve-racking prior to broadcasting networks?**
3. **Why did the success of NBC's first year make more program networks necessary?**
4. **Why is it said that the "Golden Age of Radio" served as a forerunner to television programming format?**
5. **How did radio adapt to the presence of television to retain a significant place in the lives of Americans?**

DEVELOPMENT OF TELEVISION PROGRAMMING

Television had one distinct advantage over radio at its inception in the late 1940s. The American public was already well accustomed to expecting and receiving quality entertainment on a regular basis in their living rooms. It would not take a depression or a world war to develop an eager and appreciative audience.

The reality of an audience created for television by radio worked to television's advantage in that television became an instant success. Perhaps one disadvantage, however, was that the novelty of "newness" of the box with pictures wore off much more quickly than had been the case with radio. The major program networks were developed some six years after the first broadcast on KDKA. Television programmers didn't even enjoy six months before the public was demanding more and better programs.

First Television Programs

While the quality of very early television programs outdistanced the quality of the first radio entertainment, it was still evident that the emphasis rested on the novelty of the invention rather than on creation of stimulating program content.

This author vividly recalls his first evening of television viewing. My family and I went several blocks to a friend's home to see the new picture box; we arrived thirty minutes before sign-on time. The very first television programmers followed the format of motion-picture theaters in patterning their program schedules. The first program, a children's puppet show, was on at 6:00 p.m. and was followed by a fifteen-minute newscast. With the puppet show and newsreel over, the next two to three hours were consumed with studio-produced dramas and situation comedies, each thirty minutes in duration. About 10:00 p.m. the station signed off. The visiting families then went home in awe trying desperately to rearrange finances in order to purchase a television set.

The trend, then, in early programming was for a very short broadcast schedule, following an already accepted viewing format from the motion-picture theater, consisting of short subjects followed by feature attractions.

Within one year of the first network television programming, the American public had completely accepted the new medium and began to make greater and greater demands on the programmer to provide more and better entertainment.

Almost immediately the major networks adapted 1930 radio programming concepts to the television screen. Daytime programming was directed to a specialized audience of housewives, early evening and Saturday programming was reserved for children's viewing, and the evening prime-time hours offered variety directed at all members of the family.

The early national television audience quickly built loyalties to favorite programs. Television found the same intensity of admiration that radio had enjoyed fifteen years earlier: such early hits on the black-and-white screen as "The Texaco Star Theatre" starring Milton Berle, "I love Lucy," "Toast of the Town" with Ed Sullivan, and "The Ken Murray Show" became part of the American family's routine.

Thirty Years of Television Programming

In the nearly thirty years of regular television programming, four developmental characteristics stand out as responsible for television entertainment as we know it today. Program format, use of movies on television, program flooding, and restriction of subject matter are most significant in their contribution to today's programming.

Program Format. Most early television programs were thirty minutes in duration; some were sixty minutes. For years professionals have viewed television as the medium of fast entertainment.

The theory has been that audiences desire several self-contained dramatic or humorous encounters in an evening. Thus, the practice exists to get into a show quickly and get out just as quickly thirty or sixty minutes later. If audiences wanted longer sessions of entertainment on a regular basis, they could go to the movies.

Some alteration of the early format has occurred in the past three decades: "The Virginian" was one of the earliest successful ninety-minute series. Later successes using an expanded format have been few, but some do exist. When movies entered prime-time programming in 1961–62, the program format was extended to 120 minutes to accommodate the full showing of a feature film. Some spectacular movie showings have even consumed 180 minutes or the full prime-time clock segment for one viewing evening.

Even though some innovations have occurred with success in the past, a quick check of *TV Guide* during a current telecast season will bear out the fact that television programmers still rely most heavily on the original thirty- and sixty-minute program formats. Some theorize that the traditional thirty- or sixty-minute format is no more than a carry-over from radio. To some extent this is true; however, radio was quite successful with the fifteen-minute program format. Experiments with fifteen-minute television shows met with little public favor and in the current program market such programs are just short of obsolete.

Movies on Television. Motion pictures have always been a part of television viewing. Until 1961–62, however, movies were generally shown on television only after they had been thoroughly drained of any box office appeal and, then, relegated to late-show and early-show formats.

During the 1961–62 television season NBC experimented with a regular weekly format of higher quality movies in prime-time hours. Their "Saturday Night at the Movies" became such a success that in a few years all three networks were covering every night of the week with a prime-time movie offering.

As home audiences became accustomed to viewing movies in their living rooms with commercial interruptions, another problem faced network planners. One major effect of television on the motion-picture industry since 1950 is that far fewer movies are now produced each year than in the pretelevision era. By 1970 television had begun to use movies at a rate faster than Hollywood could produce them.

Television programmers realized that they could never meet the apparently insatiable appetite of the audience for televised movies. Experimentations with ninety-minute "made for TV movies" proved so successful that within two years more than 100 movies were made for television in one season. Today's practice finds network programmers using Hollywood-produced movies at a faster rate than ever; at the same time more movies for TV are being produced than at any time in the past.

Program Flooding. As we will see in later discussion, commercial television is one of the most highly competitive industries in America today. All three major networks, ABC, CBS, and NBC, compete with each other, as well as with hundreds of independent and educational stations for the viewer's attention. The practice of program flooding is an inevitable result of such competition.

Program flooding refers to the practice employed by programmers to attempt to take quick advantage of a successful show by copying its theme. Program flooding can occur in two distinct forms: competing programs of the same type and program "spin-offs."

Throughout the history of television a successful program during one season will be followed by several of the same type the following season. The past is patterned with successful westerns followed by more westerns; popular science-fiction shows followed by more science-fiction; successful medical shows, followed by more medical shows.

Perhaps even more common today is the program spin-off. The unprecedented success of "The Beverly Hillbillies" resulted in two shows directly from its scripts—"Petticoat Junction" and "Green Acres." "The Mary Tyler Moore Show" has contributed both "Phyllis" and "Rhoda." However, the practice of program spin-off is probably best illustrated by "All in the Family." Two shows, "Maude" and "The Jeffersons" were both spawned in Archie Bunker's household. "Good Times" featuring a former maid spun off from "Maude" could in a sense be labeled the grandchild of "All in the Family."

The practice of program flooding has always been a part of television programming. Furthermore, as long as the television industry remains as competitive as it has been in the past, we can expect more of the same practice.

Restrictive Subject Matter. The nature of television as a form of family entertainment in the home has traditionally resulted in a more rigid system of restrictions on acceptable subject matter for program content. Robert C. O'Hara has declared that our culture places limitations on programmers and media communicators in the guise of formulae for acceptable content.[4] Perhaps the formula most dominant in American television to date is that virtue is rewarded and evil is punished. From the earliest crime shows throughout the television era to our current mod private investigators, crime has not paid. In fact, it pays to be good. While movies, because of the nature of the medium, might succeed at showing a "bad guy" as likeable, it is generally accepted in media theory that television is more restricted. An example of acceptance of movies showing "bad guys" as likeable characters can be seen in audience empathy with the Corleone family in *The Godfather* and *The Godfather, II.* A regular weekly television series featuring the head of a mafia family would be questioned in terms of appropriate subject matter.

Another area of restriction for television programmers is in the treatment of controversial subject matter. Until recently subjects such as prostitution, homosexuality, and abortion were considered taboo for the American living room. Recent efforts to inject controversial subject matter into prime-time television viewing have been met with varied reactions from the public. An example is the variant reactions from the public received by CBS after airing a two-part episode of "Maude" dealing with abortion. Programmers are keenly aware of the public's reaction to controversial subjects on television which emphasizes that television has always been and still is more restricted in subject matter than any other of the mass media.

THE CHRONOLOGY OF A NEW TELEVISION PROGRAM

The layman unfamiliar with broadcast media likely has little conception of the complex process of moving a television program from an idea in a creator's mind to the reality of a listing in *TV Guide.* For demonstrative purposes, let us follow a television program through a chronology of events beginning with an idea and terminating with either a successful run of several years or rapid cancellation.

To promote clarity, we will assume that you, the reader, and we, the writers, are going into partnership to launch a new television show. We will plan to create a private investigator show with a very young and attractive female as the investigator.

Converting Idea to Reality

We cannot sell an idea. Our first task is to create a pilot or trial episode of the new series, and our first major necessity is *money*. If we have collective resources, fine; if not, we have to get it. Many program ideas never go beyond this first obstacle.

Assuming that we have funding for our pilot project, we now must secure the services of a star for the title role and a good supporting cast. This may be difficult because at the pilot stage we can offer no assurances of continued employment. We must find someone willing to gamble along with us. Once we have the cast and a script for the pilot episode which thoroughly states the theme of the series and introduces all the principal characters, we must rent production facilities and crew to have our episode produced either on film or video tape.

Program Pilot

We now submit our finished pilot episode to the major networks for screening and evaluation. The odds of success for each pilot is low—the networks must reject far more pilots each year than they are able to use. We will assume, however, that luck is with us and one of the networks accepts our pilot.

Selling the Show to an Advertiser

Now we must sit and wait while the network allows representatives from their advertising clientele to screen pilots and make offers for sponsoring. Once again this step can be precarious—even if the network likes our show, they must be able to sell it to advertisers.

Selling the Show to Network Affiliates

One of the most effective sources of control on network programming is the large corps of affiliate stations across the country. After the network has sold the show to advertisers, representatives from affiliate stations are invited to screen the proposed schedule which will include our new program. We will hope that mid-American station managers agree with us that the public is ready for a female private investigator. If they don't, our program will die before it is aired.

Attracting an Audience

We meet with success. The network, advertisers, and station managers all have endorsed our idea. The show is then scheduled into a time slot, and we immediately need more money—lots and lots of money. We now must produce at least twelve more segments of the show to be ready for the fall season. Our original pilot will serve as our premiere offering.

Since the broadcast season is divided into thirteen-week segments, we are reasonably assured of a thirteen-week run. However to continue beyond thirteen weeks we must have a sufficient viewing audience. We eagerly await the results of the early Nielsen ratings to tell us what percentage of the potential television audience agrees with the merits of our idea enough to watch our show. If the audience is with us, we will continue production beyond thirteen episodes. If we haven't an audience, we will have spent lots of money—perhaps not all of it ours—and we have one pilot and twelve episodes of our show as souvenirs.

RADIO AND TELEVISION PROGRAMMING OTHER THAN ENTERTAINMENT

Our heavy emphasis in this chapter has been on entertainment programming. We do not mean to imply that radio and television exist solely for entertainment purposes. The vast majority of regular programming of both media is aimed at little more than audience entertainment. On occasion, however, the broadcast audience looks to the airwaves for more than entertainment. Now, we will explore three types of nonentertainment programming: public service programming, regular newscasts, and special event newscasts.

Public Service Programming

All radio and television stations are required to provide an established percentage of time to programming meant to serve the public rather than entertain them for commercial profit. Religious programming on Sunday morning, community bulletin announcements, tornado information films, et cetera, are examples of this type of programming.

The dominance of entertainment in broadcasting, though, is evidenced by the scheduling of most of the public service programs in times other than prime time and the tendency for public service programming to utilize formats similar to prime-time shows. In this vein, producers of public service programs make every effort to dramatize their messages for maximum effect.

Regular News Programming

Americans have grown to expect the broadcast industry to provide them with first-hand news events on a regular basis. We are all confident that at various times in the broadcast day, newscasters will tell us what is happening. We have also come to expect that if a major event occurs unexpectedly, broadcasters will interrupt our entertainment to tell us about it.

While we have learned to depend on broadcasters to provide us with news, we have also learned to expect that such material will be a small part of the total broadcast content. Most network-affiliated commercial stations limit news coverage to approximately two hours per day out of as many as nineteen hours of transmission. We expect local news at noon, evening, and bedtime, with an addition of perhaps one national network newscast per day.

Special Events News Broadcasts

We have experienced the greatest impact of the broadcast capability in special-events coverage of turning points in our recent history. Radio took on a new significance to Americans with its ability to bring World War II into American homes. For instance, all Americans within hearing distance of a radio set experienced the tragedy and drama of the FDR funeral procession.

Television simply increased the drama of live coverage of events important to Americans. Very few people complained when all three networks suspended regular programming for days when the nation reeled in shock at the murder of President John F. Kennedy. Other events such as man's first step on the moon and the intrigue of Watergate were a part of every American's life as they could never have been without the electronic media.

SUMMARY PROBES

1. **How did early television programming copy the motion-picture format?**
2. **What change occurred in 1961–62 regarding television's treatment of motion-picture feature films?**
3. **Why were "made-for-TV movies" necessary?**
4. **What is meant by program flooding? What is a spin-off program?**
5. **Why are greater subject matter restrictions placed on television than on movies?**
6. **Trace the chronological development of a new television series.**
7. **What is public service programming?**

LEARNING EXPERIENCES

1. Make an effort to obtain a tape or phonograph recording of radio programs from the 1930s. Record your reactions to the early programs and be prepared to discuss them in class.

2. For a period of at least one week record the situations when you listen to radio. Was your use of radio primary or secondary? If secondary, what was your primary activity while listening to the radio?

3. Using a current television program listing, cite instances of what you consider to be program flooding. How many of the programs cited are spin-offs?

4. Using the same television listing, cite instances of program content dealing with restrictive or controversial subjects. Have trends in this area changed in your memory?

5. View what is considered to be public service programming on television. How does it differ from evening prime-time entertainment?

References

Brown, Les. *Television: The Business Behind the Box.* New York: Harcourt Brace Jovanovich, 1971.

Head, Sydney W. *Broadcasting in America: A Survey of Television and Radio*. New York: Houghton Mifflin, 1972.

Hiebert, Ray Eldon; Unguriat, Donald F.; and Bohn. Thomas W. *Mass Media: An Introduction to Modern Communication*. New York: David McKay, 1974.

Lichty, Lawrence W., and Topping, Malachi C. *American Broadcasting: A Source Book on the History of Radio and Television*. New York: Hastings House, 1975.

Whitney, Frederick C. *Mass Media and Mass Communications in Society*. Dubuque: Wm. C. Brown, 1975.

SEVENTEEN

GOALS **After completing this chapter you will be able to:**

1. Discuss two alternatives to our system of supporting broadcasting programs by selling commercial advertising.

2. List both advantages and disadvantages to subscription television.

3. Understand the historical development of our system of commercial broadcasting.

4. Comprehend the scope of modern network advertising.

5. Identify two other sources of revenue a local station has in addition to network advertising.

6. Recognize effects on the consumer of local station reluctance to originate live programming.

7. Identify two categories of restrictions currently in force on broadcast advertising.

Broadcasting Finance

How many times have you heard someone comment, "Television commercials insult the intelligence of the viewer?" Of all aspects of broadcasting, none has received more criticism from the public over the years than the content of commercials on radio and television.

One might wonder why the public has tolerated a system that it obviously finds so objectionable. The answer to this query emerges when one considers what television costs the consumer today. Once a family has made the initial investment of the purchase of a television receiver, the entertainment that follows is free except for the pennies required daily for electricity to operate the set.

This chapter will present an overview of the American system of commercial broadcasting. Specifically, we will examine some of the alternatives to our system of "insulting viewer intelligence." The historical development of broadcast advertising will be investigated, and three sources of advertising revenue for broadcasters will be cited. We will conclude with an examination of restrictions placed on broadcast advertising.

Most of the discussion will center on television because of its relevance to the reader. Some differences exist in radio advertising; however, consumer concern usually focuses on television commercializing.

ALTERNATIVES TO OUR COMMERCIAL SYSTEM

Most consumers can accept the economic fact of life that someone must pay the tremendous cost of the top quality entertainment available to viewers on television. If advertisers did not pay the cost in return for minutes of commercial announcements, the funding would most likely come from one of two sources: Funding would have to be derived either from an agency outside the broadcast communication complex or directly from the consumer.

External Agency Funding

It is almost inevitable that any form of support for broadcasting originating from external agencies will include some level of government either directly or indirectly. At one end of a continuum, you would find complete government funding usually accompanied by government control and operation of a national broadcast system. At the opposing end of the continuum you might find a system much like some of the former educational networks in the United States, now called public radio and television networks. In most educational broadcasting systems, the lion's share of financial support is provided by some element of public monies. Government operation, however, is not usually a part of such a system. Educational and other outlets for public television in this country often function with fewer restrictions on program content than commercial television.

The major difference existing between broadcasting supported by a combination of tax monies and private funding and our commercial system is the role of public opinion in determination of content. All three major networks depend almost totally on advertising revenue for income; advertisers' primary interest is the number of people watching a program, and, consequently, their commercial announcements. A station receiving income from government sources and private foundations does not face pressure resulting from quantity of audience. Program planners for educational and public television, therefore, do not have comparable restrictions that stem from mass popularity. Fewer restrictions and lack of pressure from the audience "numbers game" normally results in a program format offering significant alternatives to network prime-time popular shows.

Consumer Funding

Most experiments with attempts to shift the cost burden of television to the consumer have sustained little lasting enthusiasm. Any such effort eradicates the major advantage to our commercial system which has traditionally been top quality entertainment and entertainers at the lowest possible price to the consumer.

The most popular form of consumer-sponsored broadcasting has been the practice of subscription programming. With such a system, the family would have a wider selection of programming available with a cost factor assigned to each program. Most such systems would use some variation of a scrambling device. The home set, when turned on to a particular channel, would be scrambled. In order to receive a specified program the family would have to "order" the program from a catalogue or listing and relay the request to some form of central control. The closed circuit set at home would then be unscrambled making it capable of receiving the desired program and the charge for the program would be assessed to the household.

Presumably a system of regular billing for each family would be utilized much in the manner of telephone billing. As long as the family paid its "television" bill, entertainment would continue to flow. A family in arrears, however, might face the prospect of having service discontinued with an additional service charge assessed for reinstatement.

Of course, not all programs would be priced at the same rate. Program cost would depend greatly on the quality of the offering. An entire family might watch a 1943 vintage late movie for five cents; however, the Super Bowl in January could cost the same family as much as three dollars.

Advantages to such a system are (1) since the consumer pays the cost, virtually any material could be made available: first-run movies, the Indianapolis 500, world heavyweight boxing matches, and other events not usually seen on television could be made available at a higher-than-average cost for those who desire to pay; (2) Less restriction on program content would exist because the consumer would have to order the program, thus assuming that the consumer had already made some qualitative evaluation of the content. Programs would no longer barge through home walls and into living rooms with no warning; (3) The consumer could determine his own costs for television.

Disadvantages to such a system have traditionally been sufficient to thwart any widespread efforts for implementation. First, such a system might mean the end of commercial television. Consumers with ability to pay would most likely opt for a greater quantity of subscription service than those with less financial ability. Advertisers are most interested in reaching those who can pay; General Motors has little interest in broadcasting commercials to an audience of which the majority are families with little discretionary purchasing power. Discretionary purchasing power—the ability of the consumer to exercise discretion in buying products after the essentials of life are provided for—is the "left-over" money that advertisers seek. (Discretionary purchasing power as it relates to television advertising is discussed in Sydney Head, *Broadcasting in America,* p. 252.) Second, success for subscription television must be preceded by a significant degree of dissatisfaction with the present commercial system. Even though Americans complain bitterly about both the quantity and quality of broadcast commercials, when given the choice of free program content or subscription service, they have traditionally opted for the status quo.

SUMMARY PROBES

1. **Why are public television stations able to operate with fewer restrictions on programming than commercial stations?**
2. **How would subscription television be similar in some respects to a telephone bill?**
3. **How would a subscription television system be a threat to commercial television?**

DEVELOPMENT OF COMMERCIAL ADVERTISING

Commercial advertising as we are accustomed to in modern broadcast media faced what appeared to be insurmountable obstacles during the 1920s. Sentiment from most strata of society opposed the use of broadcasting for any form of direct advertising. The following statement by Secretary of Commerce Herbert Hoover in 1924 stood indicative of the opinion of members of the broadcast industry and the general public:

> I have never believed that it was possible to advertise through broadcasting without ruining the industry. I don't believe there is anything the people would take more offense at than the attempt to sell goods

over radio broadcasting. The average person does not want his receiving set filled with that sort of material, and his resentment will extend to the establishments that are responsible. They will lose much more than they gain.[1]

Opposition from government and broadcasting officials delayed the advent of "hard-sell" commercials on radio; however, as early as 1922 the practice of selling time on radio to commercial concerns was evident. The first recorded purchase of time on radio occurred that year on station WEAF in New York when the Queensboro Corporation paid for ten minutes of air time.[2] The time was used to "discuss" a cooperative apartment development in Jackson Heights, New York. The Queensboro name was used only one time in the ten minutes, and absolutely no "hard-sell" advertising devices were employed.

For several years advertising that did appear on radio was completely "soft-sell" in nature. Individuals or businesses buying the time could not make mention of price on the air, nor could they suggest that the purpose of the remarks was to get the listener to buy the product. Of course, the early commercials did not interrupt the flow of programming. Commercials were either at the beginning or end of an entertainment show, or, in many cases, the commercials were the entire program.

The primary factor involved in changing the nature of early commercializing was the public demand for better quality programming on radio. Better entertainment meant more cost to the stations and eventually to the networks. More cost to broadcasters meant that those buying radio time would have to pay more for it. These events led to the philosophical conflict between broadcasters and advertisers alluded to earlier.

The primary aim of the programmers was to entertain the public in the best possible manner. The primary aim of advertisers providing funds for the entertainment was to achieve a net profit from advertising via commercial messages on the air. Both forces had to use the same means to achieve their primary aim: the program format.[3]

The programmers' point of view was that if the public was to be served at maximum efficiency, commercial announcements should appear either at the beginning of a program or after program content had been concluded. To interrupt the continual flow of program material would be an injustice to the public and to the concept of radio entertainment.

The advertiser countered that if they were to pay huge sums of money to provide quality entertainment for radio listeners, the advertiser's only method of receiving net gain from such payment is to have access to the listeners at times of peak numbers. Obviously, large numbers of listeners are not closely attending to the radio receiver before a program starts or after it concludes. Commercial announcements must be placed at strategic points of program climax to assure maximum listeners.

Had this point not been settled between programmers and advertisers, our commercial system probably would not exist today. Public demands and the lure of large profits won out, however; radio programmers eventually agreed that they could, in fact, build program content around commercials without seriously hampering effect on or benefit to the listening public. Obviously, many would disagree with the points of settlement still today.

With the major point of conflict between programmers and advertisers settled, the path was cleared for the commercial broadcast system familiar to us today. Television did not have major difficulties in adapting the commercial format from radio to its medium. Once again, radio fought and won the battles that affected television so dramatically later.

THREE SOURCES OF ADVERTISING REVENUE

Three major sources of advertising revenue centering on television will be examined and analyzed for purposes of clarity. A typical television station receives advertising revenue from the network, local merchants, and national representatives.

Network Advertising

As illustrated in Table 17.1, the greatest percentage of advertising revenue in television broadcasting is generated through the three major networks, ABC, CBS, and NBC. Each broadcast season finds the three networks competing with program content for the attention of the advertisers possessing the money. The competition has been tough and the prices for program production high. In 1975 costs to the three networks to fill prime-time hours ranged from $17,000,000 to $19,000,000 per week. The cost to produce a single epi-

Table 17.1 **Television Advertising Volume 1973–74**

Medium	**1973** **$ Millions**	**% of total**	**1974** **$ Millions**	**% of total**	**% change**
Television					
Total	4,460	17.7	4,851	18.1	+8.8
Network	1,968	7.8	2,145	8.0	+9.0
Spot	1,377	5.5	1,495	5.6	+8.6
Local	1,115	4.4	1,211	4.5	+8.6

Abstracted from an article by Robert J. Coen, "Ad Volume in '75 Expected to be 6 Percent Above Last Year," *Advertising Age.* (September 15, 1975), p. 3.

sode of an average thirty-minute series is $115,000. A sixty-minute episode costs from $270,000 to $280,000.[4] Current practice has resulted in business and industry buying time to support network television in one of three ways.

Entire Program Sponsorship. An advertiser may provide funds for an entire thirty- or sixty-minute program. In early stages of television programming, this practice was common; however, in the last decade the practice has faded until now it is very rare to see a television program with only one sponsor. The highly tentative success of most programs for any significant duration of time has made it financially unsound for a single corporation to invest the momentous sums necessary to be the sole sponsor of a show.

Shotgun Buying. The practice of shotgun buying is the practice most advertisers opt for today. Rather than spend an entire television advertising budget on a few shows, most companies prefer to spread money all across the program board and on more than one network. Some time is purchased at a higher rate in top ranked shows; time is also purchased at lower rates in less popular shows. Many companies choose to spread their dollars into time periods other than prime-time hours.

The practice of shotgun buying by advertisers has resulted in making it nearly impossible for viewers to identify a particular sponsor with a show. On the other hand, in the very early years of television programming, most popular shows were closely identified with a single sponsor. For instance, Milton Berle's early success was on "The Texaco Star Theater," "I Love Lucy" was sponsored by Phillip Morris cigarettes, and "The Ken Murray Show" was closely identified with the Anheuser-Busch Brewing Company. Today during a typical thirty-minute situation comedy, the viewer may be exposed to as many as four different services or products advertised.

Between Program Spots. Periods between programs on network television provide an additional outlet for brief spot announcements. Some time is provided for the local station during a program break. However, the major networks sell short time slots to advertisers who would desire these periods rather than during specific programs.

All time periods in the network broadcast day are not of equal worth. The most expensive periods for advertisers are what is designated as prime time, identified as "a continuous period of not less than three and one-half consecutive hours per broadcast day as designated by the station between the hours of 6:00 p.m. and midnight."[5] Advertising in any other period costs advertisers less than the same time segment would cost in prime time. (Actually, this factual statement is somewhat deceptive. Even though equal amounts of time in the two periods cost different amounts, the station and network can sell more minutes per hour in periods other than prime time. In many cases, daytime advertising may be more lucrative for the network than prime time, for in addition to selling more units of time, production costs are less in other than prime time.)

Many consumers of television mistakenly believe that local stations pay the networks for the privilege of showing their programs. The opposite is actually true. The three major networks with headquarters in New York and other major cities lack an essential item for independent survival: Networks have no broadcast licenses or transmitters apart from a handful of widely spread local stations that each owns. Thus, they have no method of distributing programs directly to the public. Networks must rely on their chain of affiliate stations to transmit programming. Networks, therefore, pay the local stations directly in proportion to the amount of network fare the local station uses. They pay local stations a percentage of the station's local advertising rate for the time period in which the program is shown. The actual percentage paid varies and is dependent on time slots, popularity of the show, and other factors.

Local Station Advertising

All local stations have advertising rate cards like that shown in Table 17.2 for use in selling time to local merchants who are not utilizing network programming. Local station advertising rates are divided into time segments much like network rates, identifying certain time segments as Class A time and more expensive to advertisers and others as perhaps B, C, or D, and less expensive, respectively. Networks pay local stations a percentage of the rate shown on the card for the time segment in which network programming is used by the local stations. Thus, a network program in prime time will result in a station being paid a percentage of its Class A advertising rate.

The management of the local television station faces the task of selling all the time not used by the networks. Even during prime-time hours when perhaps all programming originates with the network, the local station has station-break and between-program spots to sell local merchants. The presence of great quantities of time to sell by local stations has resulted in two practices not necessarily beneficial to the television viewer.

Minimal Amount of Locally Originated Programming. Most local television stations could originate several hours of programming each day. For special-occasion coverage of an event of unusual interest to the local area, the television station can, and sometimes does, preempt regular network fare to bring the viewers the special-interest event. Such happenings are rare, primarily for two financial reasons.

Let us establish a hypothetical situation involving a city of approximately 50,000 people with one major network affiliated station. Let us, also, assume that the city is the home of a major university. During basketball season it would be of special interest to most people in the community for the local station to televise all the week-night home games of the university team. The station may televise a game occasionally; however, it is doubtful that they will carry all games primarily for financial reasons. The ball games would most likely be scheduled during prime-time hours; in order for the station to carry the game, they would have to preempt at least two hours of prime-time network programming. If the station doesn't show the network schedule, they don't get paid for that time; thus, the local station would have to sell the entire two hours to local merchants at prime-time rates. It would be difficult for a station to find local sponsors in a city of 50,000 who could provide the necessary revenue on a regular basis. Faced with a choice between showing all basketball games and losing money, or going with regularly scheduled network programming, most stations opt for the latter most of the time.

Heavy Reliance on Syndicated Programming. Some times are set aside by networks specifically to promote local program origina-

Table 17.2 **Sample Rate Card**

ANNOUNCEMENTS
DAYTIME

	I	II*	III
Class A (11 am–3:30 pm, M–F; 4–6 pm, Sat & Sun) 30 Seconds	$ 60	$ 50	$ 40
Class B (9–10 am, M–F; 2–4 pm, Sat; 9 am–4 pm, Sun) 30 Seconds	$ 50	$ 40	$ 30
Class C (Sign-On–8 am, M–F) 30 Seconds or Less	$ 20	$ 15	$ 10

*Subject to Preemption on 2 Weeks' Notice
ID's: 50% of 30-Second Rate

PRIME TIME
30 Sec.—I

Class AA

	MON	TUE	WED	THUR	FRI	SAT	SUN
7:00 pm	$145	$145	$130	$145	$125	$125	$125
7:30 pm	155	130	130	175	145	140	125
8:00 pm	155	145	160	160	155	125	145
8:30 pm	155	145	160	SF	155	130	145
9:00 pm	160	145	155	SF	140	125	145
9:30 pm	160	130	145	SF	140	125	145
10:00 pm	120	110	120	SF	110	95	120

10 Seconds—One Half cost of 30-Seconds
60 Seconds—Twice cost of 30-Seconds

30 Sec.—II

Class AA

	MON	TUE	WED	THUR	FRI	SAT	SUN
7:00 pm	$120	$120	$105	$120	$100	$100	$100
7:30 pm	125	105	105	140	120	110	100
8:00 pm	125	120	130	130	125	100	120
8:30 pm	125	120	130	SF	125	105	120
9:00 pm	130	120	125	SF	110	100	120
9:30 pm	130	105	120	SF	110	100	120
10:00 pm	95	90	95	SF	90	80	95

ROS Prime: $95
Rate Protection: 3 Months for Announcements.

SPECIAL FEATURES

		SECTIONS I	II	III	10 Sec.
Dinah	M–F 8:00– 9:00 am	30	25	20	—
NEWSCENTER 10					
Noon Report	M–F 12:00–12:30 pm	$ 50	$ 45	$ 40	$ 25
Early News	M–Sat 6:00–6:30 pm (Incl. 6 & 6:30 pm Breaks)	90	75	65	40
Late News	M–Sun 10:00–10:30 pm (Incl. 10:30 pm Break)	90	75	65	40
FRINGE/ACCESS					
Jeannie	M–F 3:30–4:00 pm	40	35	30	15
Partridge Family	M–F 4:00–4:30 pm				
Bewitched	M–F 4:30–5:00 pm				
Hogan's Heroes	M–F 5:00–5:30 pm				
To Tell The Truth	M–F 6:30–7:00 pm	80	70	60	35
Nashville Music	Sat 6:30–7:00 pm	80	70	60	35
CBS Movie	Thur 8:00–10:00 pm (Incl. 10 pm Break)	145	115	—	65
Candid Camera	Sun 10:30–11:00 pm	80	70	60	35
Late Show	M–Sa 10:30 pm–Cc	35	25	20	10
Sammy & Company	Sun 11:00 pm–Cc	35	25	20	—
KIDS' SHOWS	Sat 7:00 am–2:00 pm	40 FLAT			
	Sun 8:00 am–9:00 am	40 FLAT			

SPECIAL FEATURE PACKAGES

		FLAT RATES—30 Sec.	
ACCESS PACKAGE			
	M–F 6:30– 7:00 pm	2/Wk	$100
NEWS COMBO (1 Spot in Each)			
Early News	M–Sa 6:00– 6:30 pm		$120
Late News	M–Su 10:00–10:30 pm		
ACTION PACKAGE			
Various	M–F 3:30– 5:30 pm	2/Wk	$ 95
To Tell The Truth	M–F 6:30– 7:00 pm	1/Wk	
HOUSEWIFE PACKAGE			
	M–F 9:00 am– 5:30 pm	3/Wk	$110
DINAH PACKAGE			
	M–F 8:00–9:00 am	3/Wk	$ 45

tion. Normally during the late afternoon and early evening hours a great deal of the time is so designated; however, many stations do not use the time for live local programming. They, instead, purchase syndicated series of old television shows, usually, those cancelled from regular network schedules. Choosing syndicated reruns over live local programming offers the station two financial benefits: (1) The reruns "fill" the time without the station management having to initiate the expense of creative program development. (2) The reruns of old successful series are much easier to sell to local merchants than untried local talent.

National Representatives

A third source of revenue for most television stations exists with the use of national representatives. All time segments not supported by network advertising are not filled with local advertising. Stations frequently run commercials selling nationally known products at times when the programming is originating from the local studio. For instance, during a late show featuring a movie projected by the local television station, brief commercial announcements for nationally known products such as beer, soap, dog food, and so on appear. Such brief spot commercials are sold by national representatives for the station. Filmed or video-taped commercials are supplied to the local station for a specified number of airings. Every station has a national representative or agency located in strategic cities throughout the country whose function is to sell spot announcements to national advertisers for stations.

The national representative is more vital to the independent station because such a station has only local and national representative revenue available to it. The network affiliate station, however, has all three sales forces working to ensure its financial health.

In summary, the average local station affiliated with one of the major networks has three sources of income. The advertising fed to the local stations on network lines, along with program content, results in a payment to the local station by the network. Every local station must rely on its own local sales staff to sell a certain percentage of time to local merchants. The balance of the time not covered by the first two sources is placed in the trust of a hopefully effective national representative.

The viewer may, without realizing it, see three consecutive commercials which are the results of three different sales staffs.

A network series, sponsored by a leading dog food company, may air a commercial on the network wire at the end of a show. This commercial might be followed by an announcement for a leading soft drink sold by a national representative and transmitted on film or tape from the local studio. The soft drink announcement could be followed by a thirty-second spot announcing a furniture sale by a local merchant. All three might be aired between two programs, all occurring in a time span of one minute, and all three sold by different sales staffs working for the television station.

The total amount of money spent in television advertising alone overwhelms most consumers. Perhaps, even more staggering is the estimate that both network television advertising and national television spot advertising increased by eight percent in 1975 over the amount spent in 1974.[6]

SUMMARY PROBES

1. **How did commercials in the 1920s differ from those on television today?**
2. **What was the major point of controversy between radio programmers and advertisers in the 1920s?**
3. **What is the difference between entire program sponsorship and shotgun buying?**
4. **How do local stations receive revenue from network shows?**
5. **Why are local stations reluctant to originate live television programming?**
6. **How does a national representative serve a local television station?**

RESTRICTIONS ON ADVERTISING

Broadcast advertising has been restricted with varying degrees of rigidity from the first commercial, aired in 1922, up to the present time. We mentioned earlier that the first commercials were not identified as such and in many instances comprised an entire program. Early commercials could make no direct mention of price and could not suggest that the viewer should buy the product or service discussed.

Later in the 1920s and into the next decade certain products were banned from the airwaves. Products identified as personal could not be sold air time; included in this category at the outset were such common items as tooth-paste and deodorant.

Early restrictions on advertising have liberalized significantly over the years. Most products today are judged permissible for television and radio sales. Some exceptions still exist: cigarette advertising has been made unlawful. The code of the National Association of Broadcasters also rules out hard liquor as inappropriate for radio or television advertising.

Restrictions still operative in the broadcast industry generally fall into one of two broad categories. They are either restrictions imposed internally by the industry itself or restrictions imposed by external agencies.

Industry Self-Regulation

The National Association of Broadcasters (NAB) was formed in 1923. The association emerged as a result of controversies involving payment for the use of copyrighted music.[7] It has since become the most significant source of industry-wide self-regulation. Membership in the NAB is voluntary and not all stations belong. Membership does not dictate subscription to the code of the NAB; thus, fewer stations are code subscribers. Those stations that subscribe to the code, however, earn the privilege of displaying the NAB Television Code Seal of Good Practice on the air. To retain this privilege subscriber stations must abide by the specifications in the television code.

The major concerns of the NAB involving television advertising can be categorized as quantitative and qualitative.

Quantitative Concerns. The NAB specifies how much time can be consumed using commercial material. The latest edition of the code, for instance, limits the amount of time used for commercials in prime time to nine minutes and thirty seconds for every sixty minutes of programming.[8] At other periods of the day, commercials may consume more time. Other quantitative concerns of the NAB are frequency of interruptions per program and number of consecutive commercial announcements both within programs and during station breaks.

Qualitative Concerns. The NAB recommends against the advertising of certain products such as hard liquor. Further, the concern of the NAB extends to the method of presentation of advertising. The eighteenth edition of the television code states, "Advertising should offer a product or service on its positive merits and refrain from discrediting, disparaging, or unfairly attacking competitors, competing products, other industries, professions or institutions."[9]

While the NAB code for advertising practices contains sound recommendations, serious limitations hamper its effectiveness. First, the code applies only to stations who subscribe to it, and subscription is voluntary. Secondly, if a station violates the code, the most severe penalty the NAB has at its disposal is to deny the offending station the privilege of displaying the NAB seal.

External Regulation of Advertising

Perhaps the most celebrated incident of external regulation of advertising is found in the controversy surrounding cigarette advertising. Slightly more than three years after the United States Surgeon General's announcement in 1964 that cigarette smoking was harmful to health, the Federal Communications Commission interpreted its "Fairness Doctrine"[10] to require stations to broadcast anti-smoking announcements. This act was followed by a Congressional Act prohibiting all cigarette advertising on radio and television. The role of the government in regulating advertising in this instance stands out as definitive; however, such cases are rare in the history of American broadcasting.

The most prominent external force in broadcast advertising has become the Federal Trade Commission. The FTC's most viable effect on advertisers is its program of asking advertisers to document their commercial claims. If the commission feels that an ad is misleading, a period of negotiation follows between the FTC and the advertiser.[11] An agreement can be worked out at this stage; however, if the advertiser feels the FTC is erroneous in its judgment, the matter can evolve into a lengthy court proceeding.

The major limitation faced by the FTC, as pointed out by the American Management Association, is that the FTC can take action only *after* an alleged deceptive commercial has been aired. Furthermore, the delayed action will most likely require a lengthy period of time before any corrective measures are taken by the advertisers, if, in fact, they ever are. During this delay the consumer may continue to be exposed to the alleged deceptive commercial.

Both internal and external restrictions exist on broadcast advertising. The unfortunate conclusion drawn, however, is that except on rare occasions, restrictions are either voluntary or time consuming to implement. While all this occurs, we, the consumers, continue to be at the mercy of the advertiser and his message, however unethical or erroneous, glib or gimmicky, it might be.

SUMMARY PROBES

1. **How does the National Association of Broadcasters regulate advertising? Why is the NAB's effectiveness limited?**
2. **In what way is the ban on cigarette advertising in the broadcast media a rare situation?**
3. **How does the Federal Trade Commission regulate advertising? Why is the FTC's effectiveness limited?**

LEARNING EXPERIENCES

1. Read about national systems of broadcasting other than our own. Be prepared to discuss the differences and to cite advantages and disadvantages of other systems when compared to our own.

2. Look up descriptions and accounts of past experiments in this country with subscription television. What do you feel would be the advantages and disadvantages of such a system?

3. If a public or educational television station is available to you, watch several programs that are not interrupted with commercials. Determine for yourself if programmers or advertisers were right in their beliefs in the controversy of the 1920s.

4. Keep a log of all commercials telecast during an evening in prime-time hours. How much of the advertising appeared to be shotgun buying? How much was local advertising?

5. Make an effort to obtain a rate card from a local radio or television station. Compare the cost differential for commercials in different time categories.

6. Browse through recent copies of the *Federal Trade Commission News Summary*. Look for cases involving action against media advertising. Bring the instances to class for discussion.

References

Adler, Richard S., and Baer, Walter S. *The Electronic Box Office: Humanities and Arts on the Cable*. New York: Praeger, 1974, pp. 19–49.

Head, Sydney W. *Broadcasting in America: A Survey of Television and Radio*. Boston: Houghton Mifflin, 1972, pp. 245–90.

Lucas, John T., and Gurman, Richard. *Truth in Advertising: An AMA Research Report*. American Management Association, 1972.

Smythe, Ted, and Mastroianni, George A. *Issues in Broadcasting: Radio, Television, and Cable*. Palo Alto: Mayfield, 1975, pp. 338–66.

"The Television Code." Eighteenth Edition. National Association of Broadcasters, June, 1975.

Wells, Alan. *Mass Communications: A World View*. Palo Alto: National Press, 1974.

EIGHTEEN

GOALS **After completing this chapter you will be able to:**

1. **List major pieces of legislation in the history and development of broadcast government regulation.**
2. **Understand how the Federal Communications Commission functions as our current government regulator of broadcasting.**
3. **Identify major legislative interpretations in areas of fairness and equal time.**
4. **Discern functions and procedures involved in broadcast self-regulation by the National Association of Broadcasters.**
5. **Understand the effects of the Nielsen ratings on regulation of broadcasting.**
6. **Recognize what procedures and methods to use in making personal feelings known about broadcasting services.**

Control Of Broadcasting

How many times have you heard the comment, "I wish that show had not been cancelled, it was one of my favorites." Statements such as these bring up the inevitable question in any discussion of broadcasting: Who makes the decisions affecting broadcasting? Who has control?

Broadcasting is unique in many respects. Like the newspaper, the industry enjoys protection by the First Amendment to the Constitution of the United States. Unlike the newspaper, no person or group can own a broadcasting channel of communication, since the airwaves are considered to be natural resources of the country, the property of the public, and to be used in the public interest.

Three areas of control over broadcasting will be investigated in this chapter. First, the chapter will trace the development of congressional legislation affecting broadcasting chronologically, culminating with the formulation of the Federal Communications Commission, which still rides herd over the airwaves. Second, the broadcasting industry's interest in performing a prescribed amount of self-regulation will be discussed. The final segment of the chapter will explore methods that the consumer of broadcasting can implement to exert control.

LEGISLATION AFFECTING BROADCASTING

Four major bills in the legislative history of broadcasting are most significant to the development and control of the system. The first two bills had many weaknesses which led to the Radio Act of 1927, the first serious effort to provide some vestige of government regulation of broadcasting. The 1927 act was later revised with the passage of the Communications Act of 1934 which created the Federal Communications Commission—the executive regulatory body, still in business today.

Legislation Prior to the FCC

The Wireless Ship Act was passed by Congress in 1910 and required all ocean-going vessels to have radio equipment on board. In 1910, wireless was only about sixteen years old and few people, including congressmen, possessed more than a remote knowledge of radio. Radio's potential, however, in life-saving situations involving maritime communication was obvious even as early as 1910.

Two years later a major weakness in the Wireless Ship Act demonstrated to the world the shallow thinking of the writers of the bill. A passenger ship, the Titanic, struck an iceberg and sank on its maiden voyage. The radio operator on board the Titanic transmitted constant SOS signals in an effort to save the passengers.[1] A radio operator on board a ship near enough to the Titanic to have saved most of those who eventually perished in the tragedy had gone off duty just minutes before the SOS signals were transmitted. A ship much farther away heard the signals and managed to save a small group of passengers, but the majority of those aboard went down with the ship. The Titanic radio operator died at his post.

The language of the Wireless Ship Act was complete in most respects: It required radio equipment on board vessels to be in good working order, to be operated by a person skilled in the use of the equipment and to be capable of transmitting at least one hundred miles. The bill was derelict in one crucial area, however: it did not require that the equipment be manned at *all times*.

If the government and the public had not been aware of the potential of radio prior to the disaster, they were now ready to take a keen interest in broadcast legislation. The scope of the tragedy, coupled with the apparent needlessness of many of the fatalities, prompted the passage of a new bill the same year.

The Radio Act of 1912 held more significance for broadcasting than simply establishing regulations for ships. The act required that anyone broadcasting must use call letters or identification names. Perhaps most significant, however, was that the act placed the regulation of broadcasting under the auspices of the secretary of commerce.

From 1912–20 very little activity resulted in few problems being evident in the area of broadcast regulation. However, when radio station KDKA transmitted its first entertainment programming from atop the Westinghouse factory in Pittsburgh, Pennsylvania, on November 2, 1920, the direction of broadcasting changed drastically. On that evening the weaknesses and inadequacies of the Radio Act of 1912 began to emerge.

As more and more stations appeared and requested licenses from the secretary of commerce, the airwaves became more and more cluttered. While the secretary of commerce had the authority to grant licenses to broadcasters, his office served as little more than a "license store." The 1912 act did not clearly define the secretary's powers of license revocation and renewal.

By the mid-1920s the situation became so bad that the industry itself began to request that the government take some steps to insure better control of broadcasters. Due to the absence of some type of agency with more than token authority, the airwaves were so cluttered that members of the listening audience could receive little more than interference from several stations operating near or on the same frequency.

The Radio Act of 1927 established a regulating agency for broadcasting called the Federal Radio Commission. The FRC was a five-man board with the authority to grant licenses, assign frequencies, establish operating times for stations, and renew licenses.

Section 4 of the act established many principles that are still in effect for the broadcasting industry today:

> Except as otherwise provided in this Act, the commission, from time to time, as public convenience, interest, or necessity requires, shall—
> (a) Classify radio stations;
> (b) Prescribe the nature of the service to be rendered by each class of licensed stations and each station within any class;
> (c) Assign bands of frequencies or wavelengths to the various classes of stations, and assign frequencies or wavelengths for each individual station and determine the power which each station shall use and the time during which it may operate;

(d) Determine the location of classes of stations or individual stations;
(e) Regulate the kind of apparatus to be used with respect to its external effects and the purity and sharpness of the emissions from each station and from the apparatus therein;
(f) Make such regulations not inconsistent with law as it may deem necessary to prevent interference between stations and to carry out the provisions of this Act. . . .
(g) Have authority to establish areas or zones to be served by any station;

. . .

(i) Have authority to make general rules and regulations requiring stations to keep such records of programs, transmissions of energy, communications or signals as it may deem desirable;

. . .

(k) Have authority to hold hearings, summon witnesses, administer oaths, compel the production of books, documents, and papers and to make such investigations as may be necessary in the performance of its duties. . . .

The Radio Act of 1927 developed a phrase still crucial to the broadcasting industry. By using the terminology—*public interest, convenience, or necessity*—the authors of the bill gave radio regulation its basis for solving disputes. In any broadcast controversy yet today, the fundamental question to be resolved is: Which decision will best serve the public interest, convenience, or necessity? The ever-present problem of defining the terms in a given situation has plagued both broadcasters and regulators for years.

The original intent of Congress was for the FRC to be reduced in importance after the first year of its existence. The theory was that the FRC would take a year to straighten the broadcasting maze and then the secretary of commerce could take over and provide the industry with a smooth, continuing operation. It became apparent immediately that the problem was greater than anticipated and the FRC was retained as a regulatory agency until its composition was revised seven years later by another piece of legislation.

The Federal Communications Commission

The Communications Act of 1934 re-emphasized most of the same basic philosophies of the Radio Act of 1927. The new bill changed the Federal Radio Commission to the Federal Communications Commission (FCC) and expanded the new commission's jurisdiction to forms of electronic communication other than radio.

The FCC consists of seven members who are appointed by the president with the advice and consent of the United States Senate. To guard against undue political influence in the regulation of airwaves, no more than four of the seven commissioners can be of the same political party at any given time.

While the scope of duties of the FCC is large, its major power base in broadcasting is in the issuance and renewal of operating licenses. Every broadcasting station in the United States is issued a license by the FCC, and every three years that license must be renewed. License renewal for a station may prove a routine matter; however, occasionally the FCC will order a renewal hearing at which time members of the station's community are invited to testify if they wish.

An FCC hearing for a local broadcast station may result in license renewal; however, the FCC may refuse to renew a license—a decision which the local station may appeal. The FCC may also choose to renew a station's license on a temporary basis: for one year or two with reconsideration at the end of the time. Such a procedure is similar to placing a station on probation for a specified period of time.

The Nature of Regulatory Power

It should be stressed that the nature of the power of the FCC in broadcasting is regulatory rather than power of censorship. Censorship of broadcasting implies that a program can be blocked from the airwaves before it is transmitted. For all practical purposes censorship power does not exist in broadcasting. The extent of the authority of the FCC is "after-the-fact" power. Of course, the knowledge of possible action as a result of broadcasting questionable material is normally sufficient to provide a significant amount of self-censorship in the broadcast industry.

Many broadcast consumers wrongly assume that the FCC has direct regulatory power over the major program networks. Such has never been the case. Networks do not hold broadcast licenses; they are business enterprises engaged in distributing a service to thousands of local stations in the country. The FCC has only indirect power over the networks. The commission controls the networks via its control of the local station. The indirect nature of the power can be quite effective, however, in that through establishing guidelines and controls for program content linked to license renewal, the affiliate stations of a given network may refuse en masse to air a specific program offered by the network. If affiliate stations collectively reject the controversial program, the network must back down or they will have no program distribution outlet. In such a case the FCC has indirectly controlled the major network.

The resultant pressure of local stations refusing to air network programs is financial in nature. The amount of advertising revenue generated by a particular entertainment program is directly related to the ratings of the program, which, in turn is directly related to the number of people in the potential audience. If four or five major affiliate stations in metropolitan areas refuse to show a network program, the audience is significantly reduced. Significant reduction in audience results in significant reduction of funds sponsors are willing to provide.

The end result of this maze is that even though the FCC lacks direct control over networks, the indirect control applied via local license renewals is sufficient to give network officials cause to be very much aware of what the FCC says about programming at any given time. Without the valuable distribution service provided by the local affiliates, the networks would rapidly fade into economic oblivion.

A Case Study

Let us construct a brief hypothetical situation involving the regulatory process as implemented by the FCC.

We will assume that a small local television station has been derelict in one of its functions of providing technical service of high quality to its consumers. Equipment is so poor and technical expertise at the station is so low that the station habitually goes off the air in the middle of the broadcast day for sometimes hours at a time.

A significant number of the station's consumers are disturbed enough by the practice to write the FCC registering their concern. At the time of license renewal for the station, the FCC will review its file on the station and determine that enough concern has been demonstrated by the public to warrant a hearing. The hearing is scheduled in the community where the station is located. Also it is well advertised on all media and invitations are extended to the public to attend the hearing and air opinions and concerns.

Such a hearing may result in one of the following courses of action: (1) the station may receive a license renewal; (2) the license may be renewed for a limited period of time, and when that time elapses improvement by the station will be assessed and license renewal reconsidered; (3) the station may lose its license. Whatever the result of such a hearing the FCC will attempt to answer one fundamental question: What course of action will best insure that the public interest, convenience, and necessity is served?

Legislation Since the FCC

Even though the basic concepts regulating broadcasting have not changed since the Radio Act of 1927, and though the FCC has operated fluently from 1934 to the present, some additions to government regulations have occurred since the FCC was formulated. The Communications Act of 1934 contained the widely known "equal time" concept. The FCC forbade editorializing by broadcast stations in its Mayflower Decision in 1941. On March 7, 1946, the FCC enacted the *Public Service Responsibility of Broadcast Licensees,* which became known as the "Blue Book" due to the color of its cover. Three years later the ban on editorializing was lifted with the issuance of the Fairness Doctrine.

Equal Time. The equal-time section of the Communications Act of 1934 specifies that broadcast stations providing time for a candidate for an elective office will make equal time available to all candidates for the same office. Since 1934 much litigation has transpired concerning alleged abuses of the section involving both candidates and stations. While several court decisions and interpretations have made revisions in application of equal time, the basic concept provided in 1934 remains in force.

The Mayflower Decision. The effect of this decision, which technically denied a broadcasting corporation a construction permit, was to place a ban on broadcast editorializing. The ban was to remain in force for a period of eight years.

The Blue Book. In 1946 the Blue Book, published by the FCC, proved to be extensive treatment of programming specifications. The major areas of program content discussed in the document were the carrying of sustaining programs, local live programs, discussion of public issues, and advertising excesses. The question of fairness was raised in the Blue Book discussion of public issues. Clarification of the concept of broadcast fairness was to come three years later.

The Fairness Doctrine. In 1949 the FCC issued its Fairness Doctrine reversing its earlier ban of broadcast editorializing and stating that broadcast licensees did have an *obligation* to editorialize on issues of public concern. Accompanying the encouragement for editorializing, however, was a clear statement that the obligation included giving opportunity to all sides of public controversies. The obligation of fairness was not limited to editorials or statements from political candidates, but extended to all forms of public discussion.

While the degree and extent of government regulation of broadcasting has varied greatly during the twentieth century, regulatory powers have existed from the outset of broadcasting. Attempts prior to 1927 to regulate the industry resulted in more confusion than success. Since 1927, however, the regulatory function of the government has functioned consistently in the hands of the Federal Radio Commission and, later, the Federal Communications Commission.

SUMMARY PROBES

1. **What was the major weakness in the Wireless Ship Act of 1910?**
2. **What hindered the Secretary of Commerce in his attempts to regulate broadcasting in the 1920s?**
3. **What significance does the phrase "public interest, convenience, and necessity" hold for broadcasters?**
4. **How is the FCC control over national program networks indirect in nature?**
5. **How did the FCC Fairness Doctrine in 1949 affect broadcaster's treatment of public issues?**

INDUSTRY SELF-REGULATION

One of the most significant methods of regulating broadcasting is the ever-present effort by the industry at self-regulation. Even though the evolution of government regulation was brought about in part by the industry in the middle 1920s, most broadcasters recognize the undesirability of the FCC being forced to take after-the-fact action. As a result, broadcasters are very conscious of public opinion and resultant government opinion of the worth of the service they provide the American public.

The most active source of self-regulation is the National Association of Broadcasters based in Washington, D.C. The influence of the NAB on media advertising was synthesized earlier. Program standards are the second major area of concern to the association. The following discussion and case study involving the NAB will be related to television; however, a separate code for radio also exists.

National Association of Broadcasters

Every two years the National Association of Broadcasters revises and publishes a code book for subscribers to the Television Code. Subscriber eligibility to the code includes, "any individual, firm or corporation which is engaged in the operation of a broadcast station or network.[2]

Subscribing stations are granted permission to use the NAB Television Seal of Good Practice. The seal, copyrighted and registered, is provided to member stations in the form of a certificate along with a slide or film for use on the air. As long as the subscribing station adheres to points in the code the station retains the privilege of possessing and displaying the seal of good practice.

Enforcement of the code rests solely in the possession and display of the seal. Section IV in "Regulations and Procedures of the Code" specifies procedures for suspension of subscription:

> Any subscription, and/or the authority to utilize and show the above noted seal, may be voided, revoked or temporarily suspended for television programming, including commercial copy, which, by theme, treatment, or incident, in the judgment of the Television board constitutes a continuing, willful, or gross violation of any of the provisions of the Television Code. . . .[3]

Some points in the Television Code remain stable after numerous revisions; however, one major purpose served in biannual revision is that it enables the broadcast industry to be responsive to public opinion, and, in some cases, to adapt to FCC and congressional pressure. Controversies have existed concerning television program content since the first commercial television in the 1940s; however, no issues have been discussed more by the public, government, and broadcasters than those of sex and violence.

Broadcasters find themselves on the horns of a dilemma. They must provide the public with exciting and entertaining programming if they are to sell time at premium prices. On the other hand, broadcasters are consistently reluctant to press too far in their efforts to capture the attention of a viewing public.

In Section IV of the Television Code's "Program Standards", broadcasters receive the following instructions concerning sex and violence:

> 1. Violence, physical or psychological, may only be projected in responsibly handled contexts, not used exploitatively. Programs involving violence should present the consequences of it to its victims and perpetrators.
>   Presentation of the details of violence should avoid the excessive, the gratuitous and the instructional. The use of violence for its own sake and the detailed dwelling upon brutality or physical agony, by sight or by sound, are not permissible.
> 2. The treatment of criminal activities should always convey their social and human effects.
>   The presentation of techniques of crime in such detail as to be instructional or invite imitation shall be avoided.
> 3. Narcotic addiction shall not be presented except as a destructive habit. The use of illegal drugs or the abuse of legal drugs shall not be encouraged or shown as socially acceptable.
>
> . . .
>
> 8. Obscene, indecent or profane matter, as proscribed by law is unacceptable.
> 9. The presentation of marriage, the family and similarly important human relationships, and material with sexual connotations, shall not be treated exploitatively or irresponsibly, but with sensitivity. Costuming and movements of all performers shall be handled in a similar fashion.[4]

Not all television stations subscribe to the Television Code; however, as long as the majority of them do, the National Association of Broadcasters will remain the most influential channel of industry self-control.

A Case Study

The 1974–75 television season created an unprecedented public outcry against sex and violence in the media with special emphasis on the point that such programming was not suited for family viewing.

The outcry was so great and pressure so strong from members of Congress and the FCC that the broadcast industry, led by executives of the three major networks "decided" to segment prime-time viewing hours into family hours and hours for more mature subject matter beginning with the fall 1975 season.

Such action by the major networks and broadcasters was not necessarily in their best interests. Advertisers pay more for shows with proven popularity. Detective shows, crime shows, and adult theme shows had proven to be popular in the past throughout the primetime viewing hours.

It is safe to say that the following restrictions concerning family viewing and program advisories in other than family hours were at least the indirect result of public and government pressure. The broadcast industry, however, managed to regulate itself lest it be regulated. The Television Code states:

> . . . Additionally, entertainment programming inappropriate for viewing by a general family audience should not be broadcast during the first hour of network entertainment programming in prime time and in the immediately preceding hour. In the occasional cases when an entertainment program in this period is deemed to be inappropriate for such an audience, advisories should be used to alert viewers. Advisories should also be used when programs in later prime time periods contain material that might be disturbing to significant segments of the audience. These advisories should be presented in audio and video form at the beginning of the program and when deemed appropriate at a later point in the program. Advisories should also be used responsibly in promotional material in advance of the program. When using an advisory, the broadcaster should attempt to notify publishers of television program listings.
>
> Special care should be taken with respect to the content and treatment of audience advisories so that they do not disserve their intended purpose by containing material that is promotional, sensational or exploitative. Promotional announcements for programs that include advisories should be scheduled on a basis consistent with the purpose of the advisory.[5]

Of interest in the above regulation is the warning to broadcasters that announcements informing audiences of adult content of shows should not be used in an effort to *attract* listeners, but should always be composed with the sole purpose of informing viewers.

This 1975 case in study serves as a clear example of broadcast industry efforts at self-regulation. Needless to say, pressure from outside the industry often results in such regulation; however, the National Association of Broadcasters and subscription to its Television Code remains as one significant method of broadcast regulation today.

SUMMARY PROBES

1. **What is the basis for enforcement of the NAB Television Code?**
2. **Explain the nature of the broadcasters' prime-time experiment in the 1975–76 television season.**
3. **How and why does public government pressure affect NAB policy?**

CONSUMER REGULATION

Underlying both government regulation and industry self-regulation is you, the consumer of media. You are the customer in a business transaction. As long as you are satisfied, little regulation of any kind will transpire. However, when consumers collectively express concern and discontent with the media, the media listens. Many consumers of media have no idea as to how to make their feelings known to bring about change. The purpose of this section is to detail three ways that you, the consumer, can control broadcasting. A hypothetical situation involving a consumer complaint will follow.

To Watch or Not to Watch

The effect of the A. C. Nielsen Company ratings on television programming is unimaginable to most viewers. Network executives are hired and fired based on Nielsen ratings, programs are chopped and replacements added in midseason with Nielsen ratings as a basis, advertising rates based on ratings are established, and the level of entertainment provided to consumers of the largest broadcasting system in the world is based on Nielsen ratings.

Throughout the years of broadcasting history, several rating methods and companies have played a role in content development. One of the companies that has earned a nearly spotless reputation in the broadcast industry, is A. C. Nielsen. Nielsen measures one major item: how many people watch television at a given time.

Nielsen figures are reported in terms of ratings and shares. A Nielsen rating refers to the percentage of all television households in the country tuned in to a specific program at a given time. A Nielsen share refers to the percentage of all households actually watching television tuned in to a specific program at a given time.[6] For example, a popular network series might receive a Nielsen *rating* of 17 for a particular episode. This means that of all the television households in the country, 17 percent of them watched the show in question. The same episode on the same evening might receive a Nielsen *share* of 44. This figure interpreted means that of all the television sets *in use* at that particular time, 44 percent of them were tuned to the show in question.

The first network schedule revisions are normally made after thirteen weeks of programming into a new season. The cuts are inevitably based on a program's Nielsen figures. You have probably heard someone comment (or perhaps you have commented yourself), "Why did they take that show off? It was one of my favorites." The answer to that oft-heard question is simply that not enough people agreed with you. While many have questioned the validity of manipulating program schedules based on one company's sampling, network officials and broadcasters generally accept the Nielsen method as statistically valid.

The Nielsen Company has, at any given time, 1,200 mechanical devices called audimeters attached to television sets selected randomly across the country. An audimeter is installed for a period of five years with twenty percent of the devices changing from one home to another each year. This procedure provides a regular change in the composure of the random sampling. In addition to audimeters, which mechanically record viewing habits, Nielsen has 2,200 diaries kept by homes other than the 1,200 using audimeters. Thus, 3,400 television households determine the viewing patterns of over 200 million Americans.[7]

The consumer, then, does play a major role in determining program content, and, thus, does make up a significant component in regulation of broadcasting. You as a consumer may not make much difference in the content of programming individually; however, if enough of your peers agree with you, the collective consumer choices of programs to watch or not to watch is devastating to the broadcast industry.

To Buy or Not to Buy

Advertisers assume that if numbers of people are being exposed to their commercial messages that those people are being affected and motivated to buy a product. This assumption is a sound one most of the time. On occasion, however, factors other than the numbers of people watching regulate the media; sometimes it is more important *who* is watching than *how many*.

Some programs have experienced failure not because of a low Nielsen rating or share, but because of the kind of viewing audience the program attracts. During the 1973–74 season one major network showed a series of movies based on an identical theme. Network officials were elated with the tremendous response the public gave the movies, and began plans for a regular hour-long series in the following television season. The new program, however, was cancelled after thirteen weeks presumably for two reasons. First, Nielsen figures indicated that the series was not as popular as the movies had been. The second, perhaps more important, reason was revealed by Nielsen demographic data which indicated that the majority of the viewers who were watching the show were under fourteen years of age. If all the fourteen-year-olds in the country watched a show regularly, it is unlikely that such a show could remain in prime-time hours because the advertiser was not reaching a lucrative market for its commercial messages.

Some shows, then, are unsuccessful series not necessarily because people don't watch the show, but because those who watch don't buy the products advertised.

To Speak Up or to Remain Silent

Why speak up? The consumer can be an influential force in the regulation of broadcasting. To do so, however, requires that his voice be heard by someone. Far too many viewers have come to feel that their opinion will not make a difference. Hopefully this chapter on regulation of broadcasting will convince you that collective viewer criticism can and does make an impact on the industry.

You will recall that government regulation and industry self-regulation normally result from public feedback. If the Federal Communications Commission perceives that the American public is totally satisfied with the broadcasting service, what reason could it possibly have for denying a license to a broadcaster? If the National

Association of Broadcasters perceives that the FCC is satisfied because of perceived satisfaction on the part of viewers, why should the NAB tinker with program standards that apparently have made everyone happy?

The point is that the broadcasting service is for the consumer. The FCC protects the public interest; the NAB protects the broadcaster's interest in the name of the public. Nothing happens if the public interest, convenience, and necessity as perceived by the public remains unknown.

How to Speak Up

Let's assume that you want to make your feelings known concerning broadcasting. The overriding question in an individual's mind is: How do I do it to be most effective?

1. Start with the local station. Always keep in mind that it is the local station who is directly responsible to you. Your local station possesses a license which binds it to serve your interest. If your interest is not being served, the station management may find itself without the operating license. Whether the program on which you wish to comment is network or local, let the local station know how you feel about it. The fact that a program aired in your community originates in New York does not absolve the local station of its ultimate responsibility to you for program content.
2. Write to the Federal Communications Commission. If you find your local station unresponsive to your input, write to the FCC. You may be sure that your letter will be read and filed for future review. If enough of your local community agrees with you, you may also be sure that some corrective measure will be taken.
3. Write to the National Association of Broadcasters. Again, whether the program on which you are commenting is local or network, air your views with the NAB. If your local station is a subscriber to the code and your views are valid, you may be sure that some action will result.
4. Write to the sponsor. Letting the sponsor of a program know how you feel may be less effective than other methods of speaking up; however, if enough viewers agree with you such action may produce results. Contact with the sponsor of a show can be especially effective in local programming. A local automobile dealer will most likely be keenly sensitive to discontent registered by significant numbers of local viewers.
5. Don't watch the show. Don't ever forget the momentous impact of

the Nielsen ratings in broadcast control. The feedback most easily interpreted and most sure to produce results is changing the channel selector or turning the set off altogether.

It may appear that broadcast regulation operates only on a negative basis, that the consumer should speak up only when something is wrong. Don't feel that you should speak up only when dissatisfied. All parties involved—the local station, the FCC, the NAB, and the sponsor—would like very much to hear you, the consumer, say, "I like it."

SUMMARY PROBES

1. **What is the difference between a Nielsen rating and a Nielsen share?**
2. **Explain the sampling procedure used by the A. C. Nielsen Company.**
3. **Explain how in some instances it is more important to determine who is watching television than how many are watching.**
4. **Assume that you have a complaint to register against your local television station. How would you go about it to achieve maximum effect?**

LEARNING EXPERIENCES

1. Interview a member of a local radio or television station's management personnel to ascertain the following: (1) the station's method of handling complaints made by the public, (2) their station editorial policy and interpretation of equal time and fairness policies.

2. Write for a complete copy of the most recent Code of the National Association of Broadcasters. After inquiring at local stations to discover which are subscribers to the code, monitor their programming to watch for what you consider to be violations of code standards.

3. Write to the A. C. Nielsen Company and request an explanation of their polling procedures for network television programming.

References

Head, Sydney W. *Broadcasting in America: A Survey of Television and Radio*. Boston: Houghton Mifflin, 1972, chapter 8; part IV.

Hiebert, Ray Eldon; Unguriat, Donald F.; and Bohn, Thomas W. *Mass Media: An Introduction to Modern Communication*. New York: David McKay, 1974, chapter 9.
Kahn, Frank J. *Documents of American Broadcasting*. New York: Appleton-Century-Crofts, 1968, pp. 6–16; 35–51; 54–94; 125–206; and 349–97.
Lichty, Lawrence W. and Topping, Malachi C. *American Broadcasting: A Source Book on the History of Radio and Television*. New York: Hastings House, 1975, part 8.

NINETEEN

GOALS

After completing this chapter you will be able to:

1. Identify four eras in the development of motion pictures in America.

2. List effects that the development of radio as an entertainment medium had on motion pictures.

3. List effects that the development of television as an entertainment medium had on motion pictures.

4. Understand how movies finally adapted to television, thus enabling the industry to survive.

5. Distinguish both advantages and disadvantages resulting from the motion picture producer's practice of block booking.

6. Compare and contrast control of film with control of broadcasting in the areas of government control, self-control, and consumer control.

The Motion Picture

Our primary concern in this unit has been with the broadcasting industry; however, some attention should be given to a cognate form of media—the motion picture. We will examine the medium of film as it relates, compares, and competes with radio and television.

First, the development of motion pictures will be explored with the content of film stressed. Second, methods of financing film will be examined, and, third, regulation of film will be analyzed with an effort to emphasize consumer impact on film regulation.

FILM CONTENT: DEVELOPMENT OF MOTION PICTURES

One of the first recorded experiments demonstrating the concept of moving pictures using photographs occurred in 1877 when twenty-four cameras were synchronized to photograph different stages of a horse race. When the succession of frames was projected rapidly, the image of movement occurred. While this experiment sounds rustic, the basic principle of the motion picture has not changed since this. The viewer still sees a series of still shots passing before his eyes at a rapid enough pase to present the image of movement.

The motion picture industry owes a great debt to Thomas Edison whose late nineteenth-century developments succeeded in collating earlier discoveries to enable feature-length films to begin appearing around the turn of the century.

Development of film as a commercial enterprise in the United States can be summarized in four eras leading to present-day filmmaking

Film Before Radio

In the first era of commercial film, filmmakers set up projection operations in almost any vacant space they could find. Closed stores, empty sheds, or attics served as the first theaters, often with one individual serving as projectionist, producer, and ticket seller.

Vaudeville theaters used films as supplementary entertainment with the stage shows in a later stage of the motion picture.

In the early twentieth century the nickelodeon had become part of the tradition. For five cents the public could view the latest films produced. Nickelodeons were popular, and within a few years the number of such theaters in the United States had increased dramatically.

Finally, the migration of the filmmakers to the West comprised the last era of the early film. By 1919, eighty percent of the films being made in the world were produced in southern California.[1]

EFFECT OF RADIO ON THE MOTION PICTURE INDUSTRY

During the first twenty-five years of the twentieth century, the motion picture was *the* novelty for Americans in the field of entertainment. Production of film for the silent screen flourished in the twenties and the public's growing loyalty awarded a glamorous immortality to a group of stars.

As the quality of radio programming improved, however, motion picture producers could feel the keen competition of the talking box in the living room. By 1926 major program networks for broadcasting had become a reality, and Americans could now stay home and listen to programs whose quality paralleled that of the local theater. Economic pressures building toward the Great Depression had begun to affect the average American; he found staying home and listening to the radio was cheaper entertainment than taking the family to the motion picture theater.

Movie producers concluded that it was time for some unique innovation to draw the loyal film buff back to the theater. That attraction came with Al Jolson's *The Jazz Singer;* in 1927, to the amazement of audiences across the country, he sang. The new drawing card was sound. The novelty of sound accompanying the visual stimulus of film provided a needed rejuvenation to the film industry and was a major contribution to enabling Hollywood to compete successfully with radio for the next twenty years.

The advent of sound in motion pictures had many effects on the film industry. Two of the most significant were (1) the ruination of many careers, and, (2) the birth of the musical.

The silent screen relied primarily on nonverbal means of communication for effect on audience members. Facial expression and adventuresome movement were keystones to good acting. Many of the masters in the silent era, such as Buster Keaton, found that their voices did not endear them to moviegoers. In many instances production studios were forced to reassess their talent pool completely and create new stars.

Film producers, also, found problems in trying to bring excitement and novelty to the theater patrons using the same plot material they had relied on in the silent era. Audiences were awe-stricken with music (possibly as a result of radio); therefore, the big boom in early Hollywood talkies was the musical "extravaganza." Like early programming in radio, the quality of early motion picture musicals often left much to be desired. The audience was so entranced with the new medium that what was presented in that medium was—for a while at least—of secondary consequence.

MOTION PICTURES FROM 1927–48

A synthesis of motion pictures produced from 1927–48 would lead us to conclude that the name of the game was escape. The economic turmoil of the Great Depression and the chaotic aftermath was sandwiched between the tragedy of national involvement in two major world wars. Adventure, music, and comedy allowed America to go to the movie theater and escape the realities that awaited them at home and at work. Movies stressing social significance were to appear on a large scale much later.

Perhaps one of the greatest contributions the motion picture industry made to the world of entertainment was in the area of comedy. Laughter had flourished in the silent era. However, many of the great comedy teams evolved later in the "talkies" in an effort to laugh America out of its doldrums. The thirties and forties saw the height of popularity for such teams as The Marx Brothers, The Ritz Brothers, Olsen and Johnson, Abbott and Costello, Laurel and Hardy, The Three Stooges, and many others.

Along with comedy, the war effort was dramatized during the 1940s. Most pictures dealing with World War II themes were patriotic in nature casting the Germans and Japanese as villains, and, of course, always losers.

The motion picture industry survived the threat of radio unscarred. In fact, the industry continued to grow and flourish side by side with a thriving radio industry. The big challenge was yet to come.

EFFECT OF TELEVISION ON THE MOTION PICTURE INDUSTRY

The reaction of the film industry could be summarized in one word: *panic*. The panic emerged via a gallant effort of Hollywood to fight back at the new living room threat. The effort to fight back was centered on two fronts: (1) innovations, and, (2) restraining television from using movies.

Innovations

The development of sound managed to draw Americans back to theaters in the late twenties; therefore motion picture producers immediately went to work developing new innovations to combat television. Special wide-screen devices such as Cinerama and Cinemascope were developed in the mid-1950s, and at about the same time theaters began to show films in the third dimension. Three-D movies were popular at first; however, problems existed with this and other innovations that followed. In 3-D movies the audience had to wear special glasses to receive the effect of flying objects coming right off the screen into their eyes. While the innovation received favorable response at first, audiences soon tired of Indian arrows and tomahawks heading for their faces. Wide-screen gimmicks faced similar problems. The novelty of Cinerama was that it permitted much more realistic depiction of scenery and outdoor surroundings. None of the innovations made significant changes in plot or quality of films, however.

The Late Show

Movies have always been a part of television from the days of the first local telecasts. Television listings featuring late shows at bedtime hours can be found in the late forties. The major difference in movies on television twenty-five years ago and movies today is simply that in 1950 you could be assured that a movie seen on television would not only be at least seven to ten years old, but that it hadn't been a very good movie in the first place. The tendency for film producers was to protect their best products.

Both the stature of the motion picture industry and the quality of its products were judged questionable by many film critics during the 1950s and the early 1960s. Even though changes came about much more slowly than in the radio era, the motion picture industry finally adapted to television. Today—although in a different respect—the movie industry once again thrives. The adaptation has come about in two major ways: (1) the motion picture now enjoys television as its best customer; and, (2) movies serve a purpose for the public that television cannot.

Television as a Motion Picture Customer

As public hunger grew for television programs, developers of such programs felt a need for good production facilities that the confines of a television studio could not provide. Hollywood had the expertise and the vacant film lots to offer, and, as a result, a great percentage of television programming currently is produced on old movie sets.

Another area in which motion pictures have profited from television exists in selling television rights for recent and popular motion pictures. Rather than fight television by barring recent and top quality movies from the airwaves, movie magnates today eagerly anticipate the sale of rights to a top movie to one of the three major networks. During the 1974–75 television season, for example, NBC paid

$10,000,000 for exclusive production rights on television for *The Godfather.*[2]

Unique Service Provided by the Motion Picture

The second form of adaptation to television exists in a different service provided by the Hollywood of today from that of twenty-five years ago. Motion pictures were not able to compete with television as habitual, family entertainment. So films took the obvious course: in many instances the content of modern movies is such that it could not be aired on television. Socially significant issues have found a new channel in movies. Since the motion picture does not invade the privacy of the home—the consumer must make a conscious, and expensive, effort to see a first run movie—restrictions are more relaxed for films than for television. Most movies today tend to cater to the specialized, segmented audience rather than the general family audience; the majority of filmgoers are city-dwellers who are educated and under thirty. The prominence of "adult" movie houses in most major cities gives evidence of the varied audiences.

Thus, the objective of movies has been and still is similar to that of the broadcast industry: entertainment. The motion picture as a mass medium has survived both radio and television efforts to put entertainment in the home. Movies thrived alongside radio, and in many ways the two media complemented each other. Movies finally survived the threat of television—after producers discovered how to use the competing medium to their own advantage.

SUMMARY PROBES

1. **What were the four eras in the development of motion pictures in America?**
2. **How did the introduction of sound in motion pictures have a drastic effect on the careers of some stars?**
3. **In what ways did the motion picture industry assist the American public to "escape" in the thirties and forties?**
4. **How has the movie industry changed in dealing with networks in the area of showing movies on television?**
5. **In what two ways have motion pictures successfully adapted to the threat of television?**

FILM FINANCE

Few similarities exist between financing motion pictures and financing in the broadcast industry. Movies do not rely on advertising as a major source of income. You, the consumer, support the motion picture industry. If the contemporary motion picture industry is to survive, the consumer must be motivated to leave his home and spend money.

The most far-reaching change in motion picture finance occurred in 1946 when the practice of block booking was outlawed. The ban of block booking, linked with the advent of television, changed the whole world of movie production and finance.

Block Booking

The practice of block booking displayed some similarities to the concept of broadcasting networks and affiliate stations. A major problem faced by motion picture studios in the 1930s and 1940s was getting the numerous films being produced and distributed to the consumer. Every studio had its own stars and the public was hungry for movies featuring its favorite stars.

Production companies signed up local theaters as outlets for their movies. The string attached, however, was that in order to get the studio's best movies featuring the top stars, local theaters had to agree to run a specified number of lower-quality movies called *potboilers*. The term referred to movies starring lesser-known figures, produced on a shoestring budget, quickly and in large quantities. Local theater owners had no choice but to show the lesser films if they were to receive the top movies. Consequently, movie bills in local theaters changed often during the thirties and forties to accommodate the large numbers of feature-length films streaming from Hollywood. A typical theater in a small community in 1945 might show as many as four different features per week. Sunday, Monday, and Tuesday normally featured a top quality film with a big star. A Wednesday-Thursday bill might show a single feature of lesser quality, and Friday-Saturday were reserved for the double-feature "potboilers." In order to have a good film on Sunday-Monday-Tuesday, the theater owner had to show the low quality films.

Suit was brought against the studios, and in 1946 the film producers reluctantly agreed to dissolve the chains of movie houses affiliated with a single studio.

With the financial protection that had been provided by the practice of block booking gone, the movie industry now faced the task of producing quality films attractive not only to the consumer, but also to the new breed of theater owners who could book any film desired and likewise reject any. The disappearance of block booking when combined with the new American habit of television viewing brought about two major changes in the film industry which are still evident today.

Fewer and Better Films

With the involuntary market gone for potboilers, no one wanted them. Thus, the number of films coming from Hollywood decreased and the quality of films increased. The practice of mass production of low budget films stopped because theater owners would not book them.

Higher Admission Prices

One of the great advantages of block booking to the motion picture industry was that rental fees and admission prices for quality films were kept low because the studio relied on potboilers not only to break even but earn large profits. Better films now had to be produced without the financial cushion of the potboiler; the result was larger budgets and, consequently, higher admission prices at the box office.

Financing of the motion picture industry is much more directly consumer controlled than financing of the broadcast industry. Radio and television now depend on consumer habit to watch and listen, and consequently, to hear and see and be affected by the commercial messages. All this occurs with no direct outlay of money by the consumer to receive the entertainment. The motion picture industry must present a product attractive enough to the public to break the radio-television habit and to motivate the consumer to leave home and spend a sizable amount of money.

SUMMARY PROBES

1. **What was meant by block booking in the 1930s and the 1940s?**
2. **What two results affect us today from the ban on block booking?**

FILM CONTROL

Many elements of control and regulation of motion picture film are similar to those of the broadcast industry, but remain more indirect. A significantly smaller degree of government control exists in the film industry than in broadcasting. Industry self-control exists; however, this is primarily so in terms of providing information to the consumer via ratings rather than actual content regulation. The ever-present consumer, however, once again plays as big a role as ever.

Government Regulation of Film

The most heralded area of government control of film lies in the continual controversy concerning pornography. Filmmakers and theater owners are subject to prosecution if their films are found to be pornographic as defined by law. Current legal definition of pornography is "any obscene material." Obscenity is based on three legal criteria: "(1) the dominant theme, taken as a whole, must appeal to a prurient interest in sex; (2) the material must be patently offensive and affront contemporary community standards; (3) the material must be without redeeming social value."[3]

The three criteria present a massive problem in any consistent government attempt to regulate film content in that all three criteria contain highly subjective language which is subject to different interpretation in any specific case at issue.

Self-Regulation

As movie themes became more and more mature, outcries of alarm from various service groups in the country became louder and louder. In recent years the movie industry has adopted a system of movie rating using various codes to alert the public as to suitablility of content for different members of the family.

The current code uses G to designate movies suitable for all audience members. PG indicates that the movie so labeled might not be suitable for younger audience members with parental guidance strongly advised. A rate of R communicates that individuals under a specified age (usually seventeen, but subject to change by local theater ownership) will not be admitted unless accompanied by a parent. X means that those under a specified age will not be admitted under any circumstance.

One major difference exists in this form of self-regulation when compared to the broadcast industry. The NAB code makes a direct effort to alter the actual content of programs. Movie ratings provide only a channel for information. The implication remains that almost anything goes on the screen as long as it has the appropriate rating designation.

Consumer Control

As with broadcasting, the most effective element of control in the film industry is often the consumer. Your decision to go or not to go to the movies, and, as a result, to pay or not to pay the price of admission most effectively regulates content of future films. High box-office figures mean more movies of the same genre.

Exercise of consumer control is probably more likely to occur in the film industry than in broadcasting. We are creatures of habit to the television set—we may watch something on a reasonably regular basis and not really like it. Television entertainment is easily available and cheap. We are less likely to spend a sizable amount of money to see a movie that we don't like, and, certainly, if we make the mistake once, it is not likely to happen again.

SUMMARY PROBES

1. **What massive problem exists in any legal effort to regulate movie content on the basis of pornography or obscenity?**
2. **Explain the current movie rating system.**
3. **Why is consumer control of motion pictures more likely to occur than consumer control of broadcasting?**

LEARNING EXPERIENCES

1. Make your own personal observations concerning the nature of movies since the advent of sound in 1927. Watch television listings for movies dated in the early 1930s, World War II period films, and movies produced in the 1950s after television became entrenched. Compare and contrast these films with each other and with current movies.

2. Investigate the changes brought about by the ban of block booking in your community. Determine how many theaters were operating prior to 1950 compared to the present. How many feature films were seen per week in your community prior to 1950?

3. Interview a local theater manager concerning current movie ratings. Determine whether or not the local manager applies any special interpretation on meanings of ratings.

References

Farber, Stephen. *The Movie Rating Game.* Washington, D.C.: Public Affairs Press, 1972.

Hiebert, Ray Eldon; Unguriat, Donald F.; and Bohn, Thomas W. *Mass Media: An Introduction to Modern Communication.* New York: David McKay, 1974, part II and chapter 16.

Knight, Arthur. *The Liveliest Art.* New York: New American Library, 1957.

Whitney, Frederick C. *Mass Media and Mass Communications in Society.* Dubuque: Wm. C. Brown, 1975, chapter 12.

Notes

One: Communication Theory

1. Alfred Korzybski, *Science and Sanity* (Lakeville: Institute of General Semantics, 1958), pp. 223–24.
2. Gerald Miller, *Speech Communication: A Behavioral Approach* (Indianapolis: The Bobbs-Merrill Co., 1966), p. 2.
3. Ralph G. Nichols and Leonard A. Stevens, *Are You Listening?* (New York: McGraw-Hill, 1957), pp. 6–10.
4. Wilbur Schramm, "How Communication Works," *The Process and Effects of Mass Communication* (Urbana: University of Illinois Press, 1955), p. 6.
5. David Berlo, *The Process of Communication: An Introduction to Theory and Practice* (New York: Holt, Rinehart and Winston, 1960), p. 72.
6. Gerald Miller, *Speech Communication,* p. 73.
7. Ibid., pp. 72–74.
8. Bruce H. Westley and Malcolm S. MacLean, "A Conceptual Model for Communication Research," *Journalism Quarterly* 34 (1957) 31–38.

Two: Intrapersonal Variables Affecting Oral Communication

1. Laura Crowell, Allan Katcher, and S. Frank Miyamoto, "Self Concepts of Communication Skill and Performance in Small Group Discussions," *Speech Monographs* 22 (March 1955): 20–27.
2. Dalmas A. Taylor and Leonard Oberlander, "Person Perception and Self Disclosure: Motivational Mechanisms in Interpersonal Communication," *Journal of Experimental Research in Personality* 4 (1969), 14–27.
3. Jesse Delia, "Attitude Toward the Disclosure of Self-Attributions and

the Complexity of Interpersonal Constructs," *Speech Monographs* 41 (June 1974): 119–26.
4. Milton Rokeach, *The Open and Closed Mind* (New York: Basic Books, 1960).
5. Erwin P. Bettinghaus, *Persuasive Communication* (New York: Holt, Rinehart and Winston, 1968).
6. Carolyn Sharif, Musafer Sharif, and Roger Nebergall, *Attitude and Attitude Change: The Social Judgment-Involvement Approach* (Philadelphia: W. B. Sanders, 1965).
7. Kenneth K. Sereno and David Morensen, "The Effects of Ego-Involved Attitudes on Conflict Negotiation in Dyads," *Speech Monographs* 36 (March 1969): 127–34.
8. William McGuire, "The Current Status of Cognitive Consistency Theories," in *Cognitive Consistency: Motivation Antecedents and Behavioral Consequences,* ed. Shel Feldman (New York: Academic Press, 1966), p. 1.
9. Fritiz Heider, "Attitudes and Cognitive Organization," *Journal of Psychology* 21 (1946): 107–12.
10. John Wenberg and William Wilmot, *The Personal Communication Process* (New York: John Wiley & Sons, 1973), pp. 178–80.
11. Theodore Newcomb, "An Approach to the Study of Communicative Acts," *Psychological Review* 60 (November 1953): 393–404.
12. Leon Festinger, *A Theory of Cognitive Dissonance* (New York: Harper & Row, 1957).
13. Donald C. Bryant and Karl R. Wallace, *Fundamentals of Public Speaking* (New York: Appleton-Century-Crofts, 1960), pp. 29–38.
14. Dale Miller, "The Effect of Dialect and Ethnicity on Communicator Effectiveness," *Speech Monographs* 42 (March 1975): 69.
15. Jesse Delia et al., "The Dependency of Interpersonal Evaluations on Context-Relevant Beliefs About the Other," *Speech Monographs* 42 (March 1975): 10–19.
16. Lawrence Wheeless, "The Effects of Attitude, Credibility and Homophily on Selective Exposure to Information," *Speech Monographs* 41 (November 1974): 329–38.
17. John Dewey, *How We Think,* (Lexington: D. C. Heath and Co., 1910).
18. Ralph W. Gerard, "What is Memory?" in *Contemporary Readings in General Psychology,* ed. Robert S. Daniel (Boston: Houghton Mifflin Co., 1959), p. 96.
19. Gerald A. Miller, "The Magical Number Seven, Plus-or-Minus Two: Some Limits on our Capacity for Processing Information," *Psychological Review* 63 (March 1956): 81–97.
20. Charles R. Petrie, "Informative Speaking: A Summary and Bibliography of Related Research," *Speech Monographs* 30 (June 1963): 80.

Three: Nonverbal Variables

1. Albert Mehrabian, *Silent Messages* (Belmont: Wadsworth Publishing Co., 1971).

2. Ray L. Birdwhistell, *Introduction to Kinesics* (Louisville: University of Kentucky Press, 1952).
3. Albert Mehrabian, *Silent Messages.*
4. Elizabeth McGough, *Understanding Body Talk* (New York: Scholastic Book Services, 1974).
5. Julius Fast, *Body Language* (New York: Pocket Books, 1970).
6. Edward T. Hall, *The Silent Language* (Garden City: Anchor Press, 1973).
7. John C. Condon and Fathi S. Yousef "See What I Mean: Observations on Nonverbal Communication Across Cultures," *An Introduction to Intercultural Communication* (Indianapolis: The Bobbs-Merrill Co., 1975), pp. 122–46.
8. C. F. Diehl, R. C. White and P. H. Satz, "Pitch Change and Comprehension," *Speech Monographs* 28 (March 1961): 65–68.
9. Ken Sereno and G. J. Hawkins. "The Effect of Variations in Speakers' Nonfluency Upon Audience Ratings of Attitude Toward the Speech Topic and Speakers' Credibility," *Speech Monographs* 34 (March 1967): 58–64.
10. D. W. Addington, "The Relationship of Selected Vocal Characteristics to Personality Perception," *Speech Monographs* 25 (November 1968): 492–503.
11. Ray L. Birdwhistell, *Introduction to Kinesics.*
12. Albert Mehrabian, "Significance of Posture and Position in the Communication of Attitudes and Status Relationships," *Psychological Bulletin* 71 (1969): 365.
13. Mark Knapp et al., "The Rhetoric of Good-bye: Verbal and Nonverbal Correlates of Human Leave-Taking," *Speech Monographs* 40 (November 1973): 182–98.
14. D. Efron, *Gesture and Environment* (New York: King's Crown Press, 1941).
15. Mehrabian, "Significance of Posture and Position," pp. 359–72.
16. Albert Mehrabian and M. Williams, "Nonverbal Concomitants of Perceived and Intended Persuasiveness," *Journal of Personality and Social Psychology* 13 (1969): 37–58.
17. Mark L. Knapp, *Nonverbal Communication in Human Interaction* (New York: Holt, Rinehart and Winston, 1942).
18. Hall, *Silent Language,* pp. 184–85.
19. N. Compton, "Personal Attributes of Color and Design Preferences in Clothing Fabrics," *Journal of Psychology* 54 (1962): 191–95.
20. G. Thornton, "The Effect of Wearing Glasses Upon Judgments of Personality Traits of Persons Seen Briefly," *Journal of Applied Psychology* 28 (1944): 203–7.
21. A. H. Maslow and N. L. Mintz, "Effects of Esthetic Surroundings: I. Initial Effects of Three Esthetic Conditions Upon Perceiving 'Energy' and 'Well-Being' in Faces," *Journal of Psychology* 41 (1956): 247–54.
22. H. Wong and W. Brown, "Effects of Surroundings Upon Mental Work as Measured by Yerkes' Multiple Choice Method," *Journal of Comparative Psychology* 3 (1963): 319–31.
23. William D. Brooks, *Speech Communciation* (Dubuque: William C. Brown Co., 1974), pp. 176–79.

Four: Language Variables

1. Skinner, B. F., *Verbal Behavior* (New York: Appleton-Century-Crofts, 1957).
2. J. P. Allen and Paul Van Buren, *Chomsky: Selected Readings* (London: Oxford University Press, 1971).
3. Eric Lennenberg, *New Directions in the Study of Language* (Cambridge: MIT Press, 1964).
4. Mary Ann Spencer Pulaski, *Understanding Piaget* (Evanston: Harper and Row, 1971).
5. Charles E. Osgood, *Method and Theory in Experimental Psychology* (New York: Oxford University Press, 1953), p. 695.
6. Jane Blankenship, "The Resources of Language," in *Messages: A Reader in Human Communication,* ed. Jean M. Civilky (New York: Random House, 1974), p. 59.
7. C. K. Ogden and I. A. Richards, *The Meaning of Meaning* (New York: Harcourt Brace and Co.), p. 47.
8. Stuart Chase, "Korzybski's Contribution," in *Basic Reading in Interpersonal Communication,* ed. Kim Giffin and Bobby Patton (Evanston: Harper and Row, 1971), pp. 244–57.
9. S. I. Hayakawa, *Language in Thought and Action* (New York: Harcourt Brace Jovanovich, 1972), p. 25.
10. Sanford I. Berman, *Understanding and Being Understood* (San Diego: The International Communication Institute, 1965), p. 14.
11. "The Blind Men and the Elephant," *Poet's Craft,* (New York: McGraw-Hill, 1963).
12. S. I. Hayakawa, *Language in Thought and Action,* p. 156.
13. Ibid.
14. J. R. Barclay et al., "Comprehension and Semantic Flexibility," *Journal of Verbal Learning and Verbal Behavior* 12 (1974): 471–81.
15. Francis DiVesta and S. M. Ross, "Imagery Ability, Abstractness, and Word Order as Variables in Recall of Adjectives and Nouns," *Journal of Verbal Learning and Verbal Behavior* 10 (1971): 686–93.

Five: Dyadic Communication

1. Don B. Morlan and George E. Tuttle, Jr., "A Determination of Communication Needs in Three Representative Communities," (Research paper, Eastern Illinois University, November 1974).
2. Gustav Ichheiser, *Appearances and Realities: Misunderstandings in Human Relations* (San Francisco: Jossey-Bass, 1970).
3. Dean C. Barnlund, "A Transactional Model of Communication," in *Foundations of Communication Theory,* ed. Kenneth Sereno and David Mortensen (New York: Harper and Row, 1970), pp. 83–102.
4. Robert F. Bales and Edgar F. Borgatta, "Size of Group as a Factor in the Interaction Profile," in *Small Groups: Studies in Social Interaction,* ed. A. Paul Hare (New York: Alfred A. Knopf, 1965), pp. 495–512.

5. Theodore Caplow, *Two Against One: Coalitions in Triads* (Englewood Cliffs: Prentice-Hall, 1968).
6. Transactional analysis (TA) contains new terms for some very old concepts. One journalist in a popular magazine has even equated TA with the older Dale Carnegie approach to communication. (That comparison is unfortunate for TA.) Actually, its origins go rather to the psychological notion of other-person analysis and classification. If you search hard, you will discover that the notion of concern for identity with the other is not foreign to Aristotle's teaching on rhetoric.
7. Eric Berne, *Games People Play* (New York: Grove Press, 1964).
8. Gerald Goldhaber, *Organizational Communication* (Dubuque: William C. Brown Co., 1974), pp. 192–207.
9. Elton Trueblood, *General Philosophy* (New York: Harper and Row, 1963).
10. Don B. Morlan and George E. Tuttle, Jr., "Determination of Communication Needs."

Six: Communication Process Functioning in Small Group Situations

1. E. J. Thomas and C. Fink, "Effects of Group Size," *Psychological Bulletin* 60 (1963): 371–84.
2. Dorwin Cartwright and Alvin Zander, *Group Dynamics* (Evanston: Harper and Row, 1968), pp. 461–82.
3. Clovis R. Shepard, *Small Groups* (San Francisco: Chandler Publishing Co., 1964), pp. 41, 77–94.

Seven: Creating Cohesion as a Participant

1. Dean Barnlund, *Interpersonal Communication: Survey and Studies* (Boston: Houghton Mifflin Co., 1968), pp. 421–38.
2. Joseph Luft, *Group Processes* (Palo Alto: National Press Books, 1970), pp. 11–20.
3. Dorwin Cartwright and Alvin Zander, *Group Dynamics* (Evanston: Harper and Row, 1968), pp. 461–82.
4. Jack Gibb, "Defensive Communication," *The Journal of Communication* 11 (1961): 141–48.

Eight: Creating Cohesion as a Leader

1. Charles Larsen, "The Verbal Response of Groups to the Absence or Presence of Leadership," *Speech Monographs* 38 (August 1971): 177–81.

2. Robert Tannenbaum; Irvin R. Weschler; and Fred Massarik, *Leadership and Organization* (New York: McGraw-Hill, 1961), p. 24.
3. Abraham Korman, "Consideration, Initiation Structure, and Organizational Criteria—A Review," *Personnel Psychology* 19 (1966): 349–61.
4. Joseph Chmeleck, "An Empirical Study Which Measures Principals and Teachers in Their Attitudes Toward, and Their Perceptions of the Leadership Dimensions of Initiating Structure and Consideration," (Thesis at Eastern Illinois University, 1975.
5. John C. Geier, "A Trait Approach to the Study of Leadership in Small Groups," *Journal of Communication* 17 (1967): 316–23.
6. Thomas Knutson, "An Experimental Study of the Effects of Orientation Behavior on Small Group Consensus," *Speech Monographs* 39 (August 1972): 159–65.

Nine: Effective Group Action through Preparation and Organization

1. John Geier, "A Trait Approach to the Study of Leadership," *Journal of Communication* 17 (1967): 316–23.
2. A. H. Maslow and N. L. Mintz, "Effects of Esthetic Surroundings: I. Initial Effects of Three Esthetic Conditions upon Perceiving 'Energy' and 'Well-Being' in Faces," *Journal of Psychology* 41 (1956): 247–54.
3. N. L. Mintz, "Effects of Esthetic Surroundings II. Prolonged and Repeated Experience in a 'Beautiful' and an 'Ugly' Room." *Journal of Psychology* 41 (1956): 459–66.
4. Gerald Phillips, *Communication and the Small Group* (Indianapolis: The Bobbs-Merrill Co., 1973).

Ten: An Introduction to Public Speaking

1. Kathleen Edgerton Kendall, "Do Real People Ever Give Speeches?" *Central States Speech Journal* 25 (Fall 1974): 235.

Fourteen: Delivering the Speech

1. Alan H. Monroe and Douglas Ehninger, *Principles and Types of Speech Communication* (Glenview: Scott, Foresman, 1974), pp. 316–17.

Fifteen: Historical Development of a Broadcasting System

1. Otto N. Larsen, "Posing the Problem of Effects," in *Mass Media: Forces in Our Society*, ed. Francis H. Voelker and Ludmila Voelker (New York: Harcourt Brace Jovanovich, 1975), pp. 407–11.

2. Lee Loevinger, "The Ambiguous Mirror: The Reflective-Projective Theory of Broadcasting and Mass Communications," in *Mass Media: Forces in Our Society,* ed. Francis H. Voelker and Ludmila Voelker (New York: Harcourt Brace Jovanovich, 1975), pp. 385–401.
3. Ibid., p. 396.
4. Ibid., p. 3.
5. "Trends in Public Attitudes Toward Television and Other Mass Media," (A report by the Roper Organization, Inc., April 1975).
6. Ibid.

Sixteen: The Development of Broadcasting Content

1. *New York Times,* 23 March 1924, p. 16.
2. Ibid.
3. *New York Times,* 22 December 1924, p. 20.
4. Robert C. O'Hara, *Media for the Millions* (New York: Random House, 1961).

Seventeen: Broadcasting Finance

1. *New York Times,* 18 May 1924, p. 3.
2. Sydney Head, *Broadcasting in America: A Survey of Television and Radio* (Boston: Houghton Mifflin Co., 1972), p. 264.
3. Ibid., p. 263.
4. Maurine Christopher, "Fall TV Series Costs . . . ," *Advertising Age,* 9 June 1975, p. 2.
5. "The Television Code," 18th ed. (Code Authority of the National Association of Broadcasters, June 1975), p. 16.
6. Robert J. Coen, "Ad Volume in 75 . . . ," *Advertising Age,* 15 September 1975, p. 3.
7. Sydney Head, *Broadcasting in America,* p. 169.
8. "The Television Code," p. 16.
9. Ibid., p. 13.
10. Lawrence W. Lichty and Malachi C. Topping, *American Broadcasting: A Source Book on the History of Radio and Television* (New York: Hastings House, 1975), p. 255.
11. John T. Lucas and Richard Gurman, *Truth in Advertising, An AMA Research Report,* (American Management Association, Inc., 1972), p. 8.

Eighteen: Control of Broadcasting

1. Sydney W. Head, *Broadcasting in America: A Survey of Television and Radio* (Boston: Houghton Mifflin Co., 1972), p. 155.

2. "The Television Code," 18th ed. (Code Authority of the National Association of Broadcasters, June 1975).
3. Ibid.
4. Ibid.
5. Ibid.
6. Les Brown, *Television: The Business Behind the Box* (New York: Harcourt Brace Jovanovich, 1971), pp. 32–35.
7. Ibid.

Nineteen: The Motion Picture

1. Ray Eldon Hiebert; Donald F. Unguriat; and Thomas W. Bohn, *Mass Media: An Introduction to Modern Communication* (New York: David McKay Company, 1974), pp. 247–48.
2. *New York Times,* 30 July 1974, p. 67.
3. Ray Eldon Hiebert et al., *Mass Media,* pp. 70–71.

Index